SEAFOOD LOVER'S

NEW ENGLAND

Restaurants, Markets, Recipes & Traditions

FIRST EDITION

Linda Beaulieu

gpp

Guilford, Connecticut

To all the men and women,
past and present, who
"go down to the sea in ships"
in search of great seafood.
We seafood lovers thank you.

Photo Credits: Images licensed by Shutterstock.com: pages iv, viii, 12, 15, 43, 46, 73, 99, 107, 117, 125, 131, 132, 144, 147, 157, 162, 167, 171, 177, 178, 180, 196, 199, 206, 220, 224, 229, 232, 237, 240, 247, 251, 254, 262, 265, 268, 273, 277, 300, and illustrations throughout the book. Photos by Karl Schatz © Morris Book Publishing, Inc.: pages 159, 165, 168, 173, 191, 202, and 214. Photos by Stephanie Webster © Morris Book Publishing, Inc.: pages 7, 11, and 19. Photos by Al Weems © Morris Book Publishing, Inc.: pages vii, 9, 17, 44, 48, 49, 52, 54, 59, 71, 74, 75, 87, 88, 90, and 92. Photos by Francine Zaslow © Morris Book Publishing, Inc.: pages 21, 40, 103, 120, 134, 138, 140, 143, 148, 151, 152, 153, and 204. Photos courtesy of Tracee Williams: pages 4, 24, 28, 33, and 217. Photo courtesy of Lobster Landing: p. 25. Photo courtesy of Harpoon Brewery, Boston: p. 110.

Editor: Amy Lyons
Project Editor: Lynn Zelem
Layout Artist: Mary Ballachino
Maps: Alena Joy Pearce © Morris Book Publishing, LLC

ISBN 978-0-7627-8654-1

Printed in the United States of America

Contents

About the Author

Linda Beaulieu is an award-winning food and travel writer. She is the author of *Providence & Rhode Island Chef's Table* (Lyons Press), *Providence & Rhode Island Cookbook* (Globe Pequot Press), *Divine Providence: An Insider's Guide to the City's Best Restaurants*, and *The Grapevine Guide to Rhode Island's Best Restaurants*. She received the prestigious James Beard Award for magazine writing for an article on Native American food, which appeared in the *National Culinary Review*.

•••————— ••••—————•••

Acknowledgments

I would like to acknowledge all the businesses and organizations listed in this book for providing me with detailed information, often via their websites. I especially want to thank the chefs, restaurants, and markets that provided wonderful recipes to illustrate New England's amazing seafood. A special thank-you goes out to my editor, Amy Lyons, and her entire crew at Globe Pequot who always help me be a better writer.

•••————— ••••—————•••

New England—Six States of Sensational Seafood

Superlatives abound when we talk about seafood and New England. The state of Maine is the nation's largest supplier of fresh lobster, and little Rhode Island is the squid capital of the world. The scallop industry is thriving in New Bedford, Massachusetts, with the size of the annual catch more than doubling since 1999.

Imagine how delicious a New England seafood stew would taste with all its key ingredients coming from the northeastern region of America! Can't you just smell the aroma floating out of a great big stockpot of simmering seafood? Clams and mussels, shrimp and lobster, squid and haddock—their individual flavors blending and marrying amidst traditional seasonings and fresh herbs, perhaps with a touch of cream or crushed tomatoes, depending on your ethnic leanings. And of course there has to be good bread on the table, chewy and dense, for dipping into that aromatic broth.

That imaginary stew is a symbol of all that awaits you in New England, the third most productive region of the United States in producing seafood, with the Pacific and Gulf regions leading the way. This book is your guide to all things seafood in Connecticut, Rhode Island, Massachusetts, New Hampshire, Maine, and even landlocked Vermont. Whether you are motoring from state to state on a New England vacation, or simply visiting Boston, Portland, Newport, or Cape Cod, this guide will help you find the very best restaurants known for their seafood, the finest fresh seafood markets, and the most successful sportfishing opportunities along the coast. We've also included all the truly worthwhile seafood festivals and events that you will want to experience while in New England. This book is just what a seafood lover needs, whether he's a local resident or she's a visiting tourist.

In search of that quintessential New England clam shack? Or five-star fine dining? It's all here at your fingertips.

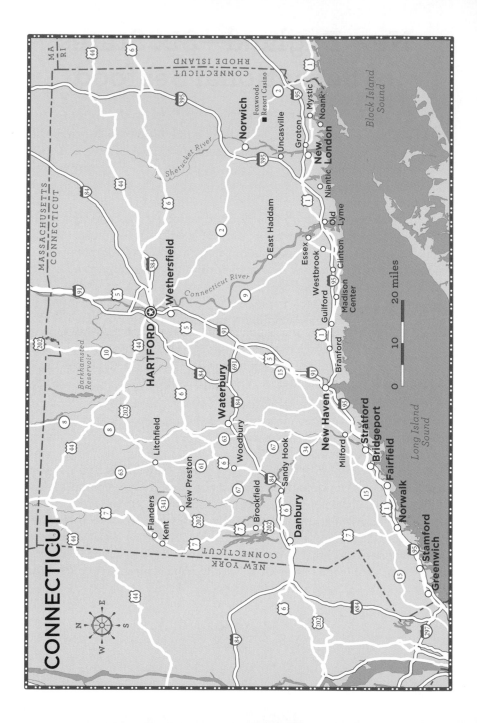

CONNECTICUT

Connecticut

Like the five other New England states, Connecticut is a colorful quilt of unique fabrics. Much of the southern and western part of the state is part of the New York metropolitan area. The northwestern region features rolling hills and horse farms, while southeastern Connecticut is known for its beaches and maritime activities. In sharp contrast to all that are the industrial cities along the coast.

Hartford may be the state capital and known as the epicenter of the insurance industry, but Mystic by the sea is Connecticut at its most charming. Water defines Mystic's past, going back to the 17th century, when this seaside village was a shipbuilding center. Since then, tourism has taken over as the area's most important industry.

Known as the Constitution State, Connecticut was one of the thirteen colonies that revolted against British rule in the American Revolution. That sense of history can still be seen in many picture-postcard towns centered around a "green," such as the Wethersfield Green (oldest in the state) and the Lebanon Green (largest in the state). Around these town greens you will still find a classic New England white church, a colonial meeting house, a tavern or inn, and restored colonial homes.

The original name of Connecticut, *Quinnehtukqut,* was derived from the Algonquin Indian word for "beside the long tidal river"—that being the Connecticut River, which runs through the center of the state. From that river comes the prized fish shad, a delicacy in this region.

Like that river, seafood is a common thread that winds through the entire state. All along the coastline there are restaurants of all kinds, from wildly popular clam shacks to four-star dining rooms within expensive resorts. Cities and towns far from the shore also have a fair share of worthy seafood restaurants and fish markets. And like the rest of New England, and perhaps all of America, food in Connecticut serves as a common language providing us not only with sustenance but with much pleasure as well. For seafood lovers this is exponentially true.

ALONG THE SHORELINE

Connecticut has more than 600 miles of shoreline, extending from exclusive Greenwich near New York City to charming Stonington on the Rhode Island state line. From Greenwich to New Haven, it's a gritty, urban stretch of industrial cities. That all changes as you continue east along the shore. A softer landscape reveals small towns, historic villages, and many beaches—as well as seafood restaurants galore.

Interestingly, Connecticut has no direct access to the sea despite its miles and miles of coastline. The jurisdiction of New York actually extends east at Fishers Island, where New York shares a sea border with Rhode Island. Although Connecticut has easy access to the Atlantic, between Long Island Sound and Block Island Sound, it has no direct ocean coast.

Seafood Restaurants

The Beach House Restaurant, 141 Merwin Ave., Milford; (203) 877-9300; beachhousemilford.com. It's pretty hard to resist any place called The Beach House. That name conjures up sweet summer memories. Relive those golden moments any time of the year at this popular restaurant near Long Island Sound. The historic building used to be a trolley station. "Fresh is best" is their motto, starting with the exceptionally fresh Blue Point oysters from a well-stocked raw bar. The seasonal menu is exciting: hand-rolled ricotta gnocchi with lobster bordelaise sauce, herb-crusted wild salmon, pancetta-wrapped scallops, and roasted black cod. A special prix-fixe menu is available Tuesday through Thursday evenings. With a prelude of littleneck chowder, typical entrees might be white shrimp carbonara or grilled golden bass. The culinary staff in the open kitchen, under the direction of Executive Chef Nicci Tripp, is devoted to serving only sustainable fin and shellfish as well as natural, hormone-free beef and organic chicken. Cocktails are served on the seasonal patio. When the nights turn cool, you can dine by the fireplace. Open for dinner Tues through Sat from 5 p.m. to closing.

Blue Lemon, 15 Myrtle Ave., Sconset Square, Westport; (203) 226-2647; bluelemonrestaurant.com. Inspired modern American cuisine in a romantic setting—that's what awaits you at this restaurant where Chef Bryan Malcarney is well-known for his seafood dishes. Before opening Blue Lemon, he spent years in the Caribbean as the chef at the Straw Hat in Anguilla. The incredibly tender grilled baby squid with a ginger and lime vinaigrette has been pleasing guests for the past decade, an appetizer the chef simply can't delete from the menu. If you're there for lunch on a Monday, try the Blue Monday special—Dover sole with lemon beurre blanc, a dish that would have made Julia Child smile. Dinner

Connecticut Food News

Some restaurants are in business for decades, while others crash and burn within a year of opening. If you're planning a trip to Connecticut and have certain restaurants on your "must visit" list, it's a good idea to call ahead to avoid any unnecessary driving and disappointment. For statewide listings check out the following websites:

connecticutmagazine.com: Statewide magazine with articles on restaurants and dining, food and drink.

ct.com: Tribune Broadcasting website covering the entire state.

ctvisit.com: The website of Connecticut's Office of Tourism.

restaurantsct.com: The official online dining guide of the state's best restaurants.

Strictly Al Fresco

Dining at the Blue Oar in Haddam is completely outdoors. Located on the banks of the Connecticut River, this seasonal restaurant offers its guests an up close water view. Arriving early guarantees you a front-row seat. People sit at colorful picnic tables to dine on fresh seafood or other landlubber options. The food is prepared on a 6-foot industrial grill manned by Chef-Owner Jim Reilly. What to expect? This is no clam shack. Seared scallops with fresh corn salad for an appetizer, grilled salmon with pesto or sautéed shrimp in coconut sauce, jasmine rice, and grilled zucchini for an entree. For a more casual lunch, try the warm lobster roll soaked in butter. This is a BYOB establishment, so bring your favorite wine or beer in a cooler. And it's cash only—no credit cards accepted. If you're getting here by boat, you can dock it next door at the Midway Marina. Open daily for lunch and dinner from Mother's Day to Columbus Day, weather permitting.

The Blue Oar, 16 Snyder Rd., Haddam; (860) 345-2994; no website.

entrees include seared king salmon over ginger spinach, seared diver scallops with orzo pasta salad, Basque-style seafood stew, and seared wild striped bass over a ragout of grilled corn, poblano peppers, leeks, tomato, and garlic with mango salsa. The *New York Times* gave the Blue Lemon a "very good" rating, calling it "a delightful oasis for diners who crave good food in cozy, conversational surroundings." In the summer you can dine on the flower-filled patio. Open daily for lunch and dinner. Lunch hours are Mon through Sat from noon to 2:30 p.m. Dinner hours are Mon through Thurs from 5:30 to 9 p.m.; Fri and Sat 5:30 to 10:30 p.m.; and Sun 5:30 to 9 p.m.

Close Harbour Seafood Market & Restaurant, 959 Meriden Waterbury Turnpike, Plantsville; (860) 621-7334; closeharbour seafood.com. This is one of those rare restaurants that serves all three classic clam chowders—New England with a cream base, clear Rhode Island clam chowder, and a silky Manhattan clam chowder with a rich tomato broth. Daily specials, such as spicy lobster chowder, can be found online. "Extremely fresh seafood, simply prepared" is their slogan. All the usual suspects can be found on the menu; steamed littleneck clams, crab cakes, mussels, and steamers. The lightly fried seafood (Ipswich clams, Gulf shrimp, fish, scallops, and calamari) is available in sandwich form or with fries and coleslaw. House specialties include pancetta-encrusted Atlantic cod, pistachio-crusted organic Scottish salmon, and Sicilian-style swordfish with pasta. With a fish market on the premises, guests can select any fresh fish in the refrigerated case to be prepared simply by the kitchen, that is, pan seared, baked, or *a la plancha* (on a special grill). This is a BYOB restaurant. Open Tues through Thurs from 11 a.m. to 7 p.m.; Fri and Sat from 10 a.m. to 8:30 p.m.; and Sun from noon to 5 p.m.

Dock & Dine, 145 College St., Old Saybrook; (860) 388-4665; dockdinect.com. One of the newest restaurants on the Connecticut coast, Dock & Dine prides itself on offering fine cuisine using the freshest local ingredients, from the sea and from the fields. In addition, the views of Saybrook Point and Long Island Sound from the waterfront dining room are simply spectacular: a feast for your eyes and your palate. Located on the Connecticut River, Dock & Dine is just that—a large restaurant where you can pull up on your yacht and have a relaxing meal. The menu offers New England clam chowder, traditional and contemporary seafood selections, as well as food for landlubbers. Al fresco dining is available in warm weather. It's Senior Citizens Day every Wednesday, when people age 62 and older with identification are given a 25 percent discount on their lunch or dinner. Open daily from 11:30 a.m. to 10 p.m.

The Fisherman Restaurant, Groton Long Point Road, Rte. 215, Noank; (860) 536-1717; fishermanrestaurant.com. This place doesn't look like much on the outside, so never judge a restaurant solely on its exterior. Just outside downtown Mystic, The Fisherman sits on Palmers Cove facing Fishers Island Sound and Esker Point Beach, providing guests with water views from every seat in the house. Live piano music is offered as well as a two-tiered patio for an al fresco experience. A favorite among locals, this coastal restaurant specializes in seafood. The local catch varies with the tides: tuna, striped bass, black back and yellowtail flounder, fluke, mahimahi, and even an occasional opah. House specialties include legendary Stonington sea scallops (from the famed Bomster family) in sherried lobster cream, Noank oysters, and a variety of seafood from Rhode Island and Maine. The signature dishes are Thai-style calamari, Atlantic codfish topped with crumbs, salads with healthy ingredients, house-made mozzarella, and sauces made from scratch. A special happy hour menu offers $5 items, such as shrimp tossed in a slightly spicy glaze. This is one of the few

Connecticut King of Clams

More clams come from Connecticut waters than anywhere else on the East Coast. The state clam is officially a *Mercenaria mercenaria,* known throughout New England as a quahog. A sure sign of summer's advent is when all the clam shacks along US 1 from West Haven to the Rhode Island line open their windows and begin their ritual deep-frying of bucketsful of ocean-fresh clams. The fried-clam season typically runs through October, depending on the weather, giving you plenty of time to work your way up the shore, searching out the best. Which is best is your call.

restaurants with a dress code, but it's a fun one: sailing casual. Open for lunch and dinner daily from 11:30 a.m. to 9:30 p.m.

Flanders Fish Market & Restaurant, 22 Chesterfield Rd., East Lyme; (860) 739-8866; flandersfish.com. Back in 1983 Cappy and Donna Formica converted a small single-family house into a fish market. Just weeks after opening, customers started requesting fish-and-chips, and a restaurant was born. Three decades later the fish market is still going strong, along with the 150-seat seafood restaurant. The menu is huge, page after page of tempting items: shellfish from the raw bar, appetizers for sharing like Parmesan calamari, chowders and the house-made lobster bisque, salads, lobster in many guises (dinners, stuffed, lobster potpie, and lazy man's style), combination platters including the fish-and-chips that started it all, shrimp dishes, fried seafood, specials such as cedar-plank salmon and Dijon swordfish tips, and seafood delicacies stuffed, flame grilled, broiled, and blackened. But wait, there's more: wraps and sandwiches including a hot lobster roll, a crispy fried fish fillet, pasta dishes such as lobster Alfredo and shrimp scampi, and a children's menu. Senior citizens get 10 percent off their purchases every Tuesday. If you just can't decide what to order, stop in on any Sunday from 11 a.m. to 3 p.m. for the seafood buffet, a feast of seafood and so much more. In addition, this casual eatery is open Sun through Thurs from 9 a.m. to 9 p.m. and Fri and Sat from 9 a.m. to 10 p.m.

The Flood Tide at the Inn at Mystic, 3 Williams Ave., Mystic; (860) 536-8140; innatmystic.com. Set high on a hill overlooking Mystic Harbor and Fisher's Island Sound, this hotel restaurant has won awards not only for its food but for its water view as well. Sweet Canadian lobster is the main ingredient in the famous lobster crepe appetizer with a Madeira wine cream sauce—a house favorite. Crab, lobster, and salmon fritters with orange, mint, and chipotle dipping sauce are another creative start to your dinner. The calamari is fried until golden, then tossed with banana peppers and Sriracha aioli. Entrees include local Stonington Bay sea scallops with baby spinach, baked local cod with pesto, baked stuffed sole with sweet pepper sauce, and grilled salmon with roasted tomato sauce. Shrimp scampi combines fettuccine with sautéed shrimp tossed in a white wine garlic sauce. Hearty appetites will love the steamed clams and mussels with chorizo sausage. You'll be dipping your toasted garlic bread in the tomato broth to soak up every drop. All this goes well with the chardonnay from the local Stonington Vineyard. Outside dining is offered during warm weather. Open for dinner every night except Tues.

Fresh Salt at the Saybrook Point Inn and Spa, 2 Bridge St., Old Saybrook; (860) 388-1111; saybrook.com. Fresh Salt boasts beautiful views of the Connecticut River and Long Island Sound. It only makes sense that seafood plays a major role on the seasonal menu, which has a simple theme—a fresh food experience. The restaurant makes every effort to use ingredients locally sourced from river valley farms, brewers, and dairy providers. Creamy New England clam chowder as well as the clear Rhode Island variety is offered. In the summer you can sit on the patio under a colorful market umbrella, and lunch on an oyster bar platter or the littleneck clams steamed in Stonington Vineyard Riesling with kielbasa, tomatoes, and *ciabatta* crostini. The food gets more serious at dinner with elegant fare: pancetta-crusted Stonington Bomster scallops for an appetizer, followed by wild striped bass, crisp sautéed soft-shell crabs, fresh cioppino with tomato saffron sauce, or cedar-plank grilled Block Island swordfish. This is creative American cuisine at its finest. Coming by boat? You can tie up at the inn's marina, which has accommodations for luxury yachts. Open for lunch and dinner daily.

Jimmie's of Savin Rock, 5 Rock St., West Haven; (203) 934-3212; jimmiesofsavinrock.com. Jimmie's is sometimes listed as a clam shack, but it's far more than that. Family owned and operated since 1925, it started

Jimmie's of Savin Rock

out as a humble hot dog stand. Today this full-service seafood restaurant is known for its fresh fish and huge portions. Just about everyone leaves with a doggie bag. The menu is massive as well, offering clams casino, the chef's special chowder, shrimp parmigiana, seafood Alfredo over linguine, platters of fried seafood, baked seafood specialties including twin lobsters, combination platters (think prime rib and baked stuffed lobster), and broiled seafood for the health conscious. A children's menu is also available. Make sure you check out the tiki bar and the early bird specials. Jimmie's is not without its critics. It gets decidedly mixed reviews. People seem to either love it or hate it. But it's a big restaurant with a panoramic view of Long Island Sound. A great deal of al fresco seating is available on a wraparound deck with an outdoor bar. Open for lunch and dinner daily.

Latitude 41 at Mystic Seaport, 105 Greenmanville Ave., Mystic; (860) 572-5303; mysticseaport.org. Right on the banks of the Mystic River near Mystic Seaport, Latitude 41 has a dining venue to suit your every mood. Enjoy a breeze off the river as you dine al fresco on New England clam chowder, crab and shrimp cakes with an herb salad, a salmon salad BLT in a spinach wrap, or day boat scallops with mushroom risotto, all from the lunch menu. Or dine at night in the Shipyard Tavern on mussels prepared with saffron, ale, and smoked bacon, and a nice slice of

Parmesan *ciabatta* for sopping up the wonderful broth. In one of the dining rooms, enjoy linguine with littlenecks, bouillabaisse, grilled swordfish, seafood stuffed lobster, beer-battered colossal shrimp, seared salmon, or lobster potpie, each with its own set of creative accompaniments. This is new American cuisine at its finest, under the watchful eye of Executive Chef D. Andrew Fine. In cooler weather linger a while near one of the fireplaces. All this makes for a true maritime experience with an ambiance that combines historical and contemporary elements. It's easy to see why Latitude 41 is called "a destination dining experience." Open for lunch and dinner Tues through Sun from 11:30 a.m. to closing.

Lenny & Joe's Fish Tale, 1301 Boston Post Rd. (Rte. 1), Madison; (203) 245-7289. 86 Boston Post Rd., Westbrook; (860) 669-0767; ljfishtale.com. Two brothers, two locations. Both are very much alike, but not identical. Lenny and Joe kicked off their restaurant careers in 1979 when they opened a roadside clam stand with just four picnic tables in a screened-in porch in Madison. Then and now they are committed to serving only the freshest seafood available in generous portions at reasonable prices with prompt, friendly service. Over the years the original location expanded, and then they opened a second family restaurant, now located in Westbrook, with a broader menu that includes baked and charbroiled items. Of the two, Madison is the more casual establishment, offering all the usual suspects when it comes to seafood, including lazy man's lobster and the super fish tale platter, a feeding frenzy of fried food. A clear broth chowder is offered at both sites. Over in Westbrook, there's just more of everything, from fried lobster as an appetizer to mahimahi. Of special note: Salt potatoes are on the menu. These are baby red potatoes boiled in a salted broth, a side dish served at county fairs in this part of New England. A children's menu is available (along with a carousel and an ice cream stand in Madison). Both locations are open for lunch and dinner daily.

Lenny's Indian Head Inn, 205 S. Montowese St., Branford; (203) 488-1500; lennysnow.com. A spiffy new waterfront dining room at Lenny's Indian Head Inn is the perfect spot for a traditional shore dinner. At Lenny's that'll get you raw cherrystone clams for starters, clear-broth chowder, steamed clams, lobster, and sweet corn. The pub room is a cozy spot, and the Back Porch overlooks a pretty tidal marsh and osprey nesting area. The inn opened in 1939 and was taken over in 1968 by Leonard Conlin, who turned it into a popular nightspot. Lenny's has now evolved into a popular family restaurant known especially for seafood. The lobsters are available steamed, broiled, and stuffed. Clams and oysters are offered raw on the half shell and fried. Other house specialties are the seafood bisque, steamers served with broth and butter for dipping, clams casino, baked stuffed clams, fried calamari, popcorn shrimp with Cajun dip, and clams zuppa with Italian bread for sopping up the spicy broth. Lenny's is also known for its fried and broiled seafood. Sandwiches include rolls stuffed with your choice of fresh lobster salad, fried clams, oysters, or scallops. A children's menu is also available. Open for lunch and dinner daily.

Liv's Oyster Bar, 166 Main St., Old Saybrook; (860) 395-5577; livsoysterbar.com. It's the little things that make Liv's Oyster Bar an outstanding restaurant. Like the bacon and chive buttermilk biscuits that accompany the chowder or the fries that are flavored with Old Bay seasoning and served with roasted garlic mayo. It's a family affair for owners John and Krissie Brascio. The popular restaurant is named after their daughter Olivia. John is also the chef, and they say he is obsessed with seafood. This neighborhood restaurant is known for its impeccably fresh seafood creations. Just consider the artful entrees: wild sockeye salmon with soba noodles, halibut with heirloom cherry tomato and basil salad, yellow fin tuna with a fennel and pepper crust, Stonington sea scallops with lemon risotto, and lump crab cakes with succotash. Tucked into the lobby of a former movie house, Liv's Oyster Bar is a dining destination with food served in the main room, at the bar, or on the patio. With exposed brick walls and romantic candlelight, the restaurant exudes warmth. The seasonal menu offers oysters from around the world as well as fresh local seafood. Open for dinner every night except Tues. Summer hours may differ—call to check.

Mansion Clam House, 541 Riverside Ave., Westport; (203) 557-4811; mansionclamhouse.com. Yet another restaurant often listed as a clam shack, Mansion Clam House has been a Westport landmark for more than 60 years. Current Chef-Owner Rigo Lino has turned it into a lovely coastal clam house serving not just clams but upscale dishes such as oysters Rockefeller and bouillabaisse. An outstanding dish is the warm salad topped with lobster, capers, and grilled mango salsa. But fear not, the restaurant's legendary fish-and-chips is still on the impressive menu as well as an award-wining clam chowder, calamari, steamers, mussels, twin lobsters, and much more. Chef Lino handpicks all the seafood served, visiting the docks of New York in the predawn hours. He uses center-cut cod for his famous fish-and-chips, dipped in a beer batter and served with extra-long fries. He is known for his fresh, simple seafood. In warm weather you can have cocktails and dine on the covered patio. A favorite with the locals, the tavern-style restaurant is located on the Saugatuck River, which adds to the nautical atmosphere. Open for lunch and dinner Mon through Sat and dinner only on Sun.

Merritt Canteen, 4355 Main St., Bridgeport; (203) 372-1416; merrittcanteen.com. Ever since 1942 the Merritt Canteen has been serving up hot dogs and burgers that generations of families have enjoyed, and now the seafood on the menu is also getting rave reviews. The hand-battered fish is deep-fried until golden brown, and fans love the light, flaky crust. That fish comes in a sandwich or with fries and the house-made coleslaw. Other sandwiches include a clam roll and a langostino roll. You can also get crab cakes, fried shrimp, clams, and scallops. Seasonal items range from clam chowder to soft-shell crabs. Technically it's fast food, but it's all made to order while you watch it being prepared. Named for the nearby Merritt Parkway, it is the go-to place especially after hours. The humble canteen has had a loyal local following for decades, but now—thanks to an appearance on *Diners, Drive-ins and Dives* on the Food Network—people from all over the country are making the trek to Bridgeport. Open for breakfast, lunch, and dinner daily (and until 4 a.m. on Fri and Sat).

Oyster River Tavern, 38 Ocean Ave., West Haven; (203) 932-0440; no website. This seafood restaurant stands out from the rest because of its delicious grilled seafood dishes. Fans rave about the grilled mahimahi and grilled tuna sandwiches with tomato basil butter on a French roll. The grilled swordfish is done simply with bread crumbs and butter. All the usual fried items are also on the big American cuisine menu that offers plenty of sandwiches, seafood, and salads. Start off with fresh shellfish from the raw bar. The pasta dishes also have seafood in a starring role as in the zuppa de mussels in a red or white sauce. Oyster River Tavern is also known for its large portions, brisk bar business, and higher-than-normal noise level, which is a trend in many restaurants these days. That's due in part to the busy jukebox. Located across the street from West Haven Beach with views of Long Island Sound, this very casual restaurant has a pub atmosphere and in the summer a popular outdoor bar. Open for lunch and dinner Mon through Thurs from 11:30 a.m. to 10 p.m.; Fri and Sat from 11:30 a.m. to 10:30 p.m.; Sun from noon to 10 p.m.

The Restaurant at Rowayton Seafood, 89 Rowayton Ave., Rowayton; (203) 866-4488; rowaytonseafood.com. Its awards are too numerous to mention. Suffice it to say The Restaurant at Rowayton Seafood is one of the very best seafood restaurants with a fresh seafood market on the premises, and that's always a good sign. Rowayton, which is part of Norwalk, is 45 miles from Manhattan, and many consider it the first New England town they come upon in Connecticut. The Restaurant is a hidden gem, a bit hard to find down quaint small streets. Locals refer to it simply as The Restaurant, tucked into an old gray-shingled house on the banks of the Five Mile River. It's a popular coastal destination for boaters as well as food lovers in search of outstanding seafood with a waterfront view. Also known for its special service, The Restaurant offers the traditional—lobsters, oysters, and chowder—as well as the innovative, such as peppadew-dusted swordfish with sweet potato-crab hash. An excellent variety of sandwiches is available at lunch. Fans rave about the lobster grilled cheese, made with multigrain wheat toast stuffed with white cheddar and a generous portion of fresh lobster, cooked in a sandwich press. The house-made potato chips just make it even better. Free valet parking is provided, and docking is available for yachts (or dinghies) by reservation. Open for lunch and dinner daily, brunch Sun.

The Restaurant at Water's Edge, 1525 Boston Post Rd., Westbrook; (860) 399-5901; watersedgeresortandspa.com. *Spectacular* is the right word to describe Water's Edge Resort & Spa, a beautiful beachfront hotel overlooking Long Island Sound. This historic gem is home to The Restaurant, known for its creative preparations of the freshest seafood. This is *the* place for romantic dinners on an escape weekend, followed by an incredible brunch the next day. Start with the colossal shrimp cocktail or the lump crab cakes and the award-winning New England clam chowder. For your main course consider the North Atlantic salmon in a light tomato broth with steamed littleneck clams, or the lightly battered pan-fried shrimp with lemon-caper sauce over house-made black pepper fettuccine. But you'll be torn with even more imaginative possibilities: the fire-grilled Canadian line-caught swordfish, the bacon-wrapped cod fillet, and the shrimp and sea scallop rosemary skewer. If that's not enough, more seafood awaits you at two other restaurants on the premises, the Seaview Bistro and the Sunset Bar & Grill, both offering more casual fare, such as shrimp pad Thai and grilled fish tacos. Outdoor dining is available in warm weather. Open for lunch Mon through Sat from 11:30 a.m. to 2:30 p.m.; brunch Sun from 9 a.m. to 3 p.m.; dinner Sun through Thurs from 5:30 to 9 p.m., Fri and Sat from 5:30 to 10 p.m.

Sandbar Restaurant, 31 Kimberly Ave., West Haven; (203) 933-3700; sandbarseafood.net. Most would agree, even its most loyal fans, that the Sandbar is a dive, but it is one of the few restaurants serving breakfast, lunch, and dinner. The small dining room has warm wood paneling with matching wooden tables and chairs. Outdoor dining is also available in warm weather. The main attraction is any of the seafood platters, especially the shrimp or the whole belly clam platter served with fries and "fantastic" coleslaw. Other noteworthy items are the lobster rolls, fried fish sandwich, and fried scallops. This is a favorite seafood restaurant for many locals mainly because of large portions, reasonable prices, and consistently good service. Open Mon through Thurs from 10 a.m. to 8 p.m.; Fri and Sat from 10 a.m. to 9 p.m.; Sun from 10 a.m. to 7 p.m.

S&P Oyster Company, 1 Holmes St., Mystic; (860) 536-2674; sp-oyster.com. It may be called an oyster company, but S&P has three other attractions—an award winning clam chowder, seafood cooked over a wood grill, and a front-row seat to the Mystic Drawbridge. From a table by the window or the patio, guests can watch the historic bascule bridge open up whenever sailboats with lofty masts travel along the river. Critics say the chowder is "perfect with a good clam-to-potato ratio and a silky broth." Other appetizers include oysters, of course, raw on the half shell and fried; seafood stuffed potato skins; blackened shrimp over creamy Pepper Jack cheese grits; and wood-grilled prosciutto-wrapped sea scallops. Much of the fish and shellfish on the menu is served both at lunch and dinner: seafood ambrosia, a mix of shrimp, sea scallops, crab, and cod topped with seafood stuffing; North Atlantic salmon, farm raised and wood grilled;

mixed grill sampler served over spring vegetable polenta; broiled seafood platter, fisherman's platter, and traditional fish-and-chips. Some of the traditional seafood is prepared with South American flair, thanks to Chef Edgar Cobena. S&P Oyster Company is just minutes from Mystic Seaport, Mystic Aquarium, and two of North America's largest casinos, Foxwoods Resort Casino and Mohegan Sun Casino. S&P is one of the most visually appealing seafood restaurants on the coast. Open for lunch and dinner daily.

Skipper's Dock, 66 Water St., Stonington; (860) 535-0111; skippersdock.com. With a view of Stonington Harbor and Fishers Island Sound, Skipper's Dock is where you want to be on a perfect summer day. Tucked inside on a rainy day isn't too bad either, because this is the place for the freshest seafood imaginable. The restaurant sits on a dock, its home since 1929. Commercial fishing is an important industry in the quaint town of Stonington, and generations of local fishermen have been bringing their daily catches to this waterfront restaurant, from local scallops to Royal Red shrimp, also known as Stonington Reds. Several menus are available, with a range of prices. On the deck you can enjoy a crock of bouillabaisse, fish sandwiches, and whole belly clam rolls. At lunch dine on beer-battered fish-and-chips or seafood penne Alfredo. In search of a lobster sandwich? Here it's done two ways: the classic cold lobster salad roll and a hot toasted lobster sandwich topped with melted gruyère cheese. At dinner start off with Cajun grilled shrimp or share an order of lobster salad sliders, followed by oven-roasted striped bass or pan-sautéed flounder. And yes, boat owners, this is a dock-and-dine restaurant. Just pull up to the main dock, secure your boat, and head into Skipper's. Open daily for lunch and dinner; brunch Sun from 11:30 a.m. to 4 p.m. Closed Tues in the off-season, from Labor Day to Memorial Day.

Skippers Seafood Restaurant, 167 Main St., Niantic; (860) 739-3230; skippersseafood.com. This coastal restaurant offers indoor seating and outdoor dining overlooking Niantic Bay. With a warm, casual atmosphere, the family-owned Skippers Seafood serves a variety of fresh seafood: fried (whole belly and strip) clams, shrimp, scallops, calamari, and hot or cold lobster rolls. Dinners come with heaping piles of fries and coleslaw; for a bit more money, you can substitute curly fries or onion rings. If you're really hungry, try the fisherman's platter. All the fried seafood is hand battered. Their top sellers include fish-and-chips, a fried fish sandwich, and an award-winning New England clam chowder. The fresh salads

come with generous scoops of tuna salad, seafood salad, and lobster salad. It's popular with families and offers a children's menu. Open daily from 11 a.m. to 9 p.m.

SoNo Seaport Seafood, 100 Water St., Norwalk; (203) 854-9483; sonoseaportseafood.com. SoNo stands for South Norwalk, and SoNo Seaport Seafood is a popular family restaurant overlooking Norwalk Harbor. It started out as a fish market in 1983, and a year later the restaurant opened its doors with a prime waterfront location and a reputation for the freshest fish around. This is a very casual, comfortable eatery with an outside bar. Everything you desire in the line of seafood can be found on the menu, from stuffed clams and scungilli salad to steamed king crab legs and fried classics such as clams, squid, oysters, shrimp, soft-shell crab, and scallops. Customer favorites include the crab cake sandwich, grilled swordfish steak, broiled seafood platter, shrimp scampi served over rice, sautéed tilapia with mushrooms, and sautéed bay scallops. Seafarer sandwiches round out the menu, which warns guests that certain items are not always available because of weather conditions or the seasonal migratory patterns of various fish. This restaurant also refuses to hold food beneath a heat lamp until the entire order is ready. So don't be surprised if your order of fried clams arrives piping hot and a few minutes ahead of the broiled scrod that someone else in your party has ordered. Open daily from 11 a.m. to 10 p.m.

Shad Shack Is a Wonderful Sad Shack

Quite possibly the oddest restaurant in the state, Spencer's Shad Shack is the last of its kind. Described as "a curious hut" and even "a sad shack" because of its dilapidated condition, it nonetheless opens for business every year during the fleeting and unpredictable shad season. The official state fish, shad and its eggs, known as shad roe, are a regional delicacy. Back in the 1800s, shad fishing was a profitable industry in Haddam, where the Shad Museum is located. Shad became scarce in the last century, and state law now mandates that shad fishing can be done only at night with drift nets. Full of small bones, shad is the largest in the herring family. Boning shad is considered an art form. Every spring, masters at "planking" shad cook the treasured fish over an open wood fire as it has been done in Haddam since 1930. Open only when the shad are running. It's wise to call before going.

Spencer's Shad Shack, 1146 Saybrook Rd. (Rte. 154), Haddam; (860) 345-4805; no website.

Turk's, 425 Captain Thomas Blvd., West Haven; (203) 933-4552; no website. In West Haven since 1939 and located across the street from Jimmie's of Savin Rock (p. 10), Turk's is another local seafood institution. Like its neighbor, Turk's also gets mixed reviews—it seems those who like Jimmie's don't care for Turk's and vice versa (people here are passionate about their fried seafood and very loyal to their favorite establishment). Turk's has a casual sit-down dining room with wait service as well as an indoor take-out area with tables that you bus yourself. Standouts include the fried whole belly clams, fried butterfly shrimp, griddled hot dogs, onion rings (fried in a light batter that makes the onion the star), and the seasonal fried soft shell crab sandwich—a large and meaty crab served between slices of buttered white bread and accompanied by a side of tartar sauce. Turk's offers some broiled seafood options as well. Early bird specials (dine in) are offered Mon through Fri from 11 a.m. to 5 p.m. Open for lunch and dinner daily.

U.S.S. Chowder Pot Restaurants, 560 East Main St., Branford; (203) 481-2356. 165 Brainard Rd., Hartford; (860) 244-3311; chowderpotiv.com. You can find a U.S.S. Chowder Pot Restaurant in Branford and another one in the south end of Hartford. Those locations are the third and fourth incarnations of what started out as a humble hot dog stand in 1977 that eventually turned into a seafood drive-in. The current Chowder Pots are big award-winning restaurants with popular lounges featuring raw bars. Live lobsters weighing up to 15 pounds swim in a tank, and you can pick the one you want for dinner. Monday night is lobster night with discounts and specials offered. The menus are virtually identical at both places, with all the seafood essentials you require, and then some. Try the crab cobb salad or the grilled tuna teriyaki sandwich at lunch. For dinner you'll be torn—may we suggest starting with the crab-stuffed mushrooms, followed by tilapia blackened with Cajun spices, or perhaps the seafood lasagna made with tender Gulf shrimp, sweet crabmeat, and scallops. Because all the seafood is delivered daily, certain fresh items may not always be available. A children's menu is available. Open for lunch and dinner daily.

Water Street Cafe, 143 Water St., Stonington; (860) 535-2122; waterst-cafe .com. Ask any local resident where to go for seafood, and just about everyone will say Water Street Cafe in the seaside village of Stonington Borough. They are especially known for an impeccable oyster bar and daily specials that rely on the local catch of the day, as well as seasonal produce (organic whenever possible). Executive Chef Walter Houlihan's multicultural menu is innovative as well. Sautéed calamari, a staple on so many menus, is served here with a Thai coconut sauce. The halibut is glazed with miso and served with a vegetable stir-fry. A house favorite, scallops are paired with duck and oyster mushrooms. Add to that a warm ambiance and friendly staff, and you have a winner. As for that oyster bar, make sure you try Connecticut's own French Kiss oysters, which have a profound salinity that gives way to a mildly sweet finish. Open for lunch and dinner daily.

Westbrook Lobster Restaurant, 346 East Main St. (Rte. 1), Clinton; (860) 664-9464. 300 Church St., Wallingford; (203) 265-5071; westbrooklobster.com. There are two Westbrook Lobster restaurants, one in Clinton and the other in Wallingford. What started out as a specialized lobster market evolved from "the shoreline's hidden gem" to being named the best seafood restaurant in the state by *Connecticut* magazine for four consecutive years. That speaks volumes in a highly competitive market. Their recipe for success is simple: top-quality seafood prepared in a variety of ways and served by a friendly staff. They promise that their fish is always fresh and never previously frozen. The lunch menu features plenty of sandwiches (try the cod bacon Reuben), soups (as in lobster bisque), salads (the seafood cobb is a winner), and low-priced complete meals such as baked stuffed sole and spice-rubbed salmon. It only gets better on the dinner menu with everything nautical and nice: seafood paella, lobster mac and cheese, and fried seafood platters. The lobsters come steamed, baked, stuffed, and pan roasted. You just might want to get a bag of clam fritters to go. Those meaty little clam-filled balls of dough are served with tartar sauce. Both locations are open for lunch and dinner daily.

The Wharf at Madison Beach Hotel, 94 West Wharf Rd., Madison; (203) 245-0005; madisonbeachhotel.com. The newly rebuilt Madison Beach Hotel is home to The Wharf, a casually elegant restaurant that offers beachfront dining and classic seaside fare. With a terrific view of Long Island Sound and its natural beauty, The Wharf offers an extensive menu that is heavy on edible sea creatures. Executive Chef John Cortesi suggests a properly chilled platter of freshly shucked oysters or a bucket of steamed clams for starters out on the covered porch or in the inviting dining room. His seasonal menu utilizing farm-to-table ingredients showcases classic New England cuisine with innovative flair. Fresh herbs are grown on the premises in the hotel garden. Popular porch seating is available only when weather permits. The Wharf is open for breakfast, lunch, and dinner daily, with a jazz brunch by the beach (in season) every Sun from 10 a.m. to 2 p.m.

Lobster Pounds & Lobster Shacks

Abbott's Lobster in the Rough, 117 Pearl St., Noank; (860) 536-7719; abbotts-lobster.com. It's a shame this place is open only during the summer—the seafood is that good. The anticipation for opening day in early May is so great that people camp out so they can be among the first to dine on a piping-hot lobster from the famed steamer at Abbott's. You also can't beat the beautiful views of Long Island Sound and Mystic River. This is yet another restaurant offering a clear broth clam chowder and hot lobster rolls, served in hamburger buns rather than hot dog rolls. The shrimp and roasted corn chowder is a real crowd-pleaser, especially on cool rainy days. Shrimp in the rough is a pile of cooked shrimp still in their shells served with cocktail sauce and fresh lemon wedges. The oysters on the half shell are purity tested from certified growing beds. Lobsters start at a pound and a quarter and go all the way up to 10 pounds. But the best buy is the New England Seafood Feast: chowder, shrimp, steamers, mussels, and a steamed lobster with all the fixings. Only serious eaters need apply. Open for lunch and dinner daily from Memorial Day weekend to Labor Day. It's wise to check their website for off-season hours of operation. While you're at it, you can print out a coupon for a free cup of chowder.

Bill's Seafood, 548 Boston Post Rd. (Rte. 1), Westbrook; (860) 399-7224; billsseafood.com. A very good lobster roll can be found at Bill's Seafood, but it's the location that puts your dining experience over the top. This lobster shack is right next door to the Singing Bridge, which spans the Patchogue River as it winds down to Long Island Sound. It's super casual with outdoor dining on picnic tables, seasonal of course. And it's fun to watch pleasure boats travel on the river while you wait for your well-buttered lobster roll served on a toasted hot dog roll. The menu also offers Russian oysters. Does not accept credit cards. Open daily for lunch and dinner.

Captain Scott's Lobster Dock, 80 Hamilton St., New London; (860) 439-1741; captscotts.com. Any restaurant that has its own fish market on the premises is bound to have the freshest seafood possible. That's the case at Captain Scott's Lobster Dock, a seasonal outdoor restaurant with its own fish market, family owned and operated. Captain Scott was indeed a sea captain who lived in New London in the late 1800s. Everyone who knew the man loved him. And today folks love the waterfront restaurant that bears his name. This scenic dining spot is right on the dock with plenty of boats on one side and an active rail line on the other. Be prepared to use GPS to find this out-of-the-way lobster shack, known for having the biggest lobster roll by far. But this king of sandwiches is not just big . . . it's also fresh tasting, succulent, and flavorful with a grilled roll that is just perfect. The lobster bisque comes in a bread bowl, if desired. The lobster dinners are served with corn on the cob, red potatoes or fries, and coleslaw. No matter what you order, it all comes with a hard-to-beat waterfront view of New London and local marinas in Shaw's Cove. Customers place their orders at walk-up windows and eat their delicacies from the deep at picnic tables on the dock. This is a BYOB establishment, so plan accordingly. Open daily for lunch and dinner. Because it is open only from spring through early fall, it's wise to call before going.

Guilford Lobster Pound, 505A Whitfield St., Guilford; (203) 453-6122; guilfordlobsterpound.com. One of the true lobster pounds in Connecticut, this is where you can purchase freshly caught lobsters and also grab a quick bite. Owner Bart Mansi heads out every day at 4 a.m. on his 42-foot lobster boat and brings his catch back to the pound, where it's weighed and sorted by size for the many customers. On the deck overlooking Guilford Harbor, you can sit at a colorful umbrella table where you can chow down on a fresh lobster roll and house-made clam chowder. This is a BYOB establishment, so you can bring your own wine and beer. After lunch you can take a one-hour scenic shore and river cruise aboard the *Charley More*, a 20-passenger Oldport launch

GUILFORD
LOBSTER
POUND

Hot Lobster Roll	$15.00
(4 oz Fresh Lobster Meat)	
Sea Dogs	$3.00
(Hot Dog on the Water)	
Clam Chowder	$4.00
(Clear Broth)	
Stuffed Clams	$3.00
(Stuffed with Scallops and Shrimp)	Each
Cole Slaw	$1.50
Soda and Iced Tea	$2.00
Bottled Water	$2.00
Chips	$1 00
Ice Cream	$3.00

(for details, visit grassislandcruisesct.com). A seasonal operation, Guilford Lobster Pound opens every Apr 1. The deck is open by Memorial Day for the summer. Open Wed and Thurs from noon to 5 p.m.; Fri, Sat, and Sun from noon to 6 p.m.

Lenny and Joe's Fish Tale, 1301 Boston Post Rd., Madison; (203) 245-7289; ljfishtale.com. It may not offer the biggest lobster roll in Connecticut, but Lenny and Joe's does have an outdoor carousel that will keep the children happy. The consistently good hot lobster roll contains a fair amount of buttery lobster in a nicely grilled roll. They also serve lobster dinners with a local favorite, salt potatoes. The lobster feast includes chowder, steamers, and a lobster. And this is one of a few lobster shacks that is open year-round, so you can satisfy your cravings even in the dead of winter. Open year-round, with limited hours in the off-season.

Lobster Landing, 152 Commerce St., Clinton; (860) 669-2005; no website. You couldn't ask for a more picturesque setting, right on the dock of a marina. The quintessential lobsterman, white beard and all, can often be seen on the premises. From a very limited menu (only three items), the hot lobster roll is the specialty. Here it is served in a toasted submarine bun, not the usual hot dog roll, with butter and a sprinkle of fresh lemon juice. The

lobster meat is cooked in small mesh bags right next to the plastic dining tables under a makeshift tent for a unique dining experience. You can also buy lobsters, steamers, clams, and oysters to take home and cook. Open late Apr through New Year's Eve for lunch and early dinner.

Lobster Shack, 7 Indian Neck Ave., Branford; (203) 483-8414; no website. In Connecticut there is only one kind of lobster roll, and there isn't a bit of mayonnaise in it as you'll find in the other New England states. It is a simple recipe: chunks of freshly picked lobster meat dunked in melted butter and piled generously into a buttered and grilled hot dog roll. The roll is then sprinkled with fresh lemon juice. That's how it is done at the Lobster Shack, one of the best shacks in the state. The picnic tables at this seasonal restaurant provide a view of nearby boats and marshes. Just look for the big red trailer on the Branford River. Open for lunch and dinner every day except Sun, weather permitting.

Clam Shacks

Chick's Drive-in, 183 Beach St., West Haven; (203) 934-4510; no website. Located across the street from West Haven Beach, Chick's Drive-in has been a long-time fixture on the local restaurant scene with second and third generations of families among its many customers. It's a popular spot to stop after a day at the beach with indoor and outdoor seating. This classic drive-in offers hot buttered lobster rolls that measure a foot long and lots of fried seafood, from soft-shell crab sandwiches and Cajun catfish to shrimp, scallops, clams, oysters, and calamari. Most of the fried seafood is available in sandwich form and as dinners with fries and coleslaw. Four kinds of chowder are on the menu: New England, Rhode Island, Manhattan, and Chick's very own chowder. Chick's Drive-in is often listed as one of the city's best seafood restaurants, but the reviews are decidedly mixed on this place. An old-time beachfront restaurant still in its original form, ideal for a trip back in time when fast food didn't have such a bad name. Does not accept credit cards. Open daily from noon to 9 p.m.

Clam Castle, 1324 Boston Post Rd. (Rte. 1), Madison; (203) 245-4911; no website. Fans say this classic roadside clam shack hasn't changed much in 30 years, and that's just how they like it. You can eat outside at picnic tables or in the small dining room with its bright yellow walls and red seats, next to the walk-up window where you can order fried whole belly clams, clam strips, and clam fritters. All that goes great with the clam chowder, brimming with ocean flavors. Local foodies claim this is the best clam shack in the state. Make sure you try the house-made lemonade. Open only in summer. Always call ahead to check on hours of operation.

Costello's Clam Company, Noank Shipyard, 145 Pearl St., Groton; (860) 572-2779; costellosclamshack.com. Costello's is the sister operation of Abbott's Lobster in the Rough, one of the state's best known lobster shacks. (Get it? Abbott and Costello?) It's a two-story clam shack rising above the docks in Noank Shipyard, offering guests an unobstructed marina view. The fresh Canadian clams are consistently delicious. The golden brown clam fritters come with a dipping sauce. The clam chowder is clear. The steamed clams come piled high with drawn butter and broth for dipping. Fried clams, whole belly and strips, are served in rolls and as a dinner with fries and coleslaw. On a clear day you'll have a postcard view of three states. Open for lunch and dinner daily from Memorial Day weekend through Labor Day.

Denmo's Snack & Dairy Bar, 346 Main St. South, Southbury; (203) 264-4626; no website. Locals call it the "Snack Shack," and the fried clams are the big draw. They come whole belly or in strips, always with a crisp crust. A dozen picnic tables offer an in-the-rough dining experience. Even when it's too cool to eat outside, the crowds still come to Denmo's, more than happy to savor the fried clams while sitting inside their cars. Cash only. Open for lunch and dinner daily during the spring and summer. Hours vary according to season. Closed in winter.

Fred's Shanty, 272 Pequot Ave., New London; (860) 447-1301; freds-shanty.com. While this place is known for its foot-long hot dogs, the folks at Fred's Shanty are also pretty proud of their fried clams, available as whole belly and as strips. You can get them as a side order or as a dinner with fries and coleslaw. Fried to perfection, the clams have a crispy, golden exterior. Don't be surprised if they run out! The fried fish sandwich is pretty good as well. And you just can't beat Fred's low prices. Celebrating its 40th anniversary, this clam shack isn't much to look at—it's really a drive-in on a busy street. But it does have a pleasing view of the marinas on the Thames River. Open daily for lunch and dinner from Mar to late Oct.

Glenwood Drive-in, 2538 Whitney Dr., Hamden; (203) 281-0604; glenwooddrivein.com. Since 1955 the Stone family has owned the Glenwood with the third generation now in the business. Their fried clams, whole belly and strips, are popular menu items. This is an old-fashioned drive-in with old-fashioned prices. There's almost always a line, but it moves quickly thanks to the ordering system. A man asks what you want, and shouts it out

Put Your Rump on a Stump at The Place

This is more than a restaurant; it's a very unusual dining experience. It has to be with a motto like this: "Put your rump on a stump." Fans say it's the coolest clambake in the state. You dine outdoors, sitting on tree stumps at bright red tables made from plywood mounted on logs. A ramshackle 18-foot grill over a crackling hickory and oak wood fire roasts the food you're about to eat. Clams, steamers, mussels, shrimp, bluefish, catfish, and lobster are your seafood options. Every ingredient is locally sourced, and it's either roasted, grilled, or steamed. Nothing is fried. Even the sweet corn is roasted and then dunked in butter. The lobsters are boiled first and then roasted, if you so desire, which gives the crustaceans a smoky flavor. The staff cuts open the lobsters and cracks the shells for your convenience. Melted butter is served on the side. Clearly this is a seasonal restaurant, open from late Apr to the end of Oct. Guests are encouraged to bring prepared side dishes, tablecloths, candles, and seat cushions. It's BYOB, so plan on bringing your own wine and beer in a cooler. And bring cash—no credit cards here. Open Mon through Thurs from 5 to 9 p.m.; Fri from 5 to 10 p.m.; Sat from 1 to 10 p.m.; Sun from noon to 9 p.m., weather permitting.

The Place, 901 Boston Post Rd. (Rte. 1), Guilford; (203) 453-9276; theplaceguilford.com.

to the cooks. By the time you get your beverage and reach the cashier, your order is ready. If you stop in on a Wednesday night (Apr through Oct), you'll think it's 1955 all over again. That's when a Cruise Night takes place with many classic cars on display. Open daily from 11 a.m. to 10 p.m.

Hub's Clam Shack, 928 Poquonnock Rd., Groton; (860) 446-2526; no website. Hub's serves American cuisine and is known for its seafood: a jumbo lobster roll and clams, whole belly and strips, in rolls, in dinners, on the side, and as fritters. The "chowda" bar offers New England clam chowder, Rhode Island–style (clear) chowder, and lobster bisque. The lobster grilled cheese special gets rave reviews, but folks seem divided on this typical clam shack. People either love or hate this place, which proves once again how subjective food can be. Hub's used to be an old ice cream store and now looks like a big drive-in on a very busy street. You can eat inside or get your food to go. Open daily from 11 a.m. to 10 p.m.

Johnny Ad's, 910 Boston Post Rd., Old Saybrook; (860) 388-4032 or (860) 388-1306; johnnyads.com. This classic gray roadside clam shack may not have an ocean view, but for more than a half a century Johnny Ad's has been cranking out exceptional fried clams. Fans love the house-made tartar sauce, unchanged all these years. There are all kinds of seafood, but clams have a starring role in dinner plates, in long toasted hot dog rolls, and as simple side orders. You can dine inside or outdoors. A children's menu is also available. Open for lunch and dinner daily.

Sea Swirl, 30 Williams Ave. (near the junction of Rte. 1 and Rte. 27), Mystic; (860) 536-3452; seaswirlofmystic.com. Another popular drive-in near the coast, Sea Swirl is known for two things—excellent fried clams, especially the whole-belly variety, and incredible sunsets overlooking the Mystic River's flood tide. The many accolades are impressive, including one proclaiming this is "the best of the best" clam shacks in Connecticut. Flawlessly fried seafood and picnic tables by a cove . . . what more could you ask for? A seasonal operation, Sea Swirl closes on Columbus Day for winter. Open daily from 11 a.m. to 8 p.m.

Sea View Snack Bar, 145 Greenmanville Ave., Mystic; (860) 245-2553; seaviewsnackbar.com. Wonderful fresh seafood from a shack by the side of the road with a view of boats sailing on Mystic River—that sums up this family-owned business. The bright blue building has a walk-up window where you can order foot-long lobster salad rolls and crab cake sandwiches that many folks rave about. Then you sit at picnic tables with colorful umbrellas with that sparkling view of the river. Other menu items include creamy chowder, plump fried clams, sea scallops, fish, and calamari. All kinds of people frequent this place, from local businesspeople to families on New England road trips, in search of the best seafood on the coast. Open Sun through Thurs from 10 a.m. to 9 p.m.; Fri and Sat from 10 a.m. to 10 p.m.

Stowe's Seafood, 347 Beach St., West Haven; (203) 934-1991; no website. The word *wacky* comes to mind at first sight of Stowe's Seafood. Totally unpretentious with a kitschy sign out front (don't be surprised if the shrubs are decorated with Christmas lights year-round) and over-flowing with pirate memorabilia, Stowe's is known for its "boats" or huge platters of seafood at different price points. Everything you'd expect to find at an authentic clam shack is on the menu, plus seafood chili and all kinds of stuffed seafood—shrimp, sole, scallops, and clams. Crab cakes and coconut shrimp are offered as interesting side dishes. Live lobsters are in a tank, waiting for you to make your selection. Picnic tables with bright red umbrellas provide al fresco dining and an ocean view. Family owned since 1927. This is beach food at its best. Cash only. Open Tues through Sun in summer. Closed Mon and Tues in winter.

Ten Clams, Olde Mistick Village, Bldg. 18, 27 Coogan Blvd., Mystic; (860) 536-1019; no website. Sounds like a clam shack, doesn't it? But the name really refers to the menu prices at this casual family restaurant. Every item offered at the economical Ten Clams is priced at $10 or less. And that includes lobster rolls. The signature dish is the fish-and-chips. Ten Clams also offers a children's menu and reduced prices for senior citizens. You can dine inside this New England–style cottage, or visit the take-out window for al fresco dining in the courtyard overlooking the quaint village. Open daily from 11 a.m. to 8 p.m.

Seafood Markets

Atlantic Seafood Market, 1499 Boston Post Rd., Old Saybrook; (860) 388-4527; atlanticseafoodmarket.com. It's almost easier to say what seafood they don't carry here. Atlantic Seafood Market's impressive website gives you a glimpse of what they offer: 6 different kinds of salmon, 14 kinds of white fish (from barramundi to trout), and 19 specialty specimens (from blackfish to wahoo); 5 kinds of shrimp, including colossal and Maine red shrimp; everything from Alaskan king crab legs to soft-shell crab; and everything between cherrystone clams and whole oysters. And then there are the prepared dishes and complete meals ready to take home for an easy heat-and-serve dinner: clam and sausage pie, lobster cakes, baked crab dip, smoked fish, mussel soup, shrimp bisque, tuna niçoise, seaweed salad, ginger tilapia, and crab-stuffed flounder—and so much more. Atlantic Seafood Market has been serving customers since 1978. The *New York Times* wrote: "To find fish any fresher, you'd probably have to throw out a line and catch them yourself." They pride themselves on never adding color, pesticides, growth hormones, or preservatives to any of their products. And if that's not enough, they bake fresh breads daily and offer fresh produce from an on-site family produce stand. Atlantic Seafood Market can ship fresh products to anywhere in the world. Want salmon delivered to your house for a delicious seafood dinner? Lobster delivered for a backyard seafood bake? No problem! Open Mon through Sat from 10 a.m. to 6 p.m., Sun from 10 a.m. to 5 p.m.

Bud's Fish Market, 4 Sybil Ave. (Rte. 146), Indian Neck, Branford; (800) 348-1019; budsfishmarket.com. Bud's reportedly has the largest selection of fresh fish and shellfish on the Connecticut shoreline, with more than 600 seafood items, including lobsters, clams, sea scallops, swordfish, salmon, tuna, haddock, Alaskan king crab legs, Icelandic arctic char, gray sole, cooked or raw shrimp, lobster tails, seafood sausage, seafood spreads, and much more. They will ship your lobster and seafood purchases anywhere in the nation. Open Tues through Sat from 10 a.m. to 6 p.m., Sun from 10 a.m. to 4 p.m. Closed Mon.

Captain Scott's Lobster Dock, 80 Hamilton St., New London; (860) 439-1741; captscotts.com. This combination lobster shack/restaurant/fish market has a picturesque view of local marinas. Live lobsters in various sizes are brought in daily and kept in tanks. Fresh fish, cod, and flounder are always available. Other favorites here are swordfish, monkfish, and salmon. Locals love the fresh yellow fin tuna and Connecticut River shad when in season. A variety of shellfish: Maine steamers, mussels, local sea scallops, and shrimp always are available as well. Clam chowder and lobster bisque are available to take home. Because Captain Scott's is seasonal, open only from spring through early fall, it's wise to call before going. Far off the beaten path, expect to use Mapquest or GPS to find this diamond in the rough. Open daily from 10 a.m. to 7 p.m.

Close Harbour Seafood Market & Restaurant, 959 Meriden Waterbury Turnpike, Plantsville; (860) 621-7334; closeharbour seafood.com. You can shop at this fish market for at-home needs, or you can select any fresh fish in the refrigerated case for your dinner in the restaurant next door. Fresh day boat–caught seafood and gourmet deli items from around the world are available, including Maine cod fillet and loins, Point Judith flounder and yellow tail sole, organic Scottish salmon fillet, dry all-natural Maine sea scallops, native swordfish, Costa Rican tilapia fillet, local littleneck clams, Prince Edward Island mussels, Maine steamers, Gulf shrimp, and their famous shrimp cocktail. The following are available when in season: halibut, wild Alaskan salmon, mahimahi, yellow fin tuna, Idaho rainbow trout, Maine shrimp, red snapper, Florida grouper, Louisiana catfish, and Italian branzino. Store-made heat-and-serve gourmet deli items are also available, including lobster-and-cheddar-cheese-stuffed potatoes, crab-and-Parmesan-stuffed mushrooms, bacon-wrapped Maine sea scallops, jumbo stuffed clams, jumbo crab-stuffed shrimp, coconut fried shrimp, coconut fried tilapia, jumbo lump crab cakes, and more. Store-made chowders and deli salads are also available. Open Tues through Thurs from 11 a.m. to 7:30 p.m.; Fri and Sat from 10 a.m. to 8 p.m.; Sun from noon to 5 p.m. Closed Mon.

Flanders Fish Market, 22 Chesterfield Rd., East Lyme; (860) 739-8866; flandersfish.com. A renovated house is the home of Flanders Fish Market. Fresh fish, seafood, and lobsters can be shipped anywhere via the online marketplace. The extensive menu includes tilapia, halibut, trout, flounder, shrimp in various sizes, chopped clams, bay scallops, sea scallops, quahogs, steamers, and oysters from Fishers Island. They also offer prepared dishes ready to take home to heat and serve. Cooking supplies are also available. There is a 150-seat restaurant on the premises. Open every day from 9 a.m. to 9 p.m.

Rowayton Seafood Market, 89 Rowayton Ave., Rowayton; (203) 838-7473; rowaytonseafood.com. Right next door to its highly acclaimed sister restaurant, Rowayton Seafood Market is housed in an old fishing shack right on the water. Don't be surprised if you see a restaurant chef ducking in to buy fresh seafood for that day's menu. Small but known as a high-quality fish and shellfish purveyor, Rowayton Seafood also serves prepared food that can be enjoyed on a small deck with bright red picnic tables and dark blue market umbrellas. On ice, there are Connecticut bluepoint oysters, littlenecks, cherrystones, and shrimp cocktail to try. Fried items include whole-belly clams, calamari, select oysters, and Gulf rock shrimp. From the steamer, you can have lobster, steamers, and Belgian mussels in a roasted garlic–white wine sauce. The limited menu also offers beer-battered fish-and-chips as well as fresh lobster rolls. All this food is posted on an old-fashioned blackboard inside the charming market. Open Mon through Fri from 9 a.m. to 7 p.m.; Sat from 9 a.m. to 8 p.m.; Sun from 10 a.m. to 8 p.m.

Saybrook Seafood, 843 Boston Post Rd, Old Saybrook; (860) 388-4600; saybrookseafood.com. The all-female staff at Saybrook Seafood has more than 100 years' experience in the fresh seafood industry. This family-owned and -operated business gets much of its fresh catch from Point Judith, Rhode Island. The fresh oysters are from Fishers Island and Whale Rock. The store is especially known for its "sweet" steamers, so clean they don't need a home washing before cooking. Customers are also advised to steam, never boil, their fresh lobsters. In addition to fresh seafood, the market has prepared foods: Robin's stuffed shrimp, Janine's shrimp spread and roasted corn chowder, stuffed clams, and crab cakes are just a few examples of what's available. Open daily.

SoNo Seaport Seafood Market, 100 Water St., Norwalk; (203) 854-9483; sonoseaportseafood.com. Opened in 1983, with an adjacent restaurant added a year later, SoNo catches its fresh fish and lobsters daily. They have it all: squid, scrod, mussels, octopus, lobster tails, cherrystones, littleneck clams, bay scallops, live lobsters, cooked shrimp, swordfish, sole, steamers, scungilli, crabmeat, imitation crabmeat, chowder clams, jumbo king crab legs, sea scallops, native bluepoint oysters, shucked oysters, shrimp in four sizes, soft-shell crabs, and a full line of fresh fish filleted daily. Open daily from 11 a.m. to 10 p.m.

INLAND

Connecticut's small towns are simply charming destinations throughout the interior of the state for shopping in boutiques, browsing in galleries, and just plain relaxing. Kent in the northeast, Litchfield in the northwest hills, and the 1634 village of Wethersfield are all worth exploring. Putnam is known far and wide for its antiques.

After a day spent in bookstores, one-of-a-kind shops, or museums, you'll be ready for a bite to eat, and there are plenty of restaurants, cafes, and bistros awaiting your arrival. More often than not, seafood plays an important role in their menus. And even though they are far from the shore, area fish markets are well stocked with seafood to satisfy all your cravings.

Seafood Restaurants

Angelico's Lake House, 81 North Main St., East Hampton; (860) 267-4276; angelicoslakehouse.com. In the countryside between Hartford and New Haven, Angelico's Lake House has so much going for it. On the banks of Lake Pocotopaug, the restaurant is housed in a beautiful old residence with an outdoor terrace on the second floor, complete with dark green market umbrellas. Right next door on the shady grounds a beer garden beckons with a water view, weekend dinners, and live music throughout the summer months. If you arrive by boat, free dock space is available. Stroll up to the lakefront Tiki Bar for classic cocktails before dinner. Seafood is the thing, with the menu offering lobster quesadilla and scallops pan seared with pineapple and white wine for starters, a classic Connecticut lobster roll (that's hot lobster meat poached in butter) on a brioche roll, and creative entrees: lobster ravioli, spicy seafood fra diavolo with linguine, and salmon lightly crusted with a mix of bread crumbs and pecans. For simpler palates the fish-and-chips is a batter-fried haddock fillet with fries and coleslaw. Everything is reasonably priced. Open daily for lunch and dinner, 11:30 a.m. to 9:30 p.m.

Carmen Anthony Restaurant Group: Carmen Anthony Steakhouse, 496 Chase Ave., Waterbury; (203) 757-3040. **Carmen Anthony Steakhouse,** 660 State St., New Haven; (203) 773-1444. **Carmen Anthony Fishhouse,** 757 Main St., Woodbury; (203) 266-0011. **Carmen Anthony Fishhouse,** 1770 Berlin Turnpike, Wethersfield; (860) 529-7557; carmenanthony.com. It all began in 1996 when the first Carmen Anthony opened in Waterbury. The Carmen Anthony Restaurant Group now consists of two steakhouses and two fish houses. All four restaurants feature fresh-daily seafood and lobsters weighing up to 5 pounds. They are especially known for their award-winning New England clam chowder and their potato-encrusted crab cake made with Maryland lump crab pan fried until golden brown and served with house-made remoulade sauce. The fresh fish selections range from scallops pan seared with artichoke hearts and sun-dried tomatoes served with delicate angel hair pasta, to grilled salmon topped with asparagus, crabmeat, and fresh diced tomatoes. Customer favorites include Chilean sea bass sautéed with Roma tomatoes, capers, garlic, and kalamata olives over pasta; lobster *fra diavolo* in a spicy red sauce over linguine; seared sesame yellow fin tuna encrusted with sesame seeds; and baked stuffed shrimp served with potato and vegetables. All this wonderful seafood pairs beautifully with selections from a wine list that year after year is awarded with the prestigious Award of Excellence from *Wine Spectator* magazine. Open daily for lunch and dinner.

David Burke Prime at Foxwoods, Grand Pequot Tower Restaurant Level, 350 Trolley Line Blvd., Mashantucket; (860) 312-8753; davidburkeprime.com. David Burke Prime is a contemporary steakhouse at Foxwoods Resort Casino that wisely offers extraordinary seafood in addition to its beef specialties. For example, one of the appetizers is a pretzel-crusted crab cake with citrus glaze, pepper jam, and beer foam. For simpler tastes the creative menu offers pan-roasted salmon with cabernet butter and Stonington scallops with caper brown butter. If you're a big winner in the casino, you can order the pricey Pequot Tower raw bar, which consists of a lobster, six jumbo shrimp cocktail, four oysters on the half shell, four littleneck clams, and jumbo lump crab with organic cocktail sauce. Lobsters weigh in at 2 to 5 pounds each. Monday night is lobster night, when you can enjoy three courses at a greatly reduced price. That special menu features the award-winning lobster bisque, lobster dumplings, and lobster tacos for appetizers. Entrees include steamed or roasted lobster, kung pao–style lobster, or lobster carbonara. A delectable David Burke signature dessert is the perfectly sweet ending to the meal. Open for lunch and dinner Mon through Thurs from noon to 10:30 p.m., Fri from noon to 11 p.m., Sat from noon to 11:30 p.m., with dinner starting at 5 p.m. Open Sun for dinner only from noon to 10 p.m.

Frank Pepe Pizzeria Napoletana, 157 Wooster St., New Haven; (203) 865-5762; pepespizzeria.com. Other locations in Connecticut include Fairfield, Manchester, Danbury, and Mohegan Sun. Why would a pizza joint be listed in any seafood lovers' guide? Because Pepe's, now with seven locations, is best known for its signature white clam pizza. Fans rave about the incredibly thin fresh clam pizza that comes out of a coal-fired brick oven with just the right amount of char on the crust. It's a huge but simple pie, topped with plump fresh clams, grated cheese, olive oil, and fresh garlic and oregano—perfect with a glass of Peroni Italian beer. It all began in 1925 in New Haven, where Frank Pepe opened a pizzeria that made true Neapolitan pizza, or as Pepe would say in his Italian dialect, "apizza" (ah-beets). The Pepe family operates the business to this day and believes the patriarch of the family created his now-famous clam pizza because raw littleneck clams on the half shell were on the menu as an appetizer. Perhaps he simply needed to use up leftover clams. No matter how it happened, loyal fans are certain that Frank Pepe's white clam pizza is the best "ah-beets" in Connecticut. This humble pizzeria is less than 5 minutes off I-95, midway between New York and Boston. Expect to stand in line. Open daily for lunch and dinner.

Jasper White's Summer Shack, Mohegan Sun Resort Casino, Uncasville; (860) 862-9500; summershackrestaurant.com. Jasper White knows seafood. One of the best seafood chefs in America, he was inspired by a traditional New England clam shack to open Summer Shack, a small chain of high-energy restaurants, offering local and regional favorites. Quirky decor is putting it mildly when trying to describe this fun place. Sit at the big circular bar that overlooks the lobster tanks, or at one of the colorful picnic tables, and let it all soak in. Check out the massive blackboard for the specials. Or watch all the action in the huge display kitchen and fish cutting room. The fresh raw bar is impressive, as is Jasper's famous pan-roasted lobster, the locally caught fish, the fried seafood baskets, the lobster rolls, and the surf and turf. Some of the more unusual menu items include lobster pot stickers with ginger, spicy Bermuda fish and crab chowder made with dark rum, cobb salad with Maine crab, Shack-style fish tacos, lobster and shrimp gumbo, and jerked fish with Jamaican spices slowly cooked over a wood grill. Open for lunch and dinner daily.

Lobster Pounds & Lobster Shacks

Blue Lobster Seafood, 376 Berlin Turnpike, Berlin; (860) 828-5833; bluelobsterseafood.com. Located far from the shore, the Blue Lobster proves you don't have to be on the water to serve impeccably fresh seafood. Munch on some clam and corn fritters while you wait for your lobster, available here in many forms: lobster bisque, lobster salad sandwich, lobster salad plate, lobster rolls, lobster dinners, and a stuffed lobster tail platter. The lobster dinners are served with chowder, fries, and coleslaw. For more than 20 years the lobster rolls have been the big draw, stuffed with lump lobster meat dripping in melted butter. The twin rolls with fries are a true bargain. Open for lunch and dinner daily.

Clam Shacks

Clamp's, Rte. 202, New Milford; no phone; no website. Folks in northwestern Connecticut say Clamp's has been there forever. Well, not quite. A sign on the side of the wood-frame cottage says it was established in 1939. Just about any time it's open, Clamp's is crowded with cars and people. Customers order their clam strips at the walk-up window, pay for the meal, wait for their names to be called, and then take their trays to a shady area where they can eat off the green wooden spool tables. Open daily from late Apr to Labor Day; 11 a.m. to 2 p.m., 5 p.m. to 8 p.m.

Hank's Dairy Bar, 1006 Norwich Rd., Plainfield; (860) 564-2298; hanksdairybar.com. Yet another clam shack with roots that stretch back to the 1950s, Hank's still has an old-fashioned walk-up counter where you can order clam fritters that are served simply in a white paper bag. These oddly shaped fritters are lightly fried, soft and doughy, filled with chunks of clams. They are also known for their secret-recipe coleslaw. A blast from the past, still family owned and operated. Hank's neon sign alone is worth the trip. Open for lunch and dinner. Closed Mon.

Seafood Markets

City Fish Market, 884 Silas Deane Hwy., Wethersfield; (860) 522-3129; cfishct.com. Longevity speaks volumes when you're looking for the best place to spend your money. City Fish has been building its sterling reputation since 1930 with four generations of the Anagnos family aiming to please all their customers. This is a big facility with plenty of room for all kinds of seafood, including live lobsters weighing as much as 10 pounds each. Like many other fish markets, this spot also has a restaurant on the premises, and they do a brisk take-out business. Their website has dozens of tempting recipes. The fish market is open Mon through Fri from 7 a.m. to 6 p.m., Sat from 7 a.m. to 5 p.m.

The Fish Market, 1307 Main St., Willimantic; (860) 423-6455; thefishmarketct.com. It's pretty hard to miss the bright turquoise building that houses The Fish Market. With plenty of free parking, this fresh seafood store doubles as a take-out restaurant with all the usual fare on the one-page lunch and dinner menu. A huge lobster tank on the premises allows customers to select the perfect crustacean, and children always enjoy watching the live lobsters climb on top of one another. With an hour's notice, they will steam cook your lobsters. Open Mon through Fri from 11 a.m. to 7 p.m., Sat from 10 a.m. to 7 p.m., Sun from 11 a.m. to 5 p.m. (The take-out kitchen is closed Sun.)

Maine Fish Market, 60 Bridge St., Warehouse Point, East Windsor; (860) 623-2281; mainefishmarket.com. You are still in Connecticut, but this market pays homage to Maine and all its great seafood. Since 1980 the Vamvilis family has been in the business of selling a wide variety of fresh seafood: live lobsters, shucked oysters, sea scallops, littleneck clams, salmon, sole, calamari, haddock, and much more. If you call ahead, your lobster can be steam cooked at no charge. With every shrimp purchase you get free cocktail sauce. Open Mon through Thurs from 10:30 a.m. to 9 p.m., Fri and Sat from 10:30 a.m. to 10 p.m., Sun from noon to 9 p.m.

Number One Fish Market, 2239 State St., Hamden; (203) 624-6171; numberonefish.com. Not far from Yale University, this first-rate fish market is especially popular with local Japanese transplants—high praise for owner Robert McNeil. He makes regular predawn trips to the famous Fulton Fish Market to inspect the fresh catch. When shad roe season begins in early spring, this market offers the boned Connecticut River shad for the short time it is available. Ready-to-cook items include Chilean sea bass in sesame teriyaki marinade and panko-encrusted tilapia. Open Mon through Sat from 9 a.m. to 6 p.m.

Solmar Fish Market, 1860 Park St., Hartford; (860) 232-5694; no website. This is the go-to place if you're cooking Portuguese dishes—they also sell chorizo sausage, and there's a Portuguese bakery next door. The staff is happy to give you cooking tips. Family run, the neighborhood market has an appealing array of whole and filleted fish and the best selection of salt codfish in the city, according to die-hard fans. Open Tues and Wed from 9 a.m. to 6 p.m., Thurs and Fri from 9 a.m. to 7 p.m., Sat from 8 a.m. to 5 p.m.

Swanson's Fish Market, 2439 Black Rock Turnpike; (203) 374-1577; swansonsfish.com. In addition to fresh seasonal seafood and shellfish, Swanson's is especially known for its full-service clam bakes and lobster bakes. The professional staff cooks the seafood on-site, along with fresh corn on the cob and red potatoes. Menu options include shrimp cocktail, steamers, stuffed clams, chowder, coleslaw, dinner rolls, and watermelon for the complete experience. The parking lot is small, and they are very busy on weekends. It's a good idea to call ahead to see what's in stock on that day. Open Mon through Thurs from 9 a.m. to 6 p.m., Fri and Sat from 9 a.m. to 7 p.m., Sun from 10 a.m. to 4 p.m.

CONNECTICUT EVENTS

Connecticut Restaurant Week, connecticutrestaurantweek.com. Restaurant Week is celebrated at restaurants throughout the state in different cities throughout the year, and seafood always plays an important role on the special prix-fixe menus offered. Check the official website for each town's schedules.

March
Old Saybrook Restaurant Week, connecticutrestaurantweek.com. Restaurant Week is celebrated at restaurants throughout Old Saybrook in March, and seafood always plays an important role on the special prix-fixe menus offered.

May

New England Lobster Days, Mystic Seaport, mysticseaport.org.
Lobster lovers won't want to miss this Memorial Day weekend event sponsored by the Rotary Club of Mystic. Lobsters "in the rough" are served with
corn on the cob, coleslaw, and plenty of melted butter for dipping. This
takes place under an open-air boat shed, which allows diners to watch the
boats cruising on the Mystic River with the music of sea shanties in the
air. Admission to the Mystic Seaport Museum is required to attend Lobster
Days. This does not include the price of food. Tickets are sold in various
packages. For more information visit mysticseaport.org.

June

Annual Essex Rotary Shad Bake, essexrotary.com. In the heart of
shad country, the Essex Rotary Club sponsors this annual shad bake, rain
or shine, on the lawn of the Essex Elementary School. Planked shad is the
main dish, accompanied by freshly shucked oysters, clams, and more. In
recent years tickets have been $20 for adults and $10 for children ages 12 to
18, with kids under 12 admitted for free.

August
**Annual Milford Oyster
Festival,** milfordoyster
festival.org. This is an
extraordinary event, not to be
missed by oyster aficionados.
Sweet and salty oysters are
available for tasting in the
East Coast Shellfish Growers
oyster garden, which attracts
tens of thousands of people
every year. Many growers
are on hand to answer your
questions. In addition there
is an oyster-shucking contest
and an oyster-eating contest.
The massive food court offers
all kinds of seafood, not just
oysters.

September

Norwalk Seaport Association Oyster Festival, seaport.org. Oysters, oysters, oysters . . . to shuck, to eat, to learn about. That's what this annual festival is all about, attracting 50,000 people every year to Veterans Park in East Norwalk. For fans of all things nautical, you can tour working vessels and an authentic seaport village. Harbor tours, entertainment, and a tempting international food court round out the schedule of activities. Just some of the seafood offered: lobster, hot-buttered lobster rolls, crab cake sandwiches, oysters and clams on the half shell, chowder, lobster bisque, fried clams, baked stuffed clams, lobster egg rolls, fish-and-chips, oyster and shrimp dinners, and oyster and shrimp po'boy sandwiches. Tickets can be purchased online at seaport.org.

Durham Fair, durhamfair.com. Ever since 1916 the Durham Fair has been a popular fall tradition. Everything you'd expect in a county fair is ready to be enjoyed, and this is now the state's largest agricultural fair. More than 200,000 people attend, when the weather cooperates. All tickets are $10; children under age 12 are admitted free. In recent years the most popular food item at the fair has been the lobster chowder.

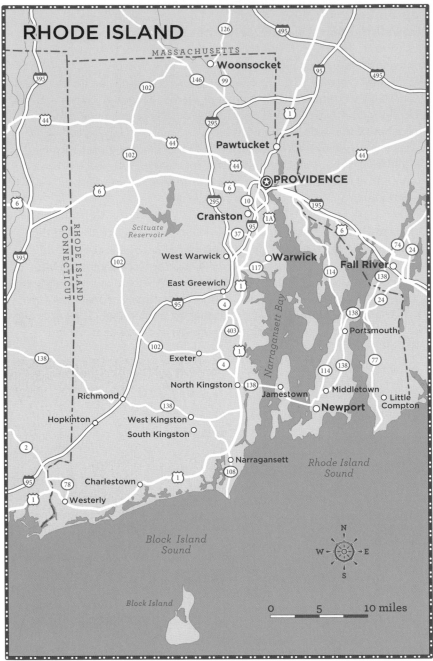

Rhode Island

In 2013 *Travel + Leisure* magazine conducted a national survey and confirmed what locals already knew: Providence, Rhode Island, has the best restaurants and best food in the nation. The unsolicited poll determined that Providence is the number one food destination in the United States, ahead of New York, New Orleans, Chicago, San Francisco, and Boston. The breadth and depth of Providence's culinary offerings are remarkable.

Rhode Island is a fascinating state on so many different levels. First of all, just take a look at the state's map. Narragansett Bay with its 38 islands nearly cuts the state in two with all of the East Bay, including trendy Newport, looking like it really should be part of Massachusetts.

Rhode Island is approximately 42 miles from east to west, and 48 miles from north to south—smaller than some major American cities. It would take 200 states the size of Rhode Island to equal the size of Texas. The state's population is just over 1 million, again smaller than many cities. New York, Los Angeles, Chicago, Houston, Philadelphia, Phoenix, San Diego, and Dallas all have higher populations. Providence is the largest city in Rhode Island and the capital of the state, with a population of only 178,000.

Despite being small, Rhode Island has a very diverse population. If you ask a native to characterize the different parts of the state in general, you would probably hear about the northern part of the state, where America launched its Industrial Revolution. The area is dotted with former mill towns. The northwest corner of the state is Apple Valley, known for its many apple orchards and rural farm stands.

The southern part of the state is called South County, although that's more a state of

Castle Hill Lighthouse, Newport

Rhode Island Food News

Thanks to the Internet, we can connect with countless restaurants almost instantly to learn about their location, menu, and hours of operation. Unfortunately not every website is as current as it should be, so we cannot emphasize this enough: Always call ahead to make sure a restaurant is open. Fortunately there are a number of reputable websites that offer the latest information on restaurants, lodging, events, and local products. For up-to-date listings check out the following online sources:

eatdrinkri.com: An excellent website with information on upcoming food events, restaurants, chefs, farms, cooking classes, and food news in general.

edibleri.com: *Edible Rhody* is a quarterly publication that celebrates the bounty of Rhode Island, season by season.

northeastflavor.com: A New England–based food, wine, and dining monthly magazine featuring interviews with local chefs, recommendations for the finest restaurants and hidden gems, local recipes, and events.

providencejournal.com: The food section of the *Providence Journal* newspaper, published every Wednesday, is an excellent source of what's happening on the Rhode Island food scene.

providenceonline.com: Monthly publications including *Providence Monthly, SO Rhode Island,* and *The Bay* with the latest news on events, food and drink, and more.

rimonthly.com: The state's hottest new restaurants are listed annually, and reviews are printed in this monthly publication.

visitrhodeisland.com: Rhode Island's guide to restaurants, lodging, and activities.

mind than an actual county. This consists of the seaside communities from Westerly heading north along the coast all the way up to Warwick, also referred to as the West Bay because this area is west of Narragansett Bay.

In between the north and south is the capital city of Providence, its suburbs, and the sparsely settled western part of the state. To the east of Providence is the East Bay, made up of well-to-do towns and historic villages located east of Narragansett Bay.

Some local residents claim that the state's intimate size is why Rhode Island has a unique cuisine that hasn't ventured far from its borders. You can find Cajun dishes in

The Breakers, Newport

restaurants that are a thousand miles away from New Orleans, but you'll be hard-pressed to find stuffies, steamers, and clear-broth clam chowder on many menus outside of New England.

It may be the smallest state in the Union, but Little Rhody, as it is called, has more than 400 miles of coastline, thanks in large part to Narragansett Bay. No matter where people live in Rhode Island, they are no more than 30 minutes from the sea, whether it's the uppermost bay or the mighty Atlantic Ocean in the southernmost part of the state. So it's no small wonder that Rhode Island is called the Ocean State. And it is in this area that Little Rhody outdoes all others. Fishermen catch flounder, cod, swordfish, tuna, and much more in Rhode Island Sound. Point Judith in Narragansett is the squid capital of the world. It's no surprise that Rhode Island has many restaurants that specialize in fresh seafood. This guide explores that culinary landscape, from shabby-chic clam shacks to high-end dining establishments. For folks who love to cook, we've also listed the state's best seafood markets. Welcome to the Ocean State!

SOUTH COUNTY (FROM WESTERLY TO WARWICK)

South County is not a real county but a nickname Rhode Islanders have given to the southern half of the state. It's a mix of farmland, suburban homes, and the oceanfront communities that line the shore from Westerly northward to Warwick. Driving along scenic Route 1A, you will come upon quaint seaside villages, miles of white sandy beaches, and marinas filled with sportfishing vessels and pleasure craft.

For information on the many towns that make up South County, visit the South County Tourism Council (southcountyri.com) or these individual websites:

Charlestown Chamber, charlestownrichamber.com
East Greenwich Chamber, eastgreenwichchamber.com
Narragansett Chamber, narragansettri.com/chamber
North Kingstown Chamber, northkingstown.com
Southern Rhode Island Chamber, srichamber.com
Westerly Chamber, westerlychamber.org

Seafood Restaurants

Westerly/Watch Hill

BRIDGE, 37 Main St., Westerly; (401) 348-9700; restaurantinri .com. *Charming* best describes BRIDGE, a fine dining restaurant overlooking the Pawcatuck River in Westerly, close to the Connecticut state line. This former wheelhouse used to power a prosperous textile mill. Today it's a stylish restaurant offering local produce and fresh native seafood traditional American cuisine. The blackboard specials reflect what has arrived on that day at the kitchen's back door. BRIDGE claims it has the largest outdoor dining area in the city and the only raw bar in Westerly. The only dog-friendly patio in town is tucked behind the restaurant on its own small island. Everything you'd expect is on the creative menu. The unexpected includes clam and corn fritters, grilled fish tacos with chipotle aioli, fried shrimp wonton chips with sweet chile sauce, shrimp gumbo, pan-roasted salmon with bacon-horseradish cream, and lobster mac and cheese. Open for lunch and dinner daily, plus Sun brunch from 9 a.m. to 3 p.m.

Nordic Lodge, 178 E. Pasquiset Trail, Charlestown; (401) 783-4515; nordiclodge.com. Imagine all the lobster you can eat . . . that's what the Nordic Lodge offers travelers from around the world who visit this out-of-the-way rustic restaurant by the busload. Of course this comes with a

Rhode Island's Unique Culinary Vocabulary

To better understand some of the descriptions in this guide, we thought it wise to offer a brief explanation of what certain culinary terms mean in Rhode Island.

Chowda: This is how many Rhode Islanders pronounce *chowder*, which comes in three versions. The clear-broth chowder is considered to be real Rhode Island chowder, especially in the southern part of the state. Adding cream or half-and-half to a clear-broth chowder transforms it into creamy New England chowder (also called white chowder), popular throughout New England and beyond. Adding tomatoes and certain seasonings turns it into a red chowder, similar to Manhattan chowder and especially popular in the northern part of Rhode Island.

Clam cakes: These aren't cakes at all but rather fritters, containing bits of chopped-up clams in a heavy batter. They are deep-fried and served with plenty of salt. The perfect clam cake has a light and fluffy interior, studded with bits of clam. Doughier varieties are called "sinkers." You order clam cakes by the dozen, and they come to the table piping hot in a small basket, or in a paper bag if they are ordered "to go" from a seaside clam shack. You simply bite into them, or you can tear them in two so you can dunk your clam cake into a bowl of "chowda."

Steamers: Clams that have been steamed open in a little water or beer. Most people use their fingers to remove the clams from their shells, dip the clams in melted butter, and eat them whole. A steamer consists of a tender, plump belly and a rubbery neck. Some people eat only the belly, biting off the neck and leaving it on their plates. Some restaurants offer fried whole-belly clams as well as clam strips (the rubbery necks that have been dipped in batter and deep-fried).

Stuffies: Short for stuffed clams. Usually served as an appetizer, these are made from the larger quahog clams that have been steamed open and then refilled with a flavorful stuffing made from ground up quahog meat, bread crumbs, and seasonings. Spicy versions also have chorizo sausage added to the stuffing mixture. One uses a fork to eat a stuffy, usually served with lemon wedges and hot pepper sauce on the side.

Chowder and clam cakes, steamers and stuffies—these unique seafood delicacies were always on the menu at shore dinner halls, a dying tradition in Rhode Island. Shore dinner halls were simply big halls on or near the seacoast, where hundreds of people could be seated at long banquet-style tables for full-course shore dinners. That typically included a boiled or steamed lobster with  drawn butter, about a pound of steamers, boiled new potatoes, corn on the cob, and usually watermelon for dessert. One of the few shore dinner halls left in Rhode Island, if not all of New England, is Aunt Carrie's in Narragansett (see page 53 for details).

hefty price and a few rules. The pricing is upward of $100 per person (with lower prices for children) and a time limit of 2 hours. And there's plenty to eat besides lobster: crab legs, fried scallops, fried jumbo shrimp, scallops wrapped in bacon, baked stuffed shrimp, shrimp and scallop scampi, steamed clams, baked cod, jumbo shrimp cocktail, fresh local oysters, littlenecks on the half shell, crab cakes, lobster bisque, clam chowder, shrimp salad, lobster salad, Cajun crawfish salad, marinated mussels, calamari salad, as well as food for land lubbers (such as filet mignon). And all this is all you can eat as well, within your allotted 2 hours. Save room for dessert—there are 18 to choose from, as well as fresh seasonal fruit for the health conscious. Everyone should go to the Nordic Lodge at least once in his or her lifetime. Open for dinner only Fri, Sat, and Sun from late Apr to mid-Dec.

Ocean House, 1 Bluff Ave., Watch Hill; (401) 584-7000; ocean houseri.com. For an extraordinary experience consider the luxurious Ocean House, perched high above Watch Hill with sweeping views of the Atlantic Ocean. This is a very special seaside resort and the first and only AAA Five Diamond hotel in the state. Dining options abound with 7 separate dining venues on the premises, and all feature native Rhode Island seafood. Seasons is fine dining at its best with a farm-to-table menu and a commitment to the ethical use of the sea. An American bistro menu that includes sustainable seafood is available in the Seasons Bar, Seasons Terrace, and the Winter Garden. On the wide veranda overlooking the croquet court, you can sit in an old-fashioned rocking chair, graze on fresh shellfish shucked to order, and sip on a creative cocktail. Adjacent to the pool, with a view of the vast Atlantic, the Seaside Terrace offers al fresco dining under stylish market umbrellas. At lunch the light fare includes salads and sandwiches; in the early evening, cocktails with a sunset view are available. Dune Cottage is an outdoor beach restaurant overlooking the dunes and the surf with a menu of hot and cold sandwiches and chilled soups. The hotel is open 365 days a year; hours vary with each restaurant.

Paddy's Beach Club, 159 Atlantic Ave., Westerly; (401) 596-2610; paddysbeach.com. Nothing says summer like Paddy's Beach Club right on the water at Misquamicut Beach in Westerly. Creative oceanfront dining, specialty drinks, and live entertainment are the big draw. In the summer watch sun-kissed bodies play volleyball just yards from your umbrella table on the deck. Seafood lovers will have their choice of Thai mussels, clam fritters, calamari, and stuffies (here they are topped with cheddar cheese, very unusual). Craving a sandwich? Try the fried tilapia or the lobster roll brightened with a citrus mayo. Tilapia also makes an appearance in the fish tacos with chipotle dressing and black bean corn salsa. Classic New England fare includes clam strips, fish-and-chips, and the sampler plate of fried haddock, clams, scallops, and calamari. Entrees include linguine and clams, oven-roasted haddock, and a lobster boil served with fingerling potatoes and fresh corn on the cob. A children's menu is also available. Open for lunch and dinner every day of the week.

Two Little Fish, Atlantic Avenue, Westerly; (401) 348-9941; no website. Fried seafood lovers, look no more. Located right across the street from the Westerly Town Beach, this is one of the best no-frills places for reasonably priced fresh seafood. You've heard of fast-food restaurants—this is a fast-fish restaurant, from sweet and tender fish-and-chips to delectable fried oysters served with fries and slaw. All the food is served on sturdy paper plates, and the plates overflow with golden fried seafood. The lobster roll also overflows with buttery chunks of lobster. In a hurry? Call ahead, and you can pick up your order at the drive-through window. Senior citizens are offered a lower-priced menu. A children's menu is also available. Open daily for lunch and dinner from May through Sept.

Matunuck/Jerusalem
Cap'n Jack's, 706 Succotash Rd., East Matunuck; (401) 789-4556; capnjacksrestaurant.com. With a serene salt marsh view, Cap'n Jack's is a comfortable, old-fashioned New England restaurant, family owned and run for more than 40 years, just a short stroll to East Matunuck State Beach. They specialize in local favorites such as clam cakes, chowder, fish-and-chips, fresh lobsters, and native steamers. To keep things interesting, they also offer creative specials such as saffron and lemon mussels, drunken littlenecks, and lemon dill swordfish. A house specialty features sautéed lobster meat and green and black olives with roasted red peppers in a cream sherry sauce, served over linguine. The menu is huge and diverse. A children's menu is also available. An on-premise pastry chef keeps the dessert case filled with freshly made cakes, pies, turnovers, and giant éclairs. The brand new Saltmarsh Pub & Raw Bar in a former dining room has a separate menu that includes seafood pizza and spicy calamari salad. Open for lunch and dinner daily in summer, Wed through Sun in the off-season.

Matunuck Oyster Bar

Matunuck Oyster Bar, 629 Succotash Rd., East Matunuck; (401) 783-4202; rhodyoysters.com. When it comes to oysters, it doesn't get any fresher than this. This waterfront restaurant evolved from the Matunuck Oyster Farm, founded in 2002 by Perry Raso. He opened a fish market, with a small restaurant on the side, to help sell his oysters. The restaurant was so successful, it edged out the market for much-needed space. On a warm summer night, be prepared to wait for hours for a table. But the waiting is lots of fun out on the deck, where people have drinks and freshly shucked items from the raw bar. Inside you can belly up to the bar, where the clams and oysters are shucked right before your eyes. Raso is committed to uniting fresh local produce with local seafood to make the freshest dishes imaginable. Dishes are kept simple to allow the natural flavors to come out. But the menu is far from boring. Specials include pan-seared mahimahi with a sweet Asian glaze. The grilled swordfish is topped with lobster tomalley butter. All the classic favorites, such as chowder and fried clams, are also available. Open for lunch and dinner daily.

Tara's Tipperary Tavern, 907 Matunuck Beach Rd., Matunuck; (401) 284-1901; tarasfamilypub.com. A classic hole-in-the-wall joint, almost more bar room than restaurant, Tara's has been making people feel good for decades. Formerly the Joyce Family Pub, this is a not-to-be-missed stop on any tour of coastal Rhode Island. It's the oldest Irish pub in the state. Don't be surprised if someone is singing "Danny Boy" when you order the Matunuck clam "chowda" and clam cakes. Pub fare straight from the sea includes beer-battered fish-and-chips, a basket of golden fried shrimp with fries and slaw, and an impressive seafood platter, very reasonably priced. You can also order a fish sandwich, a clam roll, and a scallop roll, if it's a sandwich you're seeking. A children's menu is available. If you're there in the summer, ask for a table on the rooftop deck with its amazing view of the Atlantic Ocean and Block Island off in the distance. Open for lunch and dinner daily.

Narragansett/Galilee

Aunt Carrie's, 1240 Ocean Rd., Narragansett; (401) 783-7930; auntcarriesri.com. The quintessential seaside restaurant, Aunt Carrie's is pure nostalgia. There really was an Aunt Carrie back in 1920 when the restaurant opened. Four generations of the same family have kept the business going. You enter through old screen doors to either order excellent seafood to go at the walk-up counter, or to be seated inside in one of the few remaining shore dinner halls on the East Coast. A shore dinner is a thing of beauty for seafood lovers—It starts with a bowl of clam chowder and clam cakes, followed by a full order of steamed clams with melted butter, fish-and-chips, and finally a full lobster. Those clam cakes are what have made Aunt Carrie's so famous. The demand for clam cakes is so great that they use a cement mixer to make the clam-studded batter, which is then dropped by the scoop full into hot beef fat. It's not very healthy, but fine in moderation—one of life's guilty pleasures. The old-fashioned desserts are not to be missed, especially the blueberry pie, Indian pudding, and an unbelievable strawberry shortcake available only when native strawberries are in season. A children's menu is available. This is a BYOB establishment, so feel free to bring some beer or wine to go with your seafood. Picnic tables are on the grounds if you prefer to enjoy their award-winning chowder and clam cakes outdoors with a distant ocean view. Open Apr through Sept for lunch and dinner every day except Tues.

Buster Crab's Burger Shack & Beach Bar, 265 Great Island Rd., Narragansett; (401) 284-0218. One of the newer restaurants on the local scene, Buster Crab's is getting great reviews for its laid-back vibe, fun atmosphere, and better-than-average food. Located in the heart of Galilee, a working seaport, this open-air restaurant offers a view of the Block Island ferry coming and going. Folks enjoy sitting outdoors under the fake palm trees as they dine on coconut shrimp, crab rangoon, and lobster quesadilla with tropical drinks on the side. The signature sandwiches are pricey but well worth it, stuffed with lobster or whole-belly clams. In the mood for something different? Try the scallop and bacon roll with Cajun remoulade sauce. Three kinds of chowder are available: Rhode Island clear, creamy New England, and Manhattan. This seasonal place is especially known for its "bodacious" fisherman's platter, overflowing with fried seafood. A children's menu that includes seashell mac and cheese is available. Open for lunch and dinner daily in the summer, closed in winter.

Coast Guard House, 40 Ocean Rd., Narragansett; (401) 789-0700; thecoastguardhouse.com. Steeped in history, the restaurant dates back to 1945 when it was transformed from an old Coast Guard station into a seasonal oceanfront restaurant. Present owners made it a year-round establishment and added a large deck that offers a spectacular view of Narragansett Town Beach and Newport off in the distance. The staff is trained to make customers feel as though they were on a cruise ship. Fresh seafood is procured daily from the nearby Port of Galilee. The "day boat" entree is one of their most popular. The lobster bisque is scented with vanilla. The lobster crepes are flavored with cheddar and spicy aioli. The lobster ravioli is finished in brandy cream. For simpler fare there's everything from fish-and-chips to grilled

Sweet, Sour and Spicy Shrimp at the Coast Guard House

swordfish. The menu says "all plates can surf"—that is, you can have lobster, shrimp, or scallops added to any selection. Open for lunch and dinner daily, with an award-winning brunch on Sun.

George's of Galilee, 250 Sand Hill Cove Rd., Narragansett; (401) 783-2306; georgesofgalilee.com. George's of Galilee is a Rhode Island institution. They come by the busloads to sit in this recently renovated waterfront restaurant to dine while watching boats of all sizes plying the channel that runs between Galilee and Jerusalem. There's room for everyone in the 5 dining rooms, plus the wildly popular take-out window. It's fun to take your chowder and clam cakes right over to Salty Brine State Beach, just steps away. In the summer the covered deck on the second floor is usually crowded with folks having a good time with Jimmy Buffett music playing in the background. The menu is huge, offering all the usual suspects and then some: creamy dill seafood chowder, mussels steamed in Narragansett beer, and chilled lobster artichoke dip for starters. George's specialties include seafood potpie and baked stuffed flounder topped with lobster sauce. Keeping up with modern tastes, sushi and sashimi are now also available. Open for lunch and dinner daily.

Jimmy's Portside, 321 Great Island Rd., Narragansett; (401) 783-3821; no website. Location, location, location. Jimmy's Portside is right across the street from the Block Island Ferry. A throwback to years ago, this is a quaint seasonal restaurant with an always-busy walk-up window, where you can get fresh seafood that was on one of the nearby fishing boats just hours ago. Now in its third generation of ownership by the Petrella family, the Portside is famous for its clam cakes and chowder, fried clams, steamers, and lobster. You can eat inside the simple, almost austere large dining room, which hasn't changed in years, or at picnic tables where you can watch island-bound people race to catch the ferry. Open for lunch and dinner daily from late spring to early Nov.

Mariner Grille, 142 Point Judith Rd., Narragansett; (401) 284-3282; marinergrille.com. This is the kind of place that will make everyone happy, from grandparents to children, from folks who like their food plain and simple to people with gourmet appetites. For instance, the menu offers your basic calamari, and then there's the exotic lemongrass calamari. All the seafood your heart desires is available, often with tantalizing twists, such as Tuscan clams and garlic-zapped shrimp for appetizers; strawberry balsamic salmon, jambalaya, and drunken scallops for entrees. The fish-and-chips is exceptional, as is the Down East fisherman's platter. Specials, such as sea scallops served over truffle risotto and topped with lemon buerre blanc sauce, are posted daily on the website. A children's menu is also available. The rave reviews go on and on. Tucked inside Mariner's Square, many fans say this is a hidden gem with a lively bar scene. Open for lunch and dinner daily.

Spain, 1144 Ocean Rd., Narragansett; (401) 783-9770; spainri.com. One of the most successful restaurants in the area, Spain is almost always packed with people in search of the good life. A carafe of sangria and a fine mix of French, Italian, and Spanish cuisines make that possible at Spain. Be prepared to wait for a table in their large lounge area. There are two beautiful dining rooms, one on the second floor with a distant ocean view, plus a charming flower-filled courtyard in the summer. The food is just as beautiful, especially the paella dishes, an assortment of shellfish baked in saffron rice. The varied menu offers plenty of seafood: twin lobsters, scallops in a champagne cider sauce, a spicy shrimp casserole, a simple fillet of sole, and North Atlantic salmon in a citrus saffron glaze. Highly recommended is the Basque-style fillet of sole served with clams, mussels, and shrimp in a white wine sauce. If you're lucky, you'll dine in the courtyard where an outdoor fireplace crackles and pops, keeping the mosquitoes away. Open Tues through Thurs 4 to 10 p.m., Fri and Sat from 4 to 10:30 p.m., Sun from 1 to 9 p.m.

Trio, 15 Kingstown Rd., Narragansett; (401) 792-4333; trio-ri.com. Part of the prestigious Newport Restaurant Group, Trio is a handsome restaurant just a stone's throw from Narragansett Town Beach. This is a local "chain" that is very serious about obtaining only the freshest fish with strong support for local "day boat" fishermen. They also believe strongly in the warmth and tradition of family dinners. The open kitchen creates extraordinary food that can be enjoyed inside or out on the patio. The menu offers authentic New England seafood with South County influences, such as calamari from Galilee and baked local oysters. The linguine is served with clams, the tortelloni with lobster. The fisherman's stew comes with grilled bread for sopping up the tasty broth. Jasmine rice accompanies the yellow fin tuna with a citrus *beurre blanc*. One of the most popular items is the lobster roll livened up with lemon-chive mayo. A children's menu is also available. Open Mon through Thurs from 4 to 9 p.m., Fri from 4 to 10 p.m., Sat from 3 to 10 p.m., and Sun from noon to 8 p.m.

Twin Willows, 865 Boston Neck Rd., Narragansett; (401) 789-8153; twinwillowsnarragansett.com. If you went to college in Rhode Island, chances are you've been to Twin Willows, a popular watering hole, which in recent years has evolved into a family restaurant. They pride themselves on their fresh local seafood, shellfish, and produce, so everything is fresh from the ocean and farm to plate. Signature dishes include lobster, steamers, chowder, clam cakes, stuffies, and one of the best lobster rolls in the state. Some restaurants offer twin lobsters—this is one of the very few that offers triple lobsters. Even more decadent is the lobster stuffed with scallops and served with mac and cheese. The littlenecks Italiano are worth a try, made with sausage and white beans, and bread for dipping. The Portuguese-style braised haddock is flavored with chorizo and oregano. The grilled salmon comes with a zesty horseradish-dill sauce. A children's menu is available. Outdoor seating is available, with a peekaboo view of pretty Bonnet Shores. Open for lunch and dinner daily.

East Greenwich/North Kingstown/Wickford
Duffy's Tavern, 235 Tower Hill Rd., Wickford; (401) 295-0073; no website. It's easy to miss Duffy's Tavern, an unassuming roadhouse that serves up some of the best food at reasonable prices you'll ever come upon in your travels. This fun place is known for its bar food, sandwiches, and seafood, with quahog chowder and lobster dishes being the signature dishes. The lobster is almost any way you want it—steamed or baked and stuffed with shrimp and scallops, all the way up to 3 pounds each. Duffy's is also famous for its quahog chili. The Baltimore platter is unusual for Rhode Island, crab cakes and sea scallops baked and topped with a garlicky a la mama sauce. Seasonal specials include seafood Alfredo (lobster, langostinos, and shrimp) and the baked native cod and Atlantic mussels in red basil sauce, both served over linguine. In warm weather you can dine on the patio, where live music is often offered. A children's menu is available. Open for lunch and dinner daily.

Finn's Harborside, 38 Water St., East Greenwich; (401) 884-6363; finnsharborside.com. Formerly known as Harbourside Lobstermania, this is where those in the know go for good food and good times. Located on scenic Greenwich Cove, just about every table inside and out offers a million-dollar view of yachts and powerboats. If you arrive by boat, there's free customer docking at the marina. You can enjoy lunch or dinner at the sprawling restaurant or in the comfort of your boat. Known for its lobsters and local seafood, this waterfront restaurant purchases its fish daily from local fishermen. Various menus are available. Upstairs you can dine on scallops wrapped in bacon, land and sea combinations, and the house specialty: Lobstermania, a baked lobster stuffed with shrimp and scallops. The downstairs menu is a tad more casual with swordfish when in season and sandwiches, including the popular scallop roll. On the deck start with little-necks on the half shell or stuffed quahogs, followed by fish-and-chips or fried clams. Open for lunch and dinner daily in summer; closed Mon, Tues, and Wed in winter.

Nautika, 28 Water St., East Greenwich; (401) 398-7774; nautikari .com. Its name has changed over the years, but this seasonal restaurant has never looked so good, thanks to the Micheletti family. This is where they want you to spend breezy summer days and balmy summer nights. Inside Nautika is dark and stylish. Outside there is plenty of deck seating with a spectacular view of boats of all sizes in the marinas on Greenwich Cove. A special menu of food "designed to travel" is offered to boaters. The regular menu has a definite Italian accent, from the roasted tomato and crab bisque garnished with basil oil to the pappardelle pasta with fresh lobster meat. Fish-and-chips here is called *pesce e patate* and served with a white balsamic coleslaw. The grilled seafood comes with various toppings, including scampi butter. And that classic Italian concoction, tiramisu, is always on the dessert menu. Open for dinner daily from May 1 to Sept.

Plum Point Bistro, 1814 Boston Neck Rd., Saunderstown; (401) 667-4999; no website. One of the newest restaurants in the area, Plum Point Bistro was a hit with customers on day one. It's a family affair there with Ralph Conte as the chef, wife Elisa greeting guests, and their two 20-something children serving food and drinks to an often-packed dining room. The herbs used in cooking come from Elisa's home garden, and don't be surprised if the fish you are eating was caught that morning by Ralph, an avid angler. Just some of the outstanding fare includes rosemary shrimp bruschetta, grilled octopus, tuna tartare, and spaghetti dressed up with garlicky shrimp, native clam sauce, or fruits of the sea. Typical entrees

Linguine in Clam Sauce with Summer Tomatoes at Plum Point Bistro.

are pan-seared summer fluke, cornmeal-dusted native cod, and lobster and seafood stew. In true bistro style, this is a noisy restaurant, due in part to the old-fashioned tin ceiling. For years the Contes have owned and operated award-winning restaurants. Plum Point Bistro is just another jewel in their crown. Open for dinner only every night except Mon.

Jamestown

Chopmist Charlie's, 40 Narragansett Ave., Jamestown; (401) 423-1020. Fabulous seafood at great prices—that's what Chopmist Charlie's promises its customers. Located in the heart of quaint Jamestown, this is the quintessential New England restaurant with nautical decor galore. The essentials here are the chowder, clam cakes, and stuffies. The lobster in the lobster bisque comes from Zeek's Creek, a wonderful local fish market. The menu is just big enough to please everybody, from the simple (fish-and-chips) to the complex (boneless breast of chicken with two jumbo shrimp in a light Dijonaise sauce with artichoke hearts). Pasta dinners include a creamy lobster Alfredo, shrimp scampi over linguine, and scallops Florentine over fettuccine. For lighter appetites there's an excellent array of sandwiches, including an awesome fried oyster roll. Much like the bar in the TV show *Cheers*, Chopmist Charlie's is the kind of place where everyone knows your name if you are there more than once. Open for lunch and dinner daily.

Jamestown Fish, 14 Narragansett Ave., Jamestown; (401) 423-FISH (3474); jamestownfishri.com. The newest kid on the restaurant block that runs through Jamestown is simply called Fish, for that is the specialty of the house. And what a serene and stylish house it is. The blue and white clapboard building is pure New England. Inside there's a main dining room with an intimate bar where the food is simply sublime: Dover sole, locally caught tuna seared rare on a special grill, and Maine halibut. Upstairs at the Bridge bar and deck, small plate offerings include a spicy fish soup, clams and oysters on the half shell, mussels steamed in white wine, and European cuttlefish. In the summer the patio menu includes pizza topped with clams and chorizo, and simple main dishes such as a lobster roll on a brioche bun and an amazing surf and turf combination of lobster salad and Kobe beef sliders. Equally impressive is this restaurant's wine list. Open for dinner only. Hours change with the seasons, so it's wise to call ahead.

Jamestown Oyster Bar, 22 Narragansett Ave., Jamestown; (401) 423-3380; no website. It seems like this place has been a fixture forever in the village of Jamestown. Housed in a quaint, cedar shingle–sided building, the small restaurant has a combined bar-dining area. Oysters have a starring role on the menu, supported by steamers, mussels, littleneck clams, and seafood entrees. As you step outside, look to your left. The harbor beckons, with a view of Newport off in the distance. Open for lunch and dinner daily in summer; open for lunch and dinner Thurs through Mon in winter.

Warwick

Legal Sea Foods, 2099 Post Rd., Warwick; (401) 732-3663; legal seafoods.com. Legal Sea Foods is a small East Coast chain of restaurants that got its start in Boston, Massachusetts. It is known for its New England clam chowder, which has been served at the inaugural festivities dating back to President Ronald Reagan in 1981. Legal, as it is called, is also known for having more than 40 varieties of fish and shellfish on the menu year-round. Just some of those offerings include jumbo lump crab cakes, double stuffed baked shrimp, swordfish piccata, nutty Atlantic salmon, Boston scrod, and Portuguese fisherman's stew. Fried seafood is available as well as surf and turf items and lobsters weighing up to 2½ pounds each. If you prefer, your rainbow trout or yellow fin tuna can be cooked over a wood-burning grill. Every year an oyster festival is held here from mid-September to mid-October. A children's menu is also available. In warm weather a patio offers al fresco dining. Legal Sea Foods is located very close to the state airport and local hotels. Open for lunch and dinner daily.

Top of the Bay in Warwick, 898 Oakland Beach Ave., Warwick; (401) 921-FOOD; topofthebayrestaurant.com. With a fabulous ocean view, Top of the Bay is an ideal spot for lunch or dinner when you're craving seafood. Lunch favorites include a Key West cobb salad with baby shrimp, a generous portion of lobster meat in a fresh torpedo roll, baked stuffed shrimp, and baked scrod. Dinner can start with steamed mussels served with garlic toast for dipping into the broth or littlenecks on the half shell with cocktail sauce, followed by broiled scallops Nantucket, shrimp scampi with rice pilaf, or a grilled rib-eye steak topped with sea scallops and crabmeat. In the summer you can drink and dine on the upper deck and patio. Inside or out, just about every table offers a view of Narragansett Bay. Open for lunch and dinner daily.

Clam Shacks

Champlin's, 256 Great Island Rd., Narragansett; (401) 783-3152; champlins.com. Located over Champlin's Seafood Market, you know that the food at this rustic clam shack is going to be super fresh. Sit at wooden picnic tables on the upper deck for a fascinating view of the state's biggest fishing fleet arriving with the catch of the day. Indoor seating is also available. Champlin's is known for its clear chowder, golden clam cakes, steamed clams, lobster dinners, fish-and-chips, and other fried seafood offerings. Open daily in summer from 11 a.m. to 9 p.m. Open in winter Fri through Sun from 11 a.m. to 7 p.m., Mon from 11 a.m. to 6 p.m.

Hitching Post, 5402 Post Rd. (Rte. 1), Charlestown; (401) 364-7495; hitchingpostrestaurant.com. Since 1950 this humble roadside restaurant, just minutes from local beaches, has been serving up some of the best clam chowder, clam cakes, and fried fritters in the area. In addition you can get seafood sandwiches and full dinners, including shrimp in a basket and an impressive fisherman's platter. A children's menu is available. In addition to a modest dining room, there's a pretty garden area with picnic tables. Open with seasonal hours for lunch and dinner daily in summer, in the off-season Sun only from noon to 8 p.m.

Iggy's Doughboys & Chowder House, 889 Oakland Beach Ave., Warwick; (401) 737-9459; 1157 Point Judith Rd., Narragansett; (401) 783-5608 (seasonal); iggysdoughboys.com. What's not to like about a place called Iggy's? The Gravino family, owners, likes to say, "it's always summer at Iggy's." The original Iggy's is located at Oakland Beach

Are They Clam Cakes or Clam Fritters?

Most places in Rhode Island call them clam cakes. The Hitching Post in Charlestown calls them clam fritters. It's more of a regional thing to call them cakes. Fritters, by definition, are deep-fried bits of batter that contain meat or fruit. So the folks at the Hitching Post call them fritters because it is more universally known. However, if you go to their walk-up window and order a dozen clam cakes, they won't question or correct—they know what you want!

with beautiful views of Narragansett Bay from the indoor dining room and the outdoor patio. A summer-only Iggy's can be found in Narragansett. Either place you can eat in or take out. In addition to all the usual clam shack fare, Iggy's makes wonderful doughboys, warm and dusted with sugar, the perfect dessert. Iggy's in Warwick is open daily from 11 a.m. to 8 p.m. (1 hour later on Fri and Sat) year-round. Iggy's in Narragansett is open daily from Mar to Columbus Day.

Jim's Dock, 1175 Succotash Rd., Jerusalem; (401) 783-2050; jims dock.com. A favorite with locals and boat owners, Jim's Dock is one of Rhode Island's best-kept secrets. It doesn't get any more authentic than this, sitting right on the dock, surrounded by boats of all sizes. Clam chowder, fried whole-belly clams, clam cakes, and stuffed quahogs are the big draw. At lunch you can try the crab cake sandwich. At dinner you can have the grilled swordfish or a boiled lobster dinner. This is a BYOB establishment. Later you can charter a boat with a fishing guide at the marina. Very dog friendly. Cash only. Seasonal operation from May to Oct (open for breakfast, lunch, and dinner daily in good weather).

Johnny Angel's, 523 Charlestown Beach Rd., Charlestown; (401) 419-6732; johnnyangelsclamshack.com. An authentic New England clam shack, Johnny Angel's is a bit off the beaten path but definitely worth finding. You order your fried clams from the take-out window, and you dine in nice weather on the deck at the rear of the clam shack. The clam cakes come highly recommended along with the clam chowder, lobster roll, and fried seafood platters. Wash it all down with Del's Lemonade, another Rhode Island summer tradition. Open daily for lunch and dinner June through Sept.

Monahan's Clam Shack by the Sea, 190 Ocean Rd., Narragansett; (401) 782-2524; monahansri.com. Perched right on the water next to Narragansett's famed sea wall, Monahan's often has long lines of customers ordering clam chowder and clam cakes to eat at nearby picnic tables. With a spectacular view of Narragansett Bay, this is pretty hard to beat. Monahan's claims to have Rhode Island's most affordable lobster roll. All the usual clam shack fare is on the menu, plus coconut shrimp and fried oysters. Open every day from 11 a.m. to 8 p.m. between Memorial Day and Labor Day; in early spring and late fall, Fri through Tues from 11 a.m. to 7 p.m.; closed in winter.

Seafood Markets

Captain's Catch Seafood, 1702 Mineral Spring Ave., North Providence; (401) 353-FISH; 1 Centerville Rd., Warwick; (401) 738-6762; captainscatchseafood.com. Captain's Catch brings its seafood in from Boston, New Bedford, and Point Judith. More than 300 seafood items are on display, including a varied line of prepared appetizers and entrees. Hot seafood items are available for takeout every Friday, from classic fish-and-chips to fried smelts. Open Mon through Sat from 9 a.m. to 6 p.m., Fri until 7 p.m., Sun from 9 a.m. to 1 p.m.

Champlin's Seafood, 256 Great Island Rd., Narragansett; (401) 783-3152; champlins.com. Commercial fishing vessels bring in fresh seafood daily at the landing docks at the rear of this market in Galilee, a village in Narragansett. Founded 70 years ago, Champlin's is a no-frills operation with a cement floor, tanks of lobsters you can hand select, and fresh fish and shellfish on ice. Frozen chowders and stuffies are available, as well as smoked fish and pickled herring. Open daily from 9 a.m. to 6 p.m.

Dockside Seafood Marketplace, 2275 Warwick Ave., Warwick; (401) 921-5005; docksideseafoodri.com. With its own boats bringing in fresh seafood from Narragansett Bay and the deep sea, Dockside also offers fresh live lobsters from Maine and king crab legs from Alaska. Day boat catches of fresh fish are filleted at the store daily. This market is especially known for its deeply discounted weekly specials. Open Mon through Fri from 9 a.m. to 6 p.m., Sat from 9 a.m. to 5 p.m., Sun from 9 a.m. to 4 p.m.

Ferry Wharf Fish Market, 296 Great Island Rd., Narragansett; (401) 782-8088; thelobsterguy.com. "Ship to shore to you" is their motto. This fish market is owned by Captain Timothy "The Lobster Guy" Handrigan, who has been a lobsterman for more than 30 years. They offer lobsters, crabs, swordfish, tuna, shrimp, scallops, mussels, and clams. To keep everything fresh, the staff is happy to pack your order on ice in a foam cooler. Open from May to Jan, Mon through Fri from 9 a.m. to 5 p.m., Sat and Sun from 9 a.m. to 6 p.m.

The Fishery, 271 Post Rd., Westerly; (401) 322-7700; westerly fishery.com. Fresh and freshly frozen fish and seafood is on display—

lobsters, shellfish, steamers, clams, and native fish. Prepared foods and deli items are also available. Owner Mike Pugliese is often on hand to answer all your questions, from what fish are in season to how long you should steam a lobster. Open daily from 10 a.m. to 6 p.m., with later hours in summer.

Gardner's Wharf Seafood, 170 Main St., Wickford; (401) 295-4600; 641 Warwick Ave., Warwick; (401) 781-CLAM; gardners wharfseafood.com. Live lobsters, fresh fish, and shellfish can be found in the quaint Gardner's Wharf Seafood in Wickford, where boats have been pulling right up to the back door with their fresh catch every day for 70 years. The bounty from local waters is unloaded, processed, and available for sale at both locations. They also carry grocery items related to seafood and prepared foods such as clam chowders, stuffed scallops, stuffed quahogs (mild and spicy), and seafood salads. A full-time cook named Picasso is available for custom orders. Open daily. In Wickford, Mon through Sat from 9 a.m. to 6 p.m., Sun from 9 a.m. to 5 p.m. In Warwick, Mon through Thurs and Sat from 10 a.m. to 6 p.m., Fri from 10 a.m. to 8 p.m., Sun from 10 a.m. to 4 p.m.

Market by the Sea, Rte. 1, Charlestown; (401) 322-0232; no website. For half a century the tiny Market by the Sea has been sitting by the side of Route 1, along with other charming ramshackle buildings—Henry's for fresh fruit and vegetables and Ramblin' Rose for antiques. Ever since Liz Messemger took over in 2012, this seafood market has been doing a brisk business thanks to reasonable prices and her delicious prepared foods. In addition to the fresh fish and shellfish on display, Liz offers snail salad, stuffies, stuffed scallops, salmon burgers, crab cakes, clams casino, and scallops wrapped with bacon. While browsing, you can sample her clear clam chowder and shrimp cocktail. A seasonal operation so it's wise to call ahead to check on their hours.

Ocean Catch Seafood, 566 Kingstown Rd., Wakefield; (401) 789-3474; no website. The new kid on the block, Ocean Catch specializes in fresh seafood nicely arranged in a sparkling 50-foot display case. This new gourmet seafood market offers a wide variety of fresh fish, shellfish, live crabs, marinated salads, prepared entrees, ready-to-bake appetizers, stuffed lobsters in any size, and gourmet platters (with advance ordering). Open Mon through Wed from 9 a.m. to 6 p.m.; Thurs and Fri from 9 a.m. to 7 p.m.; Sat from 9 a.m. to 6 p.m.; and Sun from 9 a.m. to 4 p.m.

Rhode Island Clambakes

An authentic Rhode Island clambake is the quintessential summer dining experience. It should take place outdoors, preferably on a beach or at least near the shore. Traditionally the key ingredients include fresh lobsters, steamed clams, potatoes, and corn on the cob. Additional items might include littlenecks, mussels, sausage or hot dogs, and brown bread. Chowder is always served as the first course, and watermelon is the preferred dessert.

The essential clambake items are placed in huge trays. A bonfire is built on-site with local hardwoods. Large stones are added, and the fire is lit. The bakemaster and his crew rake out the fire for an even spread of the burning embers and hot rocks. Seaweed from local beaches is placed on top of the stones to create steam. The huge trays of the lobsters with all the fixings are placed on top of the seaweed. Heavy tarps are placed over the trays to keep the steam in for that unique clambake flavor. When the bakemaster declares the food is all cooked, the tarps are uncovered to reveal the bright red lobsters. All the food is set up buffet style, and folks line up for their fair share of the feast.

Obviously this is an event for a crowd. If your party of two or more would like to experience a clambake, there are restaurants in Rhode Island that hold public clambakes on specific dates. Reservations are always a must.

The award-winning Castle Hill Inn at 590 Ocean Rd. in Newport offers authentic clambakes on a monthly basis in the summer, usually on Thursday. The event begins at 6:30 p.m., with cocktails and appetizers. Guests can play bocce or croquet on the lawn, or sit in classic Adirondack chairs to relax while Chef Karsten Hart and his team prepare the bake. Their fire pit sits on the far edge of the lawn on a bluff with sweeping views of the Pell-Newport Bridge.

Served on beautifully set tables on the lawn, dinner includes a traditional clam chowder with black pepper biscuits, followed by the family-style clambake: steamed local lobsters, chorizo and peppers, sweet local corn, potatoes with butter and sea salt, steamed littlenecks, crispy baguette with drawn butter, and shaved red cabbage slaw with apple cider vinaigrette. For dessert, apple crisp and watermelon aqua fresca are served. Guests may substitute a smoked chicken breast with sausage and local greens for the lobster upon request. The cost is upward of $100 per person plus tax and gratuity. For more information or to make reservations, call (401) 849-3800 or visit castlehillinn.com.

Every Friday night throughout the summer, Ocean House at 1 Bluff Ave. in Watch Hill hosts popular clambakes on its private beach, with an ever-amazing view of the Atlantic Ocean. Starting at 6 p.m., the event includes cocktails, beer, wine, and a buffet. The cost is $85 for adults, $45 for children ages 5 to 12, and free for children ages 4 and younger. For more information call (401) 584-7010 or visit oceanhouseri.com.

If you're interested in having a private clambake with your own crowd (usually the minimum is 25), there are a number of professional clambake companies that cater such events, either on their premises or yours:

The Company Picnic Company, North Kingstown; (401) 295-7420; thecompanypicnicco.com

Compton Clambakes, Little Compton; (401) 635-4114; comptonclambakes.com

Kempenaar's Clambake Club, Middletown; (401) 847-1441; newportclambakes.com

The Lobster Guy, Narragansett; (866) 788-0004; thelobsterguy.com

McGrath Clambakes, Newport; (401) 847-7743; riclambake.com

Yawgoo Bakes & Barbecues, Slocum; (401) 372-2575; yawgoobakes.clickforward.com

Smitty's Seafood Market, 641 Warwick Ave., Warwick; (401) 781-2526; no website. Known for their friendly customer service, Smitty's is happy to pack your cooler to keep your purchases fresh. Families enjoy stopping in to see the giant lobsters in the tank. Fried seafood dishes are available for takeout every Wed and Fri. Open Mon through Thurs from 10 a.m. to 6 p.m.; Fri from 10 a.m. to 7 p.m.; Sat from 10 a.m. to 5 p.m.; and Sun from 10 a.m. to 2 p.m.

Zeek's Creek Seafood Market, 194 North Rd., Jamestown; (401) 423-1170; no website. For close to 30 years, locals have been stopping in at this weather-beaten shack by the side of the road for fresh fish. And now some smart restaurant chefs have also been known to get their fish—and fishing advice—from the owner, Greg Zeke, a commercial fisherman well-known for his angler achievements. Open seasonally from late spring to early fall.

PROVIDENCE & POINTS NORTH

As the state capital, Providence is the center of activity for all of Rhode Island and is called the Renaissance City for its transformation in recent decades. It used to be a dirty and neglected city that people drove through on their way to Boston or New York. Today it is a vibrant, exciting city with preserved architecture, a thriving arts scene, a collection of well-respected colleges, and a world-class restaurant scene.

In 2013 *Travel + Leisure* magazine declared Providence the best food city in the United States. A national poll determined that this little city (population 178,000) has the best food and the best restaurants in the nation.

Dubbed "Divine Providence" in many travel articles, the city has hundreds of restaurants waiting to be experienced, from neighborhood joints known for their fish-and-chips to the famous Italian restaurants on Federal Hill serving lobster ravioli, from ethnic establishments with their exotic seafood concoctions to trendy cafes and bistros dishing up everything from down-home comfort food to cutting-edge creations. The city even has a clam shack or two (see page 80), and a bevy of seafood markets in the communities around Providence are well stocked with all your seafood needs.

For additional information visit providenceri.com, the official website of the capital city with detailed visitor information including listings for more than 100 restaurants.

Seafood Restaurants

Bluefin Grille, 1 Orms St., Providence; (401) 272-5852; marriott providence.com. Located inside a Marriott hotel, the Bluefin Grille has been serving up some mighty fine seafood for years under the direction of Executive Chef Franco Paterno. The family-friendly restaurant is known for its large portions at competitive prices. A traditional cream-style chowder is on the menu, as well as the signature pan chowder swimming with littleneck clams and smoked mussels, along with Point Judith calamari in a ginger-lime soy sauce. Sandwiches include an unusual tuna Reuben. The specialty dishes range from Georges Bank scallops over corn and lobster pudding to seared halibut with tarragon vinaigrette. With a focus on simplicity, four types of fish (tuna, arctic char, haddock, and salmon) may be prepared in four ways (pan seared, cast-iron blackened, oven roasted, or fire grilled) with a choice of four sauces (spicy mustard, ponzu sauce, grilled pineapple salsa, and brown butter almondine) and a choice of four sides. In addition, a 3-course prix-fixe menu is offered. Open for breakfast, lunch, and dinner daily.

The Capital Grille, One Union Station, Providence; (401) 521-5600; thecapitalgrille.com. Known primarily for its extraordinary steaks, The Capital Grille is also an outstanding location for impeccably fresh seafood, especially from its award-winning raw bar. Think icy cold Gulf Coast jumbo shrimp and freshly shucked oysters. The seafood is flown in from both coasts and obtained locally whenever possible. At lunch the lobster and crab burger on brioche is pretty hard to beat. A light entree might be the grilled swordfish with lemon-shallot relish. For dinner start with the lobster bisque drizzled with sherry, followed by seared tenderloin with butter-poached lobster tails, or the seared citrus-glazed salmon. Now a national chain, the very first Capital Grille is this one in Providence. It's as handsome as ever with its rich African mahogany paneling and art deco chandeliers. With more than 5,000 bottles of wine in their cellar, there's bound to be one that will please you. Open for lunch Mon through Fri, for dinner daily.

Carrie's Seafood & More, 1035 Douglas Ave., Providence; (401) 831-0066; carrieslobsterri.com. If Carrie's is known for anything, it's the 3-pound lobster that's always on the menu. This massive crustacean can be boiled, stuffed and baked, grilled, or served over linguine. The time-honored offerings include all the basics: chowder, fried Point Judith calamari, crab cakes, clams casino, steamers, littlenecks on the half shell, steamed mussels, and award-winning stuffies. Also known for Italian cuisine, Carrie's makes an excellent clam zuppa (red or white), served with grilled bread for dipping in the zesty broth. Entrees include baked and fried seafood dishes, such as baked stuffed fillet of sole and good old fish-and-chips. The most popular dish on the menu is the baked seafood sampler with clams casino, stuffed mushrooms, scallops, sole, and baked stuffed shrimp. This is a family restaurant through and through; it's been family owned and operated for more than 30 years. An abbreviated to-go menu is available at Carrie's Seafood Express. Open for lunch on Fri only, for dinner Wed through Sat.

CAV, 14 Imperial Place, Providence; (401) 751-9164; cavrestaurant .com. Not a seafood restaurant per se, but without a doubt, the seafood on CAV's menu is sublime. And there is so much to sample, starting with a silky lobster bisque that has a hint of vanilla. Other appetizers include coconut shrimp, calamari with garlic, mussels with a fragrant red curry sauce, pistachio-crusted crab cake (large enough to serve as lunch), and butter-poached lobster over crispy noodles in a lobster sherry fumet. It only gets better with the entrees: sautéed lobster meat over fresh pap-pardelle in a beurre blanc, sashimi quality tuna with wasabi aioli, North Atlantic salmon with a coconut-spinach sauce, and jumbo diver sea scal-lops over lemon zest risotto. The lunch menu is more casual. What does CAV stand for? Cocktails, antiques, and victuals. This historic restaurant is almost magical, and all the antiques and artifacts on display are for sale. Open for lunch and dinner daily, with brunch on Sat and Sun.

Hemenway's Seafood Grill & Oyster Bar, 121 S. Main St., Provi-dence; (401) 351-8570; hemenwaysrestaurant.com. Hemenway's is one of a handful of Providence restaurants that are known for their impec-cably fresh raw bars. This is a very cool restaurant with soaring ceilings, neon signage, and sophisticated nautical decor. The service is outstanding. All the seafood is either locally sourced or flown in daily from around the world. For lunch it's hard to pass up the lobster BLT or the grilled tuna on a toasted sweet roll. At dinner so many options tempt the seafood lover: fried oysters with corn relish for starters, a simple baked scrod, or the complex pan-roasted mahimahi with banana aioli. Other chef specialties include grilled salmon with beluga lentils, pan-roasted arctic char, chili-lime

swordfish, herb-rubbed halibut, prosciutto-wrapped whole
trout, and a classic paella
loaded with seafood and saffron rice. Pasta lovers can
choose between the lobster
ravioli and the lobster mac and
cheese. Open for lunch and
dinner daily.

**McCormick & Schmick's
Seafood Restaurant,** 11
Dorrance St., Providence;
(401) 351-4500; mccormick
andschmicks.com. Located
in the historic Biltmore Hotel,
McCormick & Schmick's has
a mostly seafood menu with
some intriguing dishes, such
as the shrimp kisses appetizer
with Pepper Jack cheese and
wrapped in crispy bacon.
Lunch entrees include shrimp
mac and cheese, salmon riga-

Hemenway's Paella

toni, and crispy fish tacos. For a light entree, try the lobster cobb salad.
Fresh fish simply grilled or broiled is offered at lunch and dinner, especially nice when topped with tropical fruit relish. Signature fish dishes are
the almond-dusted rainbow trout, seared ahi tuna, cashew-crusted tilapia,
and pan-roasted Alaskan halibut. House specialties include shrimp either
buttermilk fried, Cajun barbecued, or stuffed with crabmeat; seared sea
scallops with crab-potato hash; or Maine lobster with roasted potatoes. The
mixed grill selections provide plenty of variety: shrimp paired with grilled
salmon and seared scallops, or filet mignon teamed up with stuffed shrimp.
The happy hour menu from 3:30 to 6 p.m. daily at the bar only can't be
beat. Open for breakfast, lunch, and dinner daily.

Providence Oyster Bar, 283 Atwells Ave., Providence; (401) 272-
8866; providenceoysterbar.com. This is one of the few places in the
city where you have a choice of three chowders: creamy New England,

Fish-and-Chips in the Ocean State

Just about every city and town in Rhode Island has a restaurant that is known for its fish-and-chips, a dish that can be traced back to Great Britain. A regular meal for the working classes, it consists of fish that is battered and deep-fried and served with deep-fried potatoes, called chips. The first fish-and-chip shop was opened in London in 1860. Fish-and-chips became a popular take-away food in England, Ireland, Scotland, and Canada, where it is usually accompanied with tartar sauce and peas. It also is sprinkled with salt and malt vinegar. Years ago the fried fish and potatoes were wrapped in newspaper, but today it is traditionally wrapped with white paper. As people immigrated to the United States, they brought this food tradition with them. Here in the States, most restaurants serve fish-and-chips on paper plates with tartar sauce and coleslaw.

Ye Olde English Fish & Chips, 25 S. Main St., Woonsocket; (401) 762-3637; no website. This is the oldest fish-and-chip restaurant in Rhode Island. In business since 1922, the family-owned Ye Olde (as it is locally known) has a wood-paneled dining room decorated with New England memorabilia. It's also known for its fish cakes, fried scallops, and chowder bar. Open for lunch and dinner Tues through Sat.

Stadium Fish & Chips, 1079 Park Ave., Cranston; (401) 944-0971; no website. A true hole-in-the-wall, the Stadium is another family operation, in business since 1942. There are a

Manhattan red, or clear Rhode Island. The raw bar is top-notch. For something a little different, try an oyster shooter spiked with Bloody Mary mix, vodka, and horseradish. The essentials are all there on the menu, plus some tasty twists, such as the wasabi ginger calamari, shrimp tacos, and po' boy sandwiches at lunch. The dinner menu seems to have it all: coconut shrimp and lobster wontons for starters, followed by East Coast classics such as baked native cod, fried whole-belly clams, and

few tables for dining in, but this is mostly a take-out operation. Everything is made on the premises, from the chowder to the coleslaw. Open for lunch and dinner Wed through Sat.

Whistle Stop Restaurant, 119 Main St., Albion; (401) 333-1143; no website. This place is off the beaten path, but definitely worth discovering with its small-town atmosphere and huge portions. Aficionados say this is the best place for fish-and-chips in the state. The chowder and clam cakes are also excellent for an inland operation. Open for breakfast, lunch, and dinner Wed through Fri; breakfast and lunch Sat and Sun.

a crab cake dinner. The pasta dishes are very tempting: fresh lobster meat over linguine with saffron cream, spicy shrimp puttanesca, and lobster mac and cheese. The chef's specials range from grilled Atlantic swordfish to Chilean sea bass. Sushi is also available. The lower-priced bar menu is worth checking out, with super cheap raw bar items from 4 to 6:30 p.m. every day. Open for lunch Tues through Sat, for dinner Mon through Sat.

Seafood Markets

Captain's Catch Seafood, 1702 Mineral Spring Ave., North Providence; (401) 353-FISH. 1 Centerville Rd., Warwick; (401) 738-6762; captainscatchseafood.com. Captain's Catch brings its seafood in from Boston, New Bedford, and Point Judith. More than 300 seafood items are on display including a varied line of prepared appetizers and entrees. Hot seafood items are available for take out every Friday, from classic fish-and-chips to fried smelts. Open Mon through Sat from 9 a.m. to 6 p.m., Fri until 7 p.m., Sun from 9 a.m. to 1 p.m.

Northern Lobster & Seafood, 1450 Hartford Ave., Johnston; (401) 272-6378; no website. Fans rave about this unassuming market located in a strip mall. The seafood is the freshest around, and prices are affordable, they say. A family operation, the staff is superfriendly to boot. Fish-and-chips and clam cakes are available for take out on Friday. Open Mon through Thurs and Sat from 9 a.m. to 6 p.m., Fri from 9 a.m. to 7 p.m., Sun from 9 a.m. to 1 p.m.

R&D Seafood, 652 Smithfield Rd., Woonsocket; (401) 769-1078; rdseafood.com. R&D stands for Raymond and Doris Charest, who started this market in 1968. The second generation of Charests is now in charge. Daily deliveries of high-quality fish and shellfish ensure customer satisfaction. The knowledgeable staff is another plus. Just about every kind of fresh and frozen seafood product is available, as well as prepared chowders, appetizers, and salads. Open Tues through Thurs from 8 a.m. to 5:30 p.m., Fri from 8 am. to 6 p.m., and Sat from 8 a.m. to 4 p.m.

Wilfred's Seafood, 805 Cumberland Hill Rd., Woonsocket; (401) 769-6260; wilfredseafood.com. Generations of families have been shopping at Wilfred's, where delicacies of the deep are offered at competitive prices. Just about every kind of fish and shellfish is on display, plus an oven-ready line of products made in house, including a deluxe baked stuffed lobster. Open Mon through Wed from 7 a.m. to 5:30 p.m., Thurs and Fri from 7 a.m. to 6 p.m., and Sat from 8 a.m. to 4 p.m.

EAST BAY

As Narragansett Bay extends from the Atlantic Ocean northward to Providence, it nearly slices the state in two with the East Bay area bordering Massachusetts. From gritty East Providence southward to the seaside towns of Tiverton, Bristol, Warren, Barrington, and Middletown, the East Bay is completely different from the rest of the state. *Quaint* and *charming* best describe these historic towns. The nation's oldest Fourth of July parade takes place in Bristol every year. Just about every home along the lengthy parade route has a backyard party, and seafood is always high on the menu.

Many of the restaurants and fish markets in these areas have a Portuguese accent in honor of local residents. And all have a serious appreciation for the bounty of the sea.

For more information contact the Newport & Bristol County Convention & Visitors Bureau at (401) 845-9123 or visit visitrhodeisland.com.

The Boat House in Tiverton

Seafood Restaurants

Boat House, 227 Schooner Dr., Tiverton; (401) 624-6300; boat housetiverton.com. It started out as a seafood shack, evolved into an open-air eatery, and is now a handsome year-round restaurant that celebrates New England's fresh seafood and local produce. Sophisticated, yet still charming, the romantic Boat House is perched high above the Sakonnet River with a panoramic view of Mount Hope Bay. In the summer there is no better place to watch the sunset than from an Adirondack chair on the patio. Part of the prestigious Newport Restaurant Group, the Boat House offers a seafood-centric menu that includes everything you'd expect, plus some creative fare including lobster fritters with chipotle aioli, pork and clams in a Vinho Verde broth, and baked oysters with Parmesan cream, and that's just for starters. Imaginative entrees include native fluke with lobster-vegetable ragout and pan-roasted scallops with pea risotto. The service matches the fine cuisine. Open for lunch and dinner daily with brunch on Sun from 11 a.m. to 2 p.m.

DeWolf Tavern, 259 Thames St., Bristol; (401) 254-2005; dewolftavern.com. DeWolf Tavern has everything going for it. Located in a renovated stone warehouse, the two-level restaurant overflows with historic charm. You can have a cool summer cocktail on the patio, or light fare in the romantic tavern with its massive stone walls. Upstairs, with a serene water view, you'll dine on contemporary American cuisine prepared by the very talented Sai Viswanath, a chef-owner who has refined his cooking skills as he traveled around the world. Sai is most famous for his lobster popovers, light and airy and filled with lobster sautéed in a light sherry sauce. Other seafood delights are his chorizo-crusted cod with tomato cream, tandoori-marinated swordfish with tamarind vinaigrette, and seafood stew with coconut broth. A 3-course prix-fixe menu is offered Sunday through Thursday nights. DeWolf is located next door to the Bristol Harbor Inn. Open daily for breakfast, lunch, and dinner.

Horton's Seafood, 809 Broadway, East Providence; (401) 434-3116; hortonsseafood.com. It started out in 1945 as a fish market, and then in 1963 the Horton family began serving fish-and-chips and fried clams for take out that customers raved about. In 1988 the place was remodeled for eat-in business, and folks today are still raving about the food. This is a cozy neighborhood restaurant with friendly service and affordable prices. The clam chowder (clear, red, or white) makes for a nice lunch with clam cakes. In addition to seafood sandwiches, there are baked and fried dinners. On the baked side you can have scrod, scallops, stuffed shrimp, swordfish, stuffed sole, mahimahi, tilapia, salmon, or the baked seafood platter. Fried items include all the usual plus oyster plates and even a smelt plate. Grab a copy of their online menu, and you'll find coupons for some real meal deals. Open for lunch and dinner Wed through Sat.

Lobster Pot, 119-121 Hope St., Bristol; (401) 253-9100; lobsterpotri .com. One of Rhode Island's premier waterfront restaurants, the Lobster Pot overlooks Bristol Harbor and Narragansett Bay in the charming historic town of Bristol. Traditional New England fare has been served here since 1929. Quahog chowder, lobster bisque, and lobster stew make for a fine lunch, as does the grilled shrimp and scallop salad with smoked Gouda. Dinner gets off to a good start with the oysters Rockefeller and the steamed mussels with saffron cream. Fried seafood is offered, as is as broiled scrod and fillet of sole. The Atlantic salmon and swordfish can be grilled, broiled, or blackened. Specialties include pepper-seared tuna steak, bouillabaisse, tempura shrimp with coconut, and curried salmon fillet. Lobster lovers have their choice of lobster done up 10 different ways. Open year-round, you can have a summer lunch on the patio or a winter dinner by the fireplace. Open for lunch and dinner daily.

Persimmon, 31 State St., Bristol; (401) 254-7474; persimmon bristol.com. One of the very finest restaurants in the state, Persimmon is the creation of Champe Speidel, the award-winning chef-owner. This is a modern American bistro with a seasonal menu. The food here is clearly on a higher plane. Warm oysters on the half shell are served with wakame seaweed butter and ginger oil. Agnolotti is paired with buttered lobster and grilled native sweet corn. Sea scallops and octopus marry in a seviche with Meyer lemon—and those are just the appetizers. For the main event, a crispy skin striped bass fillet comes to the table with a ragout of mussels and littleneck clams in a smoky tomato-shellfish broth, and a pan-seared halibut fillet swims in a red wine sea sauce. Persimmon is pricey, but definitely worth it. With only 38 seats, reservations are a must. Open for dinner Tues through Sat (Jan through Apr) and Tues through Sun (May through Dec).

Keep on Truckin'

The profusion of food trucks in Rhode Island gives new meaning to the term "road food." New vendors seem to pop up every week, especially in downtown Providence. Everything from house-made sausages and meat loaf sandwiches to gourmet grilled cheese and Korean barbecue are on the various menus. Down in South County, the food trucks specialize in seafood. There are no set schedules or permanent locations for these mobile eateries. Most trucks use social media to let their fans know where they can be found on a particular day.

Blue Lobster: Specializing in all things lobster, especially lobster rolls. Connected to the Coast Guard House in Narragansett. Can be followed on Twitter @Coastguardhouse.

Clam Jammers: Specializing in seafood fresh off the boats in Galilee. The bright red truck is often seen in downtown Providence, especially in the off-season. Can be followed on Facebook or call (401) 783-9600 for latest location.

Plouf Plouf Gastronomie: Specializing in rustic French cuisine, this truck is known for its lobster brioche and grilled salmon steak with citrus balsamic glaze. Based in Bristol. For the menu visit ploufploufgastronomie.com or call (401) 236-1937.

Roxy's Lobster: Specializing in lobster rolls, fish sandwiches, clam cakes, clam chowder, and lobster bisque, Roxy's Lobster is connected to Monahan's in Narragansett. Can be followed on Twitter @ROXYSLobster.

Shuckin' Truck: Specializing in oysters and other shellfish served raw on the half shell, this truck is based in Wakefield but can be found in multiple locations. Call (401) 741-5953, or send an e-mail to dave@saltpondoysters.com.

Stella Blues, 50 Miller St., Warren; (401) 289-0349; stellabluesri
.com. Casual sophistication best describes this upscale pub, a true neighborhood restaurant. Located in the heart of historic Warren, near the waterfront, Stella Blues has an enclosed porch with a view of the Warren River.
You'll find a great deal of seafood on the menu, beginning with crab-stuffed
portabello mushrooms and a trio of seafood (fresh lobster salad, jumbo
lump crab seviche, and shrimp cocktail) for appetizers. The more exciting
entrees are the seafood jambalaya, salmon with dill butter, and swordfish
Roma. Artisan ciabatta sandwiches are on the lunch menu along with a
couple of entrees: jumbo shrimp scampi and zesty mussels zuppa, both
served over cappellini. Not surprisingly the color scheme is blue at Stella
Blues. In warm weather you can sit outside at pub-height tables. Open for
lunch and dinner Tues through Sun.

Tyler Point Grille, 32 Barton Ave., Barrington; (401) 247-0017;
tylerpointgrille.com. Stylish inside and out, the Tyler Point Grille is
tucked behind busy boatyards and the Barrington Yacht Club. Arriving
by boat? Call the Striper Marina (401-245-6121) to reserve a spot for docking. In warm weather you can dine on the patio in the shade of a market
umbrella. The interior has nautical touches, and the menu celebrates the
bounty of the sea. Appetizers include seafood chowder, baked littlenecks,
fried calamari, steamed mussels, and fried oysters. House specialties feature stuffed sole, Atlantic haddock, stuffed lobster, pistachio salmon, and
seared sea scallops, each with its own set of accompaniments. A mixed
seafood grill and red snapper are also available. Pasta dishes range from
lobster ravioli to linguine with clams. For lighter appetites small plates of
several dishes are offered as early bird specials Mon through Fri. A children's menu is also available (and kids under age 10 eat free on Sun). Open
for dinner daily.

Wharf Tavern, 215 Water St., Warren; (401) 245-5043; thewharf
tavernri.com. The venerable Wharf Tavern has been serving New England fare since 1955. Perched right on the docks overlooking the Warren
River, the building dates back to the 1700s. Almost every table in the restaurant has a water view. The atmosphere says fine dining, but this is a
casual family eatery. You can arrive by car or boat. You can dine inside or
out in nice weather. The lunchtime favorites include the stuffies, oysters
Rockefeller, steamed mussels, and seafood pizza. At dinnertime the seafood linguine is popular, as is as the pan-seared salmon with a Dijon cream

sauce and the grilled swordfish with herb butter. The house specialty is
lobster Thermidor served with mushrooms and cheese in a tangy sauce,
and the signature dish is the lobster sautéed in butter. A children's menu is
available. Open for lunch and dinner daily.

Clam Shacks

Blount Clam Shack, 335 Water St., Warren; (401) 245-3210. 684
Bullocks Point Ave. Riverside; (401) 628-0485. 371 Richmond St.,
Providence; (401) 228-7746; blountretail.com. You can now find
Blount Clam Shacks in Warren, Riverside, and Providence. Blount offers
the quintessential clam shack experience. It is home of the giant lobster
roll, a full half-pound of all lobster meat. Chowder, clam cakes, stuffies, fried
whole-belly clams, and fish-and-chips round out the basic menu. The more
unusual dishes are the clam cakes made with chorizo, fish Reuben, fish taco
wraps, haddock BLT, and the clambake chowder swimming with clams,
potatoes, chorizo, and corn. A children's menu is also available. Blount
Clam Shack in Providence is open year-round Mon through Thurs from 11
a.m. to 3 p.m. and Fri from 11 a.m. to 8 p.m.; the other locations are seasonal
and open from 11:30 a.m. to 8 p.m. daily beginning on Memorial Day.

Flo's Clam Shack, 4 Wave Ave., Middletown; (401) 847-8141; no
website. A big, sprawling, seasonal two-level restaurant with an ocean
view, Flo's has outdoor seating on the upper deck. On perfect summer days
folks just love to dunk their clam cakes into the creamy chowder as they
watch the waves crash onto the beach. Great for families and takeout with
picnic tables on the grounds. The menu is fixed on the wall, and the fried
clams and other seafood delights are heaped onto paper plates. Open for
lunch and dinner daily from Mar 1 to late Nov.

Evelyn's Drive-In, 2335 Main Rd. (Rte. 77), Tiverton; (401) 624-
3100; evelynsdrivein.com. This is one of those wonderful seasonal
restaurants that you can get to by boat. On the banks of the always-calm
Nannaquaket Pond, Evelyn's has been serving up seaside dishes for more
than 40 years. They are especially known for their lobster chow mein, but
most folks go there for the succulent fried clams. Chowder, clam cakes, and
everything else you'd expect are on the menu. You can dine indoors, out on
the sunny patio, or on picnic tables in the shade. Open from spring to fall
daily from 11:30 a.m. to 8:30 p.m.

Quito's, 411 Thames Rd., Bristol; (401) 253-4500; quitosrestaurant .com. It started out as a fish market in 1954 and soon became a very popular clam shack with a view of scenic Bristol Harbor. Typical clam shack fare and a whole lot more is on the menu. Fans rave about the food, but good service seems to be an ongoing problem. Beautiful sunsets can be seen from the patio. In the summer expect to wait for an outdoor table. Open for lunch and dinner daily Mar through Nov.

Seafood Markets

Anthony's Seafood, 963 Aquidneck Ave., Middletown; (401) 846-9620; anthonysseafood.com. This is where the locals go, which is always a good sign. It started out in 1956 as a wholesale lobster company, undergoing many changes over the years. Today it is a wholesale and retail operation, with a popular restaurant on the premises. Check the website for a detailed list of what's available in the retail market: fish, scallops, shellfish, shrimp, and prepared entrees, including stuffed lobsters ready for baking. Four chowders are offered (creamy New England, clear Rhode Island, tomato-based Manhattan, and Portuguese fish chowder). Open Mon through Sat from 10 a.m. to 7 p.m., Sun from 11 a.m. to 7 p.m.

Atlantic Fish Market, 127 Waterman Ave., East Providence; (401) 400-2266; no website. Specializing in fresh fish from Portugal, this market also offers some prepared foods. Open Mon through Fri from 7 a.m. to 8 p.m., Sun from 7 a.m. to 2 p.m.; closed Sat.

Blount Market, 406 Water St., Warren; (401) 245-1800; blount retail.com. When it comes to seafood in Rhode Island, Blount is one of the most respected names. Fish and shellfish arrive daily via Blount's own lobster and scallop boats. Ten seafood chowders and bisques are also available, as are prepared foods. Open Tues through Thurs from 10 a.m. to 5:30 p.m., Fri from 9 a.m. to 6 p.m., Sat from 9 a.m. to 4 p.m.; closed Sun and Mon.

Bridgeport Seafood, 2117 Main Rd., Tiverton; (401) 624-4411; no website. A family business since 1937, Bridgeport Seafood sells locally caught lobster, shellfish, scallops, cod, haddock, and halibut. Native tuna and swordfish are also available in the summer. From afar the market brings in shrimp and sockeye salmon. Open Mon through Fri from 9 a.m. to 5 p.m., Sat and Sun from 9 a.m. to 6 p.m.

Scott's Fish Market, 334 Metacom Ave., Warren; (401) 245-3063; no website. This is the place to go when you're looking for not just local seafood but something more exotic—crawfish, for example. Hard-to-find varieties of fish are sometimes available. Take-out seafood specials are offered every Friday. Open Tues through Thurs from 9:30 a.m. to 5:30 p.m., Fri from 9 a.m. to 6 p.m., Sat from 9 a.m. to 3:30 p.m., Sun from 9:30 a.m. to 1 p.m.

BLOCK ISLAND

Block Island is located in the Atlantic Ocean approximately 13 miles off the coast of Rhode Island and 14 miles east of Montauk Point on Long Island. A bit more than 1,000 people are year-round residents, and the island population swells to many thousands during the summer as vacationers arrive by ferry, private boat, and airplane to spend a day or more. This is a simple New England getaway known for its bicycling, hiking, sailing, fishing, and beaches. There are no fast-food restaurants on the island.

For such a small island, there are many restaurants that offer a full range of dining opportunities, from inexpensive takeout to elegant gourmet fare. Many places are open only from May to Oct; most are open for lunch and dinner daily. It's wise to call ahead to check on the hours of operation, especially if you are on Block Island in the spring or fall seasons. These are some of the best places for seafood.

Seafood Restaurants

Aldo's Italian Restaurant, 130 Chapel St., Block Island; (401) 466-5871; aldosrestaurantblockisland.com. It started out as a small pizzeria and sub shop more than 30 years ago, and now it's a large family restaurant with plenty of outdoor seating under blue and white market umbrellas. Pizza is still on the expanded menu, as well as all kinds of seafood specialties: mussels Provençal, seafood pesto over linguine, shrimp fra diavolo, and even a white clam pizza. A children's menu is available.

Atlantic Inn Restaurant, Block Island; (401) 466-5883; atlanticinn .com. "Amazing" is how fans describe this picturesque inn that occupies a premier spot on the island, the perfect place to watch the sunset from the old-fashioned wraparound porch. Or sit in an oversize white lawn chair and enjoy the tapas that get rave reviews. Typical items include lobster sliders, tequila-lime shrimp tacos, Korean spicy fried calamari, and seared Point Judith scallops with tarragon cream sauce. Open only for dinner.

Ballard's Inn, 42 Water St., Block Island; (401) 466-2231; ballards inn.com. A restaurant with its own beach with its very own beach bar, what more could you ask for? The big menu has something for everyone, from the affordable to the extravagant. You can graze on chowder, clam cakes, fish sandwiches, and fish-and-chips. And then you can dine on lobster prepared 12 different ways: steamed, twins, fire grilled, baked stuffed, in ravioli, scampi, Alfredo, in rolls, in a BLT, and in surf and turf dishes.

The Beachhead, 455 Ocean Ave., Block Island; (401) 466-2249. Quaint inside and out on the porch of this gray and white restaurant, The Beachhead offers all the seafood you expect and a few interesting variations: lobster Rockefeller, seafood nachos, New Orleans shrimp wrap, littlenecks in Madeira wine, Portuguese mussels, white clam and lobster piccata, and fresh haddock served with sautéed lobster. A children's menu is available.

Dead Eye Dick's, Ocean Avenue, New Harbor, Block Island; (401) 466-2654; deadeyedicksbi.com. This is where you want to be on a perfect summer day, on the shaded deck overlooking New Harbor. Since 1940, Dead Eye Dick's on Payne's Dock has been serving its signature lobster and swordfish dishes. The eclectic menu offers salt and pepper calamari, crispy jumbo shrimp with pineapple salsa and toasted coconut dipping sauce, lobster avocado BLT, and lobster truffle fettuccine. A great place to watch the sunset.

Finn's Seafood Restaurant, 212 Water St., Old Harbor, Block Island; (401) 466-2473; finnsseafood.com. The name has changed over the years, but the focus remains the same—the freshest seafood, simply prepared. All of it comes from Finn's Fish Market right next door. You can dine on the upstairs deck overlooking Old Harbor or indoors. Beyond the basics, the menu offers spicy Cajun calamari, smoked fish, broiled bluefin tuna, baked flounder with seafood stuffing, and baked shrimp with lobster stuffing.

Hotel Manisses Restaurant, Block Island; (401) 466-2421; block islandresorts.com. Elegant and intimate, this hotel restaurant is said to have the nicest bar on the island with especially friendly bartenders. The fine dining menu includes jumbo scallops with potato pancakes, mussels in coconut milk, prosciutto-wrapped jumbo shrimp, shrimp and crab ravioli, and miso-glazed codfish. More casual fare is available at The Oar, a sister operation at the Boat Basin in New Harbor with a deck view of Great Salt Pond.

Mohegan Cafe & Brewery, 213 Water St., Block Island; (401) 466-5911; moheganbi.com. The reviews are in, and they are overwhelmingly positive for this cozy brewpub close to the Old Harbor ferry landing. The menu is supremely simple: fried calamari, coconut shrimp, crab cakes, seviche, steamed mussels, and clam chowder for appetizers; fish-and-chips and fried clams for lunch; pad Thai with shrimp, seafood scampi, blackened mahimahi, baked stuffed flounder, and scallop ravioli for dinner.

Narragansett Inn, Ocean Avenue, Block Island; (401) 466-2626; narragansettinn.net. Set a spell in an old-fashioned rocking chair on the wraparound porch with a beautiful view of the harbor. Then move indoors for a special dining experience, beginning with the grilled lobster pizza or the conch fritters. Seafood specialties include steamed lobster, seafood stuffed shrimp, broiled sea scallops, sesame-crusted tuna, fish-and-chips, pistachio-crusted cod, paella, lobster and fennel ravioli, and linguine with clams. Open for dinner only.

National Hotel Tap & Grille, Water Street, Block Island; (401) 466-2901; blockislandhotels.com. A grand old hotel dating back to 1866, the National will take you back to a kinder, gentler time. This is the island's only steak house, but it is also known for its fresh seafood delivered daily. Signature dishes include crab and shrimp spring rolls, fish-and-chips, and seared diver scallops. Other tasty treats are the wild-caught tuna salad sandwich on sourdough and the pesto salmon sandwich on grilled artisan bread.

Payne's Harbor View Inn, Beach and Ocean Avenues, Block Island; (401) 466-5758; paynesharborviewinn.com. Built in 2001, this is a modern inn with charming New England ambiance overlooking New Harbor. The island's newest inn, yet filled with antique furnishings and historic photos, Payne's is especially known for its Sunset Bistro. The sushi is "amazing" according to fans. Light fare, fine wines, and beer round out the menu.

Rebecca's Seafood, 435 Water St., Block Island; (401) 466-5411; no website. Quick and easy, and very affordable, Rebecca's can be your last stop before hopping on the ferry to head home. If you're in a big hurry, there's a take-out window. If you have the time, the picnic area is perfect for people watching. Clam chowder, clam cakes, lobster rolls, and Rebecca's famous wraps are on the down-home menu every day. If you're spending the day at the beach, check out Rebecca's on the Beach.

Spring House Hotel, 52 Spring St., Block Island; (401) 466-5844; springhousehotel.com. One of the island's most elegant historic landmarks, the Spring House has an impressive wraparound veranda with sweeping views of the Atlantic Ocean. For more than 150 years, this hotel has been host to celebrities and the site of Kennedy weddings. With a farm-to-table philosophy and three dining venues, the menu offers high-end cuisine: grilled calamari, crab-crusted cod loin, seared diver scallops, and lobster mac and cheese.

Winfield's, Corn Neck Road, Block Island; (401) 466-5856; winfieldsrestaurant.net. The sophisticated dinner menu is influenced by French, Italian, Asian, and New American cuisines. Dishes include seared scallops with pan gravy and tasso ham for an appetizer; grilled swordfish with grilled squash and pan-seared salmon with beurre blanc for entrees. Located next door to the long-famous McGovern's Yellow Kittens, a very popular nightclub with live music every night in the summer.

Seafood Markets

Finn's Seafood, 212 Water St., Block Island; (401) 466-2102; finns seafood.com. A seasonal operation, Finn's offers a wide selection of fresh fish, smoked fish, and shellfish—local whenever possible. The lobsters are caught by Finn himself (aka Fred Howarth, owner and lobsterman). Located across from the Block Island ferry landing, Finn's Seafood Restaurant is also on the premises. Open from mid-June to mid-Sept daily from 10 a.m. to 7 p.m.

NEWPORT

Called the City by the Sea, Newport is known around the world for its magnificent mansions of the Gilded Age and America's Cup yacht racing. No visit to Newport would be complete without a drive down ritzy Bellevue Avenue and Ocean Drive, or a stroll along the waterfront where million-dollar yachts are docked. Many of the city's finest seafood restaurants offer up close views of these rich and famous lifestyles.

The heart of Newport is always humming with its many shops and boutiques. Music is a major part of the city's nightlife, and summer weekends are when the renowned jazz and folks festivals are held.

For more information call the Newport & Bristol County Convention & Visitors Bureau at (401) 845-9123 or visit gonewport.com.

Seafood Restaurants

Anthony's Seafood, 963 Aquidneck Ave., Middletown (401) 848-5058; anthonysseafood.com. Established in 1956 and still operated today by the Bucolo family, this is of those delightful fish market/restaurant combinations with big comfy booths for those who choose to eat in. They claim to have the largest selection of seafood in Newport County. They offer family-style dining with everything you'd expect, from chowder and clam cakes to fried classics and baked dinners. On the unique side, they offer Portuguese fish chowder, kung pao calamari, king crab legs, a grilled swordfish steak sandwich, and a grilled salmon burger. The fish tacos feature fried flounder with black bean salsa in a flour tortilla. It's located just minutes from downtown Newport with plenty of free parking. A children's menu is available. Open for lunch and dinner daily.

Barking Crab, Brick Marketplace II, 151 Swinburne Row, Newport; (401) 846-CRAB; barkingcrab.com. A riot of colors awaits you inside the Barking Crab in Newport (the original BC is in Boston). Bright reds and yellow and lots of wonderfully tacky nautical decor set the lively scene. You can sit at the big bar or at a wooden picnic table. A slightly more sophisticated dining area is also on the premises. Crab, of course, plays a major role on the mostly seafood menu: crab cakes, crab dip, and crab Louie for starters. Crab lovers can have local whole Jonah crab, Alaskan legs, Pacific Dungeness legs, Atlantic snow crab clusters, and the pricey crab bowl with a little bit of everything. Lobsters also star in this show—boiled, fire grilled, baked, and stuffed. The lobster BLT sounds interesting, as does the lobster scampi. There's plenty of fresh fish too, including cedar-planked salmon and fried platters. From a simple grilled mahimahi sandwich to a full-blown clambake, there's something for everyone at the Barking Crab. A children's menu is available. Open daily for lunch and dinner.

Black Pearl, Bannister's Wharf, Newport; (401) 845-5264; blackpearl.com. The Black Pearl has three distinct personalities—the

Commodore's Room is elegant, the Tavern is steeped in history, and the waterside patio and bar is pure fun. Each venue has a menu to match its mood and ambiance, created by the very talented executive chef, J. Daniel Knerr. Fine china and silverware await you in the pricey Commodore's Room, where you can dine on twin lobster tails paired with jumbo lump crab cakes, soft-shell crabs, and gray sole. In the Tavern, the restaurant's famous clam chowder is a must (it's sold online), followed by lobster salad on a crois-sant at lunchtime or salmon with mustard-

dill hollandaise for dinner. Out on the lively patio, summer cocktails go well with the impeccably prepared shellfish from the raw bar. The sprawl-ing building right on the wharf dates back to the 1920s, and it was turned into the Black Pearl by a local yachtsman who liked to eat well. Don't we all? Open for lunch and dinner daily (closed from early Jan to mid-Feb).

Castle Hill Inn, 590 Ocean Dr., Newport; (888) 466-1355; castle hillinn.com. The crown jewel in the Newport Restaurant Group, Castle Hill Inn is the epitome of fine dining. Executive Chef Karsten Hart's food is extraordinary, crafted from local fish and produce. A seasonal menu is served in four dining rooms. Typical menu items include pan-roasted Georges Bank scallops with spring peas, native fluke with lobster sausage, grilled swordfish with lemon salt, and salmon with poached artichokes. With its own menu, the immaculate lawn that rolls down to Narragansett Bay is the perfect place to be on a Sunday afternoon in the summer. There the food is more casual: chowder served with a black pepper–thyme bread-stick and a native fish wrap sandwich with avocado and corn salsa. If you care to experience the quiet luxury of 18th-century seacoast life, Castle Hill has guest quarters for overnight accommodations. It is one of Newport's most charming landmarks. Open for lunch and dinner daily, with brunch on Sun.

The Deck, 1 Waites Wharf, Newport; (800) 960-4573; waiteswharf .com. Right on the water, The Deck has a spectacular view of a world-class marina and beyond that, Newport Harbor, just beautiful, especially at sunset. There's outdoor seating on the patio for the summer. Inside, this waterfront oasis is cozy and warm in the cooler months. Chef Matthew Holmes offers an upscale menu based on Nouvelle Cuisine. Midday you can dine on fisherman's chowder, lobster stuffies, and mussels steamed in beer. For dinner start with the baked oysters stuffed with lobster claw meat. Entrees include locally caught swordfish, linguine with garlicky littleneck clams, pan-seared tuna or jumbo sea scallops with wasabi aioli, lobster mac and cheese, salmon with baby shrimp, and over-the-top lobsters weighing 4 to 10 pounds each. If you want to see the chef in action, ask for a seat at the bar overlooking the exhibition-style open kitchen. The Deck is known for its warm ambiance, outstanding service, and lively entertainment, especially in the summer. Open for lunch and dinner daily in the summer; closed Tues and Wed in the off-season.

Fluke Wine Bar & Kitchen, 41 Bowen's Wharf, Newport; (401) 849-7778; flukewinebar.com. Exciting modern American cuisine is what Fluke is all about, the creation of Jeff and Geremie Callaghan. This stylish restaurant overlooks bustling Bannister and Bowen's Wharves in the heart of Newport, with harbor and sunset views to enjoy, exotic cocktail in hand. Known especially for lobster and seafood prepared with local ingredients, Fluke offers a casual and comfortable atmosphere. The food

Fluke's Fluke!

is very creative: Jonah crab cakes, scallop crudo, grilled octopus, grilled sausage-stuffed squid, roasted coconut shrimp, steamed mussels with fennel, and crispy fried oysters with mango pepper relish, all on the small plate menu. Large plates feature striped bass with broccoli rabe, Georges Bank flounder with miso vinaigrette, and pan-seared scallops with sesame-ginger glaze. The menu changes very often. Open for dinner nightly May through mid-Nov; Wed through Sat Nov through Apr.

Marina Cafe & Pub, 3 Marina Plaza, Goat Island, Newport; (401) 849-0003; marinacafepub.com. Especially popular with local boaters, the Marina Cafe & Pub serves good grub, mostly New England fare with a touch of the Caribbean. In the surrounding marina yachts worth millions of dollars are nestled in their slips. The vibe is definitely laid-back and casual. Appetizers include crab cakes with fried capers, steamers with drawn butter, fish tacos made with swordfish, mussels in a garlic-miso broth, calamari with a tropical dipping sauce, and chowder, of course. Sandwiches showcase lobster, grilled or fried fish, and whole-belly clams. Luncheon items include lobster (grilled, boiled, or baked), fish-and-chips, and a fried clam platter. Entrees feature the catch of the day, grilled swordfish, lobster ravioli, shrimp and pasta, and baked cod. For smaller appetites there's a small plate menu that offers a spicy stuffie—great with a glass of white wine on the patio. Open for lunch and dinner daily from early May through fall; closed in winter.

Working Waterfront Tour

Seafood lovers appreciate all the hard work that goes into getting that lobster or bowl of steamers onto their dinner table. So it's not surprising that these fans of fish and shellfish are interested in working waterfronts. To provide answers to their many questions, **Newport History Tours** offers regular tours starting from the Whitehorne Museum, 416 Thames St. in Newport. Every Friday at 11 a.m., the curious get to walk in the footsteps of the men and women—sailors, merchants, and immigrants—who once lived and worked in the lower Thames neighborhood. Prepare to have your senses engaged. Reservations are recommended. For more information call (401) 841-8770 or visit newporthistorytours.org.

Mooring Seafood Kitchen & Bar, Sayers Wharf, Newport; (401) 846-2260; mooringrestaurant.com. For more than 25 years, the Mooring has enjoyed a sterling reputation as one of the finest seafood restaurants not just in Newport but throughout the state. Another member of the Newport Restaurant Group, the Mooring is a multilevel waterfront restaurant with a spectacular view of yachts of all sizes. It's a terrific spot for people watching—don't be surprised if you see a celebrity or two. The new American menu opens with offerings from a well-stocked raw bar and the award-winning scallop chowder. This is a big menu, sure to please everyone in your party. Graze on the lobster, crab, and shrimp fritters. Save room for the seafood stew, sole francaise, or seafood pie, swimming with crustaceans in a cognac cream sauce. Open for lunch and dinner daily.

Muse, Vanderbilt Grace Hotel, 41 Mary St., Newport; (401) 846-6200; vanderbiltgrace.com. For quite possibly the finest food in the state, the very special Muse is located inside the Vanderbilt Grace. This

is most definitely for the gourmet seafood lover. The lobster bisque is touched with cognac crème fraîche. The day boat scallops are dressed with a champagne froth. The open ravioli shows off its poached lobster with a spring vegetable ragout. The local halibut is paired with spring fennel. The restaurant is as gorgeous as the food, with its ocean blue walls, grand fireplace, and chandeliers. This is fine dining at its finest. Al fresco dining is offered in the beautiful garden terrace during the summer. A special bar menu is also available, with oysters on the half shell and crab sliders to go with your signature Grace cocktail. Open for dinner Mon through Sat.

Muse's Lobster Bisque

Pineapples on the Bay, Hyatt Regency Newport, Goat Island; (401) 851-1234; newport-hyatt.com. The best-kept secret in Newport is Pineapples on the Bay, the al fresco dining venue at the Hyatt Regency with a spectacular view of Narragansett Bay and the Newport Bridge. This seasonal hot spot has entertainment on weekend nights and sunset celebrations that include a champagne toast and cannon salute. The menu offers crab fritters with a spicy remoulade, crispy calamari, thick and creamy clam chowder, peel-and-eat shrimp, and steamers. There's a build-your-own raw bar, and the sandwiches have fried fish and grilled swordfish in starring roles. From the lobster shack comes a lobster quesadilla large enough to share. The lobster and brie BLT is served with crispy fries. You can sit by the outdoor fireplace in old-fashioned rocking chairs or make s'mores in the outdoor fire pit. Specialty drinks, such as the Narragansett Pirate made with Newport's own Thomas Tew rum, are served at the waterfront bar. A children's menu is available. Open for lunch and dinner daily (summer only).

Scales & Shells Restaurant and Raw Bar, 527 Thames St., Newport; (401) 846-FISH (3474); scalesandshells.com. You'll find nothing but seafood on the menu at Scales & Shells, where their goal has always been to serve the freshest, highest-quality seafood to their customers. Their fish buyer makes the rounds daily to procure seafood that meets their high standards. With an open kitchen, it's easy to ask the chefs what's cooking. The specials change nightly, but you can always count on the fried calamari, clam pizza, grilled shrimp, and pasta with a red or white clam sauce. Littlenecks and mussels are done up Sicilian style. The scampi can feature shrimp, scallops, or calamari. Some of the more unusual dishes are the lobster fra diavolo for two, monkfish piccata or Marsala, and mesquite grilled fish, from bluefish to tautog (two Rhode Island favorites). Broiled seafood is also served. Open for dinner daily.

Spiced Pear, The Chanler at Cliff Walk, Newport; (401) 847-2244; thechanler.com A destination restaurant, the elegant Spiced Pear is located within The Chanler, a boutique hotel with a sweeping ocean view and access to Newport's famous Cliff Walk. You can sit by the grand fireplace and watch the chefs at work in the open kitchen, or graze on lighter fare at The Bar or The Veranda. In the summer, lunch can be had on the Cliff Walk Terrace, where a children's menu is also available. The Spiced Pear is known for its New England tasting menu of 6 to 9 courses. From the a la carte menu, the continental cuisine includes ahi tuna carpaccio with ginger-wasabi vinaigrette, butter-poached Maine lobster with truffled leeks and petite artichokes, Gulf shrimp and diver scallops with baby bok choy, and king salmon with hedgehog mushrooms. This is fine dining on the highest level. Open for dinner daily (lunch is offered on the Cliff Walk Terrace only in summer).

22 Bowen's Wine Bar & Grille, Bowen's Wharf, Newport; (401) 841-8884; 22bowens.com. Another member of the prestigious Newport Restaurant Group, 22 Bowen's is a very handsome restaurant known for its steaks and the finest seafood available. Located right on Bowen's Wharf, this waterfront restaurant has outdoor seating in the summer with a separate portside menu of appetizers, soups, salads, and sandwiches. Indoors and year-round, typical menu items include shellfish from the raw bar,

Bucket of Clams from 22 Bowen's

chowder, a blackened salmon sandwich, lobster grilled cheese on brioche, lobster salad on soft rolls, fried clam strip roll, fish-and-chips, fish tacos, and steamed lobster. At dinnertime a more sophisticated menu is offered: bacon-wrapped scallops with pineapple chutney, Maine lobsters weighing 2 to 3 pounds, roasted cod clambake, grilled yellow fin tuna with sweet red chile glaze, chipotle shrimp and linguine, and grilled Atlantic salmon with arugula. Open for lunch and dinner daily.

Lobster Shacks

Aquidneck Lobster Bar, 31 Bowen's Wharf, Newport; (401) 847-4514; aquidnecklobsterbar.com. Grab a stool and a pub-height table with a view of Newport Harbor and take a look at the menu for this rustic restaurant. This is casual dining to the nth degree with a contemporary twist here and there. A bag of crisp clam fritters comes with roasted chile tartar sauce. The crunchy yellow fin tuna appetizer has a wasabi pea crust and a teriyaki-ginger glaze with a little seaweed salad on the side.

Sandwiches include a spicy shrimp po' boy. The Caesar salad can be topped with shrimp cocktail, lobster salad, or calamari. Classic fried seafood platters are there for the asking. All sorts of fresh fish are hot off the grill. A well-stocked raw bar and steamed lobsters round off the menu. Outdoor seating is available, a lovely way to watch the sunset. Open seasonally, reopening every year in Apr.

Newport Lobster Shack, 2 Washington St., State Pier #9 at the end of Long Wharf, Newport; (401) 225-7746; thenewportlobster shack.com. This is where you can buy your local lobster, crab, and conch direct from local fishermen at "right off the boat" prices. That's all they sell: lobster, crab, and conch. Everything is guaranteed to be caught locally. Nothing fancy, this shack is a cooperative of the Newport Fisherman's Association and is staffed by local fishermen to keep costs down. If you are far from home, they will pack your purchases on ice for their safe transport. They take cash only. Open daily during summer; it's wise to call for current hours and pricing.

Seafood Markets

Aquidneck Lobster Company, 31 Bowen's Wharf, Newport; (401) 846-0106; no website. This is the real deal, no frills, right on the waterfront. You walk through an old wooden building past the massive lobster tanks and lots of shellfish on ice. You can stop in, pick out a lobster, and tell them what time you will be back. When you stop back in, they will pack it up on ice for free. They'll even steam it for you, if you like, at no charge. If you walk through this retail market, you'll find a rustic restaurant in the back. Open daily from 6 a.m. to 5:30 p.m.

Long Wharf Seafood, 17 Connell Hwy., Newport; (401) 846-6320; longwharf.info. A no-frills operation (with a no-frills website), Long Wharf offers fresh native fish and shellfish as well as prepared foods. Items include bass, calamari, clams, cod, crabs, flounder, haddock, halibut, littlenecks, lobster, mussels, oysters, salmon, scallops, shrimp, swordfish, and tuna. Open Wed through Sat from 11 a.m. to 6 p.m., Sun from 11 a.m. to 3 p.m.

Newport Lobster Shack, Long Wharf and Washington Street, Newport; (401) 225-7746; thenewportlobstershack.com. One of the best-kept secrets in Newport, this is a cooperative of the Newport

Fisherman's Association. The tanks are full of fresh lobster, conch, and crab. They will package your purchases for travel. They accept cash only. Open with seasonal hours—it's a good idea to call ahead. In summer, Fri through Sun from 10 a.m. to 6 p.m., Mon through Thurs from 1 to 6 p.m.

RHODE ISLAND EVENTS
March
Newport Restaurant Week, discovernewport.org/events-calendar /newport-restaurant-week-spring. Restaurant Week is celebrated at restaurants throughout the city in late March, and seafood always plays an important role on the special prix-fixe menus offered.

June
Great Chowder Cook-off, (401) 846-1600; newportwaterevents .com. The granddaddy of seafood celebrations is the Great Chowder Cook-off held on the first Saturday in June on the waterfront in Newport. For more than 30 years, this has been the go-to event for chowder aficionados. Held rain or shine, this event kicks off the summer season in Newport. Thousands of people attend, going from booth to booth, sampling all kinds of chowder from local and even national competitors. With your paid admission, you get to sample as many chowders as you desire and then vote for your favorite. Discounted tickets are available in advance. Children under age 12 are admitted free with an adult.

Spring Taste of Block Island, (800) 383-2474; blockislandchamber .com/taste-block-island. A true taste of Block Island's restaurants and so much more is offered during this three-day celebration, held on the first weekend in June. All kinds of discounts are offered to persons wearing special buttons that are bought in advance. A chowder contest and oyster festival are part of the festivities. Beer and wine tastings are also held. By the end of the weekend, they guarantee you will fall in love with Block Island. Taste of Block Island buttons are available for purchase at the Chamber of Commerce or aboard any Interstate Navigation Block Island Ferry or the Block Island Express Ferry for $5 per button.

July
Providence Restaurant Week, goprovidence.com/RW. Restaurant Week is celebrated at restaurants throughout the city in mid-July, and seafood always plays an important role on the special prix-fixe menus offered.

Seafood Festival in Narragansett, narragansettri.com. Thousands of people turn out for this three-day multifaceted seafood event. Held on a weekend in late July, the festival offers culinary delights from the sea (and from land) with live music so you can dance away all those calories. A raw bar, lobster dinners with all of the traditional fixings, pasta with clam sauce, barbecued shrimp, stuffies, and much more are available under a large tent next to the famous Narragansett Towers. The weekend kicks off with a major road race, and the colorful Blessing of the Fleet takes place on Saturday at noon in the fishing village of Galilee.

Warren Quahog Festival, (401) 247-2188; eastbaychamberri.org. Fresh seafood dishes are the headlining act at this annual festival, sponsored by the Warren/Barrington Rotary Club. The two-day event takes place at Burr's Hill Park on South Water Street across from Warren Town Beach.

August
Charlestown Seafood Festival, (401) 364 4031; charlestownri chamber.com. A seafood extravaganza of Rhode Island's best seafood, lobsters, steamers, chowder, fish-and-chips, clam cakes, and a raw bar is delivered without fail every year on the first weekend in August in Ninigret Park. Continuous entertainment and events are on the schedule, including a lobster raffle and fireworks display. Sponsored by the local Chamber of Commerce, this event is held rain or shine. Children under the age of 10 are admitted free with an adult.

Lobster Week at 10 Prime Steak & Sushi, (401) 453-2333; tenprimesteakandsushi.com. One of the hottest restaurants in Providence, 10 Prime Steak & Sushi at 55 Pine St. celebrates the season's bounty with its Lobster Week, held in mid- to late August. Chef David Jackson offers a prix-fixe menu at lunch and dinner featuring inspired lobster dishes as well as 10's full menu.

September
East Greenwich Restaurant Week, eastgreenwichchamber.com. Restaurant Week is celebrated at restaurants throughout the town in mid-September, and seafood always plays an important role on the special prix-fixe menus offered.

Fall Taste of Block Island, (800) 383-2474; blockislandchamber
.com/taste-block-island. The Spring Taste of Block Island is so successful, they've added a fall version of this event, held every year on a weekend
in late September. The tourists are gone from the island, and the weather is
generally perfect. Restaurant specials, farm tours, and wine and beer tastings are on tap. Taste of Block Island buttons are available for purchase
at the Chamber of Commerce or aboard any Interstate Navigation Block
Island Ferry or the Block Island Express Ferry for $5 per button.

Newport Mansions Wine & Food Festival, (401) 847-1000;
newportmansionswineandfood.org. One of the most sophisticated
food events held on the East Coast, this festival takes place in Newport's
famous mansions on a weekend in late September. Extraordinary food,
especially seafood, is served at various venues with celebrity chefs in
starring roles. The affair kicks off with a gala on Friday night at Rosecliff.
Grand tastings take place on Sat and Sun. Tickets for individual events and
seminars, as well as several weekend packages, are available for purchase.

Oyster Fest at Hemenway's, (401) 351-8570; hemenways
restaurant.com. For one Saturday in late September, Hemenway's Seafood Restaurant in Providence opens its doors and spreads its hospitality
outside into the nearby Market Square Park. Oysters from local waters and
beyond are there for the tasting during this afternoon of food and family
fun, all to benefit charities such as the Ronald McDonald House. Admission is free. Food and drink tickets are available for purchase.

Oyster Festival at Legal Sea Foods in Warwick, legalseafoods
.com; (401) 732-3663. From mid-September into mid-October, oyster
season is in full swing at this popular restaurant on Post Road in Warwick.
For four weeks the menu offers oyster specials and special events, such as
a shellfish shindig on the terrace and a 4-course oyster dinner paired with
craft beers.

Rhode Island Seafood Festival, (845) 222-7469; riseafoodfest.com.
It may be the end of summer, but mid-September in Providence means one
thing—the Rhode Island Seafood Festival, where some of the very best restaurants show off their signature dishes. Every kind of seafood, from oysters on the half shell to grilled shrimp, is offered. And what a setting: India
Point Park, right on the water, with live music. Admission is free.

Wickford Harbor Fest, northkingstown.com. The quaint seacoast village of Wickford draws thousands of people on a Sunday in late September for its annual harbor fest. Local restaurants offer their unique cuisine, and a lobster raffle is held. For pure fun you can charter a toy boat and set sail off Town Beach to earn a cash prize or new car. Admission is free.

October
Fall Restaurant Week in Westerly, westerlychamber.org. Restaurant Week is celebrated at restaurants throughout the city in early October, and seafood always plays an important role on the special prix-fixe menus offered.

Bowen's Wharf Seafood Festival in Newport, bowenswharf.com/bowens_wharf_events.html. Described as "fabulous," this fall seafood festival takes place in the heart of Newport on historic Bowen's Wharf on a weekend in mid-October. A celebration of the sea and its harvest, this gala event offers up tons of food and family fun under colorful tents, rain or shine. Local restaurants and fisherman's associations serve their signature seafood dishes: clam chowder, stuffed quahogs, clam cakes, lobster dinners, and more. Sea shanties fill the air. Admission is free. Food and beverages can be purchased from the vendors.

Newport Food Truck Festival, foodtruckfestivalsofne.com. More than 20 food trucks, including Go Fish and Lobsta Love, from throughout New England offer a variety of cuisines in mid- to late October at the Newport Yachting Center. Sampling tents, children's activities, and live music are also featured. Taste tickets are sold online in advance. There is no additional admission fee.

November
Newport Restaurant Week, discovernewportrestaurantweek.org. Restaurant Week is celebrated at restaurants throughout the city in early November, and seafood always plays an important role on the special prix-fixe menus offered.

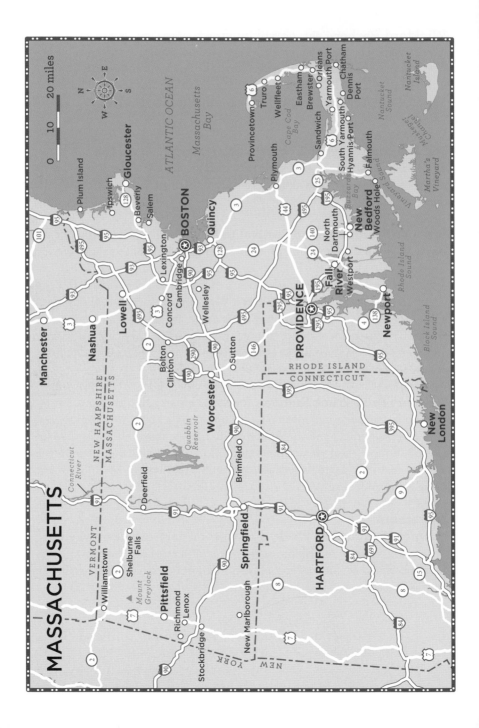

Massachusetts

Massachusetts is simply a marvelous state to visit and a magnificent part of New England in which to live. What comes to mind when one thinks of Massachusetts? From the Berkshires in the western part of the state, where you can go cross-country skiing in the winter, to Cape Cod and its miles of beautiful beaches for sun and fun in the summer—that's just part of the mystique of Massachusetts. And there in the middle you have the capital city of Boston, historic and cosmopolitan at one and the same time.

Gloucester Fisherman's Memorial

The history of Massachusetts is America's history, from the Pilgrims landing in Plymouth to the shot heard 'round the world in the American Revolution. Marvelous museums and symphony orchestras, quaint country inns and luxurious city hotels, prestigious colleges and universities, metropolitan culture and seaside villages, five-star gourmet dining and old-fashioned seafood shacks—these are just some of the many facets of Massachusetts.

The Bay State, as it is called, has approximately 1,500 miles of saltwater coastline. So it shouldn't come as any surprise that this is "the home of the bean and the cod," as the official state song proclaims, referring to Boston's famous baked beans and the fish proudly served in so many restaurants throughout the state.

GREATER BOSTON

Boston is made up of neighborhoods that are incredibly different from one another. If you were to follow the red stripe of the Freedom Trail embedded in the city's sidewalk, you'd see Paul Revere's House, Old North Church, and other monuments to America's Revolutionary War. That historic trail would lead you into Boston's oldest neighborhood, the North End, settled in 1630. By 1900 it became the city's Italian neighborhood, and even now

Boston Food News

Here are some information sources that may have an opinion-ated point of view but speak with authority about the food scene in and around Boston.

BostonChefs.com: Almost all the news of interest about the Boston restaurant scene appears first on BostonChefs.com. Track all the events, find out about soft openings, and see where the jobs are. (When a place is advertising for a head chef, you might want to eat elsewhere.)

***Boston Globe*:** Restaurant reviews and "cheap eats" reviews of casual spots are published in the Wednesday food section. About a year of these reviews are archived on the free *Globe* website, Boston.com. Many years of reviews are archived on the *Globe*'s pay site, BostonGlobe.com.

***Boston Herald*:** The paper and its website cover the local food scene closely, noting openings and closings and changes of personnel and often writing feature pieces on folks in the food trades. Most useful for paper readers is the Fast Food column. Online, the Fork Lifts blog (bostonherald.com/blogs/lifestyle/forklift) features posts by staff and by such luminaries as Roger Berkowitz of Legal Sea Foods and Chef Lydia Shire.

the North End is clearly the Little Italy of Boston, although residents are more mixed today. Most of the restaurants in the North End have an Italian accent; many of them are wonderful, with seafood playing a major role in their popularity. Parking is always a challenge, but to stroll around the North End, stopping to buy authentic Italian bread and pastries, pausing for an espresso, dining in a sidewalk *caffe*—that really is "la dolce vita."

The Freedom Trail continues on into gentrified Charlestown with its smattering of good spots to eat and drink. Over the harbor to East Boston and over the Mystic River to Chelsea, you will find restaurants serving the cuisine of the city's Spanish-speaking residents. Beacon Hill is a handsome part of the city with the gold-domed State House towering over Boston Common and the even prettier Boston Gardens. Tourists inevitably find themselves at Faneuil Hall Marketplace and Quincy Market, amazing

Boston magazine: Boston's city lifestyle magazine may be best known for bestowing Best of Boston awards, but it also features solid restaurant criticism. For lively, contemporary dish on the dining scene by talented younger writers, see *Boston*'s dining blog, Chowder, at blogs.bostonmagazine.com/chowder.

Dishing: This free column by *Boston Globe* staff appears on the Boston.com website (boston.com/lifestyle/food/dishing). Many of the posts are devoted to recipes and cooking news. Many others are behind-the-scenes notebook pieces by some of the reviewers. Restaurant news also appears frequently on Dishing.

Edible Boston magazine: Chances are that it won't be news by the time this quarterly publishes, but feature coverage of restaurants, growers, and producers tends to be insightful and thought provoking on occasion. This magazine is given away free at foodie locations and can be found online at edible communities.com/boston.

Grub Street: The coverage of Boston restaurant openings and closings and chef changes on *Grub Street* (boston.grubstreet .com) can be surprisingly good for a publication whose heart is in New York.

examples of economic development and filled with restaurants of every type, every cuisine, every price point. Close by is Boston Harbor, another area of the city where hotels and restaurants are transforming a once-gritty waterfront into an upscale neighborhood now called the Seaport District.

Since the 19th century the Back Bay has been a rather elite part of the city, with posh brownstone residences that are now being refurbished to meet real estate demands. Copley Square beats like the heart of the city, with its restaurants and bars filled with tourists and conventioneers who are out to drink and dine. The adjacent Fenway area is dominated by two giants: Boston University and the Boston Red Sox, whose legendary ballpark is now in the center of a year-round entertainment district. The Fenway is full of bars, clubs, cafes, and restaurants that appeal to both college students and sports fans.

There almost seems no end to Boston's many faces. The residential South End just might be home to more foodies per block than any other part of the city. Sunday brunch is serious business there. On one side of the South End, Roxbury has become a magnet for new arrivals from the Caribbean and east Africa. On the other side, Chinatown seems to be almost stuck in time. Venerable Chinese restaurants continue to serve their delectable dim sum to appreciative audiences.

Jamaica Plain, or JP as it's called by locals, is a slightly more affordable suburb of Boston, where young couples are buying Victorian homes and dining in cafes and restaurants of every ethnic cuisine imaginable. It's really a funky mix there—art school and college students, young professionals, Central American and Caribbean families, a strong gay population, and an unusually high percentage of vegetarians.

Rounding out the city is South Boston and Dorchester, predominantly Irish neighborhoods with Irish pubs on almost every corner. Neighborhood bars, bakeries, and cafes serve solid comfort food, while an influx of Vietnamese have brought pho restaurants to every block. Ethnic and cultural diversity seems greater there than anywhere else in Boston.

With thousands of restaurants of all kinds in business at this time, Boston has an impressive restaurant culture. The dining scene is big news—what chefs are cooking and where they're cooking, what's the hot new dish, who makes the best whatever, where are the coolest bartenders. It seems when friends or families gather, it's only a matter of time before their conversation turns to food, where they've eaten lately, and where they're planning to go next.

Boston also is an amazing place to shop. You can dicker over fresh produce with vendors at Haymarket Square on a Saturday morning, buy fresh seafood at the Boston Fish Pier, wander through dazzling Asian markets, and purchase extraordinary ingredients from Italy in the North End.

Boston can easily hold its own with any other major city when it comes to restaurants, markets, food in general, and especially seafood. After all, this is the Bay State.

Seafood Restaurants

B&G Oysters, 550 Tremont St., South End, Boston; (617) 423-0550; bandgoysters.com. More than a dozen different types of oysters are available on any given day at this subterranean restaurant in the city's trendy South End. The knowledgeable staff will guide you through your oyster tasting and wine selection. Lobster rolls, fried clams, and Mediterranean-inspired dishes are also on the menu. You can sit at the white marble bar that surrounds the open kitchen. In warm weather there's a lovely stone-walled patio for an al fresco experience. This is a Barbara Lynch property, one of eight under her direction in Boston; her name is synonymous with excellence on the local food scene. Open for lunch and dinner daily.

Chart House, 60 Long Wharf, Waterfront, Boston; (617) 227-1576; chart-house.com. Part of a reputable national chain, this is the only Chart House in New England. Housed in a building that dates back to 1760, this white-tablecloth restaurant has a handsome interior with exposed brick and towering ceilings. Famous for its whole Maine lobster cracked open right at your table, the Chart House offers fresh seafood from local waters and beyond, classic fare, and contemporary offerings—from lobster bisque and herb-crusted salmon at lunch to sweet and spicy swordfish at dinner. A gluten-free menu featuring a seafood cobb salad and king crab is also available. Open for lunch and dinner daily.

Citizen Public House and Oyster Bar, 1310 Boylston St., Fenway, Boston; (617) 450-9000; citizenpub.com. The main reason to stop in here is for the impeccably fresh shellfish—lots of oysters, littlenecks on the half shell, cocktail shrimp, and smoked mussels—and the gastropub cuisine. Entrees will please just about everyone, especially the family-style pig roast. For seafood lovers, Chef Brian Reyelt offers an oyster BLT as a bar snack and dinners of seared scallops, Atlantic salmon, and freshly ground tuna for a burger with an Asian twist. This modern neighborhood tavern is located behind Fenway Park, a great spot to try after a Red Sox baseball game. Open Mon through Sat from 5 p.m. to 2 a.m. and Sun from 11 a.m. to 2 a.m.

Court House Seafood Restaurant, 498 Cambridge St., East Cambridge, Cambridge; (617) 491-1213; courthouseseafood.com. It's always a good sign when a restaurant has a retail fresh fish market right next door. The market's been in business since 1912. The Damaso family, originally from Portugal, added the restaurant in 1987. More than half their business is takeout, with most dishes being simple fried, broiled, or baked fish with fries and onion rings. The restaurant may be small, but the menu is big. The family's ethnic heritage shows up with the offerings of fried smelts and mackerel dinners. Open Mon 11 a.m. to 3 p.m., Tues through Thurs 11 a.m. to 7 p.m., Fri 11 a.m. to 8 p.m., Sat 11 a.m. to 6 p.m.

Daily Catch, 323 Hanover St., North End, Boston; (617) 523-8567. 441 Harvard St., Brookline; (617) 734-2700. 2 Northern Ave., Waterfront, Boston; (617) 772-4400; dailycatch.com. From the day it opened in 1973, the original Daily Catch in the North End—with only 20 seats—has had a line out the door. Why? For its Sicilian-style seafood and pasta and very affordable prices. This was the North End's first restaurant to serve fried calamari, which has become wildly popular. A no-frills operation, look for the menu to be on a chalkboard and be prepared to sit communally with strangers. The Brookline location also has but 20 seats and is open nightly for dinner only. At the much larger Waterfront location, you can sit at outdoor tables even in the rain (you'll be protected under a large overhang) and watch the boats in Boston Harbor. Accepts cash only. The North End and Waterfront sites are open for lunch and dinner daily.

D'Amelio's Off the Boat, 26–28 Porter St., East Boston, Boston; (617) 561-8800; offtheboatseafood.com. The freshest seafood with an Italian accent, that's what the D'Amelio family promises its guests. The hand-painted murals on the dining room walls will transport you to the Adriatic Sea. Start off with the grilled octopus over mixed greens, followed by one of the extraordinary pasta dishes: shrimp, crabmeat, and a lobster tail sautéed with a special lobster-based sauce and tossed with freshly made fusilli pasta. All kinds of fish and seafood can also be baked, broiled, grilled, and fried. The house specialties venture beyond seafood. They also do a brisk take-out business. Open Tues through Sat from 11 a.m. to 10 p.m.

Durgin-Park, 340 Faneuil Hall Marketplace, Downtown, Boston; (617) 227-2038; durgin-park.com. For more than a century, Durgin-Park has been a top tourist destination for its classic Yankee fare—such as clam chowder, fish cakes, Boston scrod, and fried seafood dinners—and for an unusual dining experience, thanks to the sassy waitresses who are just rude enough to leave you laughing. Customers sit at long communal tables covered with red and white checkered tablecloths. This is one of the oldest continuously running establishments in the country, famous for its Boston baked beans. If you're thirsty, you can visit the Gaslight Pub or The Hideout, a beer garden. A children's menu is available. The main dining room is open Mon through Sun from 11:30 a.m. to 9 p.m.

East Coast Grill, 1271 Cambridge St., Inman Square, Cambridge; (617) 491-6568; eastcoastgrill.net. Since 1985 the East Coast Grill has been dazzling customers with delicious food—much of it seafood and most of it cooked over a wood grill—in a casual, fun setting. After all those years, there is still a line of diners waiting for a table, especially on weekends. Crowded and noisy, they don't take reservations. Everything is just a little different here—the clam and corn chowder is made with sweet potatoes, and fried shrimp comes with buffalo sauce. Entrees include snow crab legs, grilled tuna with wasabi, and grilled mahimahi with pineapple salsa. If you like really hot food, stop in on "Hell Night," when customers are served dishes like Pasta from Hell (but not before they sign waivers promising not to sue the restaurant). Open for dinner nightly, for lunch Sat, for brunch Sun from 11 a.m. to 2:30 p.m.

East Ocean City, 25–29 Beach St., Chinatown, Boston; eastocean city.com. Connoisseurs of Cantonese-style seafood should make a beeline to this full-service Chinese restaurant in Boston's Chinatown. The formal dining room has white tablecloths and pink napkins at each place setting. Every day 600 pounds of fresh seafood is delivered to the kitchen. Most dishes are large enough to share. These are just some of the seafood offerings: lobster with ginger and scallions, whole bass or sole, stir-fried fish with seasonal vegetables, Szechuan spicy shrimp, and clams with black bean sauce. If you're brave enough, you can order a live fish from the tanks near the entrance to be prepared in a variety of ways. Open for lunch and dinner daily.

Harvest, 44 Brattle St., Harvard Square, Cambridge; (617) 868-2255; harvestcambridge.com. When Julia Child lived in Cambridge, this was her favorite restaurant, and it was the first in the area to adopt the now-popular farm-to-table philosophy. The food is simply amazing, especially the seared Scituate scallops with wild mushroom and smoked bacon hash and the roasted lobster with saffron risotto. Lunch is a tad more casual—crispy Jonah crab cakes, Point Judith calamari, and an impressive lobster roll. In the summer the outdoor courtyard bar area is delightful. Open for dinner nightly, for lunch Mon through Sat, for brunch Sun from 11:30 a.m. to 2:30 p.m.

Island Creek Oyster Bar, 500 Commonwealth Ave., Fenway, Boston; (617) 532-5300; islandcreekoysterbar.com. You've heard of the farm-to-table movement in restaurants. This is an example of oyster farm-to-table, a bringing together of the oyster producer in Duxbury, the restaurant chef, and the diner. Fish and oyster selections change daily, depending on what is fresh and available. That means more than a dozen different oysters and creative entrees such as Nantucket Bay scallop carbonara, Maine lobster risotto, and Rhode Island fluke. People are raving about this Kenmore Square restaurant, especially Chef Jeremy Sewall's seared halibut,

Fishing boat leaving Boston Harbor.

lobster roll, and fried oyster sliders. Insider tip: Reservations are hard to come by so book your table as far in advance as possible. Open for dinner Mon through Sat, lunch and dinner Sun.

J. P. Seafood Cafe, 730 Centre St., Jamaica Plain, Boston; (617) 983-5177; jpseafoodcafe.com. It doesn't sound very Asian, but this neighborhood restaurant has a menu that offers everything from bento boxes for lunch to grilled teriyaki salmon for dinner. The interior has a minimalist design, and the prices are equally modest. Fans rave about the incredibly light tempura and the Double Dare Maki with extraspicy sauce. For a really different experience, stop in on Sunday for brunch and dine on the P-Town omelet stuffed with shrimp. Just one of the exciting restaurants on Jamaica Plain's exploding restaurant scene. Open for lunch Tues through Sat from 11:30 a.m. to 2:30 p.m.; dinner Mon through Fri from 5 to 10 p.m., Sat and Sun from 2:30 to 10 p.m.; brunch Sun from 11 a.m. to 2:30 p.m.

Legal Sea Foods, 270 Northern Ave., Liberty Wharf, Boston; (617) 477-2900. 26 Park Plaza, Back Bay, Boston; (617) 426-4444. 255 State St., Boston; (617) 742-5300. Legal Test Kitchen, 225 Northern Ave., Boston; (617) 330-7430. Charles Square, 20 University Rd., Cambridge; (617) 491-9400; legalseafoods.com. With 19 locations in

Massachusetts and more sites in East Coast states as far south as Georgia, Legal Sea Foods has designated its Liberty Wharf site as its flagship property with three floors of different dining concepts on the Boston waterfront. An old-fashioned fish market, casual dining at picnic tables, patio seating, private special occasion dining, and a rooftop deck with retractable walls and ceiling for al fresco dining in warm weather—Legal Harborside at 270 Northern Ave. has it all. You can count on Legal Sea Foods's famous clam chowder at every location, as well as an impressive menu—more than a dozen oysters on the half shell, seafood prepared on a wood-burning grill, and fun food such as a shrimp corn dog. Open for lunch and dinner daily.

Lineage, 242 Harvard St., Brookline; (617) 232-0065; lineage restaurant.com. The menu changes daily in order to serve the best from local seasonal markets, especially when it comes to seafood. This is fine dining, pricey but definitely worth it. Dinner might start with spicy lobster tacos offset by avocado mousse or Point Judith calamari over arugula. The grilled Scottish salmon is paired with caramelized fennel. The seafood tasting is extraordinary: salmon tartare, Prince Edward Island mussels, and roasted Gloucester day boat cod with Meyer lemon brown butter. Open for dinner nightly, for brunch Sun from 10:30 a.m. to 2 p.m.

Mare Oyster Bar, 135 Richmond St., North End, Boston; (617) 723-MARE; mareoysterbar.com. *Mare* (pronounced MAH-ray) is the Italian word for the sea, a good name for a restaurant that serves almost nothing but seafood. In season you can expect a dozen oysters on the raw bar menu. Lobster rolls come hot and buttery or cold with lemon mayonnaise on fresh brioche buns. Chef Greg Jordan's food is spectacular—check out their website for gorgeous food shots. Not to be missed: the jumbo shrimp cocktail, linguine with clams, truffle-crusted tuna served rare, zuppa di mare (seafood soup), and the grilled whole Mediterranean sea bass. Every dish seems to spill over with generous servings. Open for dinner nightly.

Neptune Oyster, 63 Salem St., North End, Boston; (617) 742-3474; neptuneoyster.com. It's so true that good things come in little packages. In this case the restaurant is small with 26 seats plus another 18 at the long raw bar, and the menu has but six entrees, including striped bass, cioppino, grilled whole bronzino, seared scallops, and butter-poached lobster. But there's no shortage of oysters from both coasts, shellfish, and delightful appetizers, including grilled cuttlefish, fried Ipswich clams, and mussels in a red curry broth. Nightly specials put more seafood into the spotlight, from lobster spaghettini to fish tacos. Arrive early or expect to wait in line for a seat. Open for lunch and dinner daily.

No Name Restaurant, 15½ Fish Pier, Waterfront, Boston; (617) 423-2705; nonamerestaurant.com. Back in 1917, when local fishermen would ask Nick Contos what was the name of his humble fish stand, he would say "no name, come eat." The name stuck as did its reputation for serving fresh seafood in a friendly atmosphere. The simple menu consists of broiled and fried fish and shellfish, steamed lobster, seafood sandwiches, and a fish chowder that never tastes quite the same since it's made with the daily catch. Best bets: the broiled smelts and the seafood plate overflowing with oysters, scallops, shrimp, and scrod. Large parties are advised to call ahead so they can accommodate your group. Open for lunch and dinner daily.

Pescatore, 158 Boston Ave., Ball Square, Somerville; (617) 623-0003; pescatoreseafood.com. A hidden treasure best describes this Italian neighborhood restaurant and seafood grill, owned by Anna and Luigi Buonopane, who were born in the Lazio region of Italy. Anna makes all the pasta from scratch, and that includes fusilli with shrimp, sea scallops, and lobster, and fettuccine with smoked salmon. A light hand is used to make all the seafood dishes, from simply seasoned swordfish steak to the haddock sautéed in extra virgin olive oil—both with generous portions of fresh vegetables on the side. The Pescatore pizza is pure heaven. Bring your own vino—this is a BYOB establishment. Open for dinner Tues through Sun.

Rabia's Italian Seafood & Oyster Bar, 73 Salem St., North End, Boston; (617) 227-6637; rabias.com. Creative Italian fare, mostly seafood, in a warm and colorful setting—that's the promise at Rabia's in the North End. An express lunch is available if you're in a hurry, but you'll want to linger over dinner, starting with the baked Maine lobster meat dip with crostini as an appetizer. Entrees include linguine with Cape Cod littlenecks, lobster ravioli, seafood risotto, and Alaskan king crab legs. Lobster makes an appearance in a number of classic dishes: lobster ravioli, lazy man's lobster, frutti di mare, zuppa del pescatore, and of course a fresh Maine lobster steamed and served over angel hair pasta. Open daily for lunch and dinner.

And It Goes So Well with Seafood

The return of breweries to Boston in the 1990s was cause for celebration among beer drinkers across New England. The products of South Boston's Harpoon Brewery have become the standby beers for many Boston pubs and bars, especially those in Southie (South Boston). Harpoon makes 8 year-round beers, 4 seasonal brews, and occasional specials in its 100-barrel limited edition series and its high-alcohol Leviathan series. Complimentary tastings are held twice each weekday afternoon, while guided tours and tastings for a fee are offered on weekends.

Harpoon Brewery, 306 Northern Ave., South Boston, Boston; (617) 574-9551; harpoonbrewery.com

Rowes Wharf Sea Grille, Boston Harbor Hotel, 70 Rowes Wharf, Waterfront, Boston; (617) 856-7744; roweswharfseagrille.com. The award-winning Chef Daniel Bruce knows seafood and wine probably better than anyone else in Boston. His equally respected restaurant offers unbeatable views of Boston Harbor. Both traditional and adventurous dishes can be found on the menu: New England clam chowder is served with griddled white corn bread, and flash-fried calamari is paired with ginger mayonnaise and fresh kimchee salad. Dinner might start with crispy peektoe crab rangoon and lobster arancini, a prelude to the simply grilled daily catch and the pan-roasted halibut. In warm weather al fresco dining is available by the water. Open for breakfast, lunch, and dinner.

Skipjack's, 199 Clarendon St., Boston; (617) 536-3500. 226 Patriot Place, Foxborough; (508) 543-2200; skipjacks.com. An innovative menu full of seafood from around the world, which includes an extensive raw bar and first-class sushi—that's what Skipjack's has to offer in two terrific locations—Boston's trendy Back Bay and Patriot Place, the world-class mall that surrounds the playing field of the New England Patriots football team, out in the suburbs. The only problem here is that it is very hard to decide what to order. The Chinatown salmon or the Baja fish tacos? The seafood cobb salad or the gingered sea bass? Even that most basic dish, fish-and-chips, is excellent. Insider tip: Children under 10 eat free at brunch. Open for lunch and dinner daily, for a jazz brunch Sun.

Thelonious Monkfish, 524 Massachusetts Ave., Central Square, Cambridge; (617) 441-2116; theloniousmonkfish.com. Sushi and Asian fusion are what this spot is all about. Of course there's a smooth jazz soundtrack playing in the background. The menu is massive with more sushi and sashimi than one could ever eat. Forge on until you get to the seafood section, and then try to decide: cranberry-teriyaki salmon? ginger cod? tilapia with pikking glaze? So much exciting food, so little time. Open for lunch and dinner daily.

Tia's on the Waterfront, 200 Atlantic Ave., Waterfront, Boston; (617) 227-0828; tiaswaterfront.com. Fans can't wait for Tia's with its huge patio to reopen every spring. What shall it be? The lobster cobb salad perhaps, or the crabmeat encrusted baked scrod. House specials include the baked stuffed lobster and the Red Dragon Seafood Sizzler, a mound of swordfish, scallops, and shrimp in a soy-ginger hoisin barbecue sauce. It's no surprise that this outdoor waterfront cafe has won so many prizes and accolades. A children's menu is available. Tia's is a seasonal operation, open Apr through Oct. It's recommended that you call for hours of operation.

Union Oyster House, 41 Union St., Downtown, Boston; (617) 227-2750; unionoysterhouse.com. There's something to be said about sitting at the same semi-circular oyster bar where Daniel Webster ate dozens of oysters on a daily basis. If only those walls could talk at the Union Oyster House, America's oldest restaurant. If you're lucky, you'll land in "The Kennedy Booth" on the second floor, where President John F. Kennedy used to feast in private. Of course there's so much more on the menu,

How to Shuck an Oyster

You will need a real oyster knife found in any local hardware store or fish market. Gloves are advised, at least one on the hand that is holding the oyster, but a towel will work just as well. Putting the oysters in the freezer for about 15 minutes before shucking is best.

1) If using a small towel, drape it in your hand over the oyster, flat side up, or place it on a firm surface. Make sure to hold the oyster firmly. Slip the point of the knife between the top and bottom shell between the hinge.

2) Using a twisting motion, pry the two shells apart, making sure not to lose any of the liquid inside.

3) Run the knife around the top shell until you get to the other side. This will sever the tendon on the top of the shell.

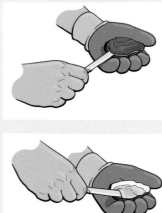

4) Slide the knife under the oyster to cut it free from its shell (it will be connected by a tough knob). Place the oyster on a bed of crushed ice and serve with your favorite topping.

including hearty portions of Boston scrod, seafood Newburg, and platters of seafood fried and broiled. Modern-day dishes range from lobster ravioli to lobster scampi over linguine. A children's menu is available. Open for lunch and dinner daily.

Clam Shacks

Barking Crab, 88 Sleeper St., Waterfront, Boston; (617) 426-2722; barkingcrab.com. The bright red and yellow colors get customers in a festive mood before they even sit down at indoor and outdoor picnic tables (weather permitting) for a seafood feast. All the seafood that New England is known for is on the menu, and the daily specials are just that—special: mussels Gorgonzola for an appetizer, shrimp and mussel étouffée for an entree. Perched on the edge of the city's historic Fort Point Channel, this is one of the few restaurants in Boston where you can arrive by boat. This coastal clam shack in a funky urban setting is very popular with tourists. A second Barking Crab can be found in Newport, Rhode Island (see page 86). Open for lunch and dinner daily.

Jasper White's Summer Shack, 149 Alewife Brook Pkwy., Alewife, Cambridge; (617) 520-9500. 50 Dalton St., Back Bay, Boston; (617) 867-9955. 850 Providence Hwy., Dedham; (781) 407-9955. 96 Derby St., Hingham; (781) 740-9555; summershackrestaurant .com. With its 350 seats and super-bright colors, the original Summer Shack seemed outrageous when it opened in Cambridge, but now with similar "shacks" in other locations, including Mohegan Sun in Connecticut (see page 36), it's become a wonderful norm. These super casual restaurants are fun places to dine, with all the basic seafood fare plus chicken, steaks, and even a mean meat loaf to make everyone happy. The Summer Shack in Boston offers Red Sox baseball fans something more than a Fenway frank, namely a choice in chowders, fish tacos, and all kinds of fish dinners, from bacon-wrapped local hake to pan-roasted arctic char. Open for lunch and dinner daily.

Seafood & Specialty Markets

Captain Marden's Seafoods, 279 Linden St., Wellesley; (781) 235-0860; captainmardens.com. This is the purveyor favored by most fine restaurants and gourmet shops in Boston, a well-respected wholesale fishmonger with a comprehensive retail operation. The seafood party platters are very popular with home cooks who entertain during the holidays. Online shopping is offered. An on-site restaurant offers breakfast, lunch, and dinner. Watch for their seafood truck on the streets of Boston. Open Mon through Fri from 8 a.m. to 6 p.m., Sat from 8 a.m. to 5:30 p.m., Sun from 10 a.m. to 5 p.m.

C-Mart Supermarket, 692 Washington St., Chinatown, Boston; (617) 338-1717. 109 Lincoln St., Boston; (617) 426-8888. 50 Herald St., Boston; (617) 338-8811; no website. Unassuming on the outside, almost overwhelming on the inside, this Chinatown market stocks everything you might expect in dry goods. The market exceeds expectations when it comes to fresh fruits and vegetables, fresh fish on ice, and giant fish tanks filled with live eel, codfish, shrimp, rock lobster, and crab. Open daily from 8 a.m. to 8 p.m.

Court House Fish Market, 484 Cambridge St., East Cambridge, Cambridge; (617) 876-6716; courthouseseafood.com. The verdict is in, and the Court House has been found guilty . . . of having the freshest seafood available. "Quality fresh fish since 1912" is the motto at this fish market that caters to the local Portuguese community. Especially for that audience, fresh sardines and small stickleback fish are flown in from Portugal every week. Fresh seafood is delivered there daily. It's wise to call ahead to see what's on hand. Next door is the Court House Seafood Restaurant. Select a fish fillet at the market, and they'll cook it for you at the restaurant while you wait. Open Tues, Wed, Thurs, and Sat from 8 a.m. to 6 p.m., Fri from 8 a.m. to 7 p.m.

The Fishmonger, 252 Huron Ave., Huron Village, Cambridge; (617) 661-4834. For more than 20 years, Cheryl Williams has been winning over customers with an impressive display of fish on ice and an open kitchen where prepared foods are created to be cooked at home. Some of the most popular dishes are an old-fashioned tuna noodle casserole, poached salmon, and the Mediterranean fish stew. Open Tues through Fri from 10 a.m. to 6:30 p.m., Sat from 10 a.m. to 5:30 p.m.

Hong Kong Supermarket, 1 Brighton Ave., Allston; (617) 787-2288. This Asian food emporium offers more than 20 varieties of fresh fish, including eel, and everything else you'll need if you're an adventurous

Whole Foods

It all started in Brookline in 1975 when the first Bread & Circus store opened. By 1992, it was acquired by Whole Foods, which has a sterling reputation for the highest-quality seafood available. Ten Whole Foods stores now serve the Boston area:

15 Washington St., Brighton; (617) 738-8187

181 Cambridge St., Beacon Hill, Boston, (617) 723-0004

15 Westland Ave., Fenway, Boston, (617) 375-1010

200 Alewife Brook Pkwy., Fresh Pond, Cambridge,
    (617) 491-0040

115 Prospect St., Central Square, Cambridge, (617) 492-0070

340 River St., Cambridgeport, Cambridge, (617) 876-6990

413 Centre St., Jamaica Plain, (617) 553-5400

916 Walnut St., Newton, (617) 969-1141

647 Washington St., Newton, (617) 965-2070

442 Washington St., Wellesley, (781) 235-7262

home cook. The store's adjoining food court (the Food Connection) abounds with quality Asian street food, good for a cheap meal on the run. Fans rave about the Korean bibimbap. Open daily from 8:30 a.m. to 11 p.m.

James Hook + Co., 15–17 Northern Ave., Waterfront, Boston; (617) 423-5501; jameshooklobster.com. Since 1925 this business has been shipping lobsters to restaurants and home cooks across the nation—these days it amounts to more than 50,000 pounds a day. The retail market is known for its shellfish and finfish, depending on the daily catch. You also can get lobster rolls, clam chowder, lobster bisque, lobster pie, and lobster mac and cheese. Open Mon through Thurs from 9 a.m. to 5 p.m., Fri from 9 a.m. to 6 p.m., Sat from 9 a.m. to 5 p.m., Sun from 9 a.m. to 2 p.m.

Morse Fish Company, 1401 Washington St., South End, Boston; (617) 262-9375; morsefish.com. A neighborhood fish market in business since 1903, Morse always stocks the local fresh catch. They also have a few tables where you can dine on fried fish dishes, or you can order your food to go. The fried haddock sandwich is the number one request. Open Mon through Thurs and Sat from 11 a.m. to 8 p.m., Fri from 11 a.m. to 9 p.m., Sun from noon to 8 p.m.

New Deal Fish Market, 622 Cambridge St., East Cambridge, Cambridge; (617) 876-8227; newdealfishmarket.com. In business since 1928, the New Deal offers the daily catch in Boston and Chatham, a full range of seafood from other New England ports, and squid from Point Judith in Rhode Island (the squid capital of the world). Open Mon from 3 to 7 p.m., Tues through Fri from 10 a.m. to 7 p.m., Sat from 9:30 a.m. to 6:30 p.m.

North End Fish–Mercato del Mare, 99 Salem St., North End, Boston; (857) 362-7477; northendfish.com. This subterranean shop features the local catch as well as select imports. The staff is always willing to give customers a recipe idea or cooking tip. At the front window you can watch fresh sushi being assembled. This boutique shop validates parking. Open Mon through Fri from 10 a.m. to 8 p.m., Sat from 10 a.m. to 6 p.m., Sun from noon to 5 p.m.

Boston Harbor

Reliable Market, 45 Union Sq., Union Square, Somerville; (617) 623-9620. If you love to cook Asian food, this is the market for you, especially when it comes to fresh produce, fresh local seafood, and exotic western Pacific fish. Open Mon through Sat from 9:30 a.m. to 9 p.m., Sun from 10 a.m. to 7 p.m.

Sakanaya Japanese Fish Market, 75 Linden St., Allston; (617) 254-0009; sakanayaboston.com. Excellent sushi at bargain prices—that's the big draw here. They also sell impeccably fresh fish so you can make your own sushi at home. Many Japanese people shop here, and their website is in Japanese—that speaks volumes. Open Tues through Sun from 10:30 a.m. to 7:30 p.m.

Waltham Fresh Fish & Prime, 36 Spruce St., Waltham; (781) 891-1515; walthamfreshfishnprime.com. This market does it all—fresh fish plus fried seafood, subs, salads, wraps, gyros, and even baklava for dessert. A veritable smorgasbord of ethnic cuisines is available. Open Mon through Sat from 9:30 a.m. to 9 p.m., Sun from 9:30 a.m. to 7 p.m.

Wulf's Fish Market, 407 Harvard St., Brookline; (617) 277-2506. In business since 1926, they must be doing everything right at this tiny shop, including getting their fish daily from the Boston Fish Pier. It's a treat to watch the enthusiastic fishmongers in crisp white aprons fillet the whole fish out in the open. Open Mon through Fri from 9 a.m. to 6 p.m., Sat from 9 a.m. to 5 p.m.

Yankee Lobster Company, 300 Northern Ave., Boston; (617) 345-9799; yankeelobstercompany.com. It's hard to say this is just a fish market. For more than half a century, Yankee has been a lobster wholesaler. But the retail arm of this operation is where you can also get the freshest affordable seafood on the waterfront. The thick chowder, lobster bisque, lobster roll, and fried scallops are highly recommended. Open Mon through Sat from 10 a.m. to 9 p.m., Sun from 11 a.m. to 6 p.m.

Boston Events

January
Dorchester Restaurant Week,. restaurantweekboston .com/?neighborhood=Dorchester. For the last two weeks of January, participating restaurants in Dorchester and adjoining Milton offer fixed-price dinner menus Sun through Thurs. Many restaurants feature their signature seafood dishes.

March
Restaurant Week Boston, restaurantweekboston.com. More than 200 restaurants in Boston and surrounding towns offer specially priced menus at lunch and dinner. Many restaurants feature their signature seafood dishes.

April
Taste of Dorchester, mahahome.org/tasteofdorchester. Sample a wide range of cuisines from Italian to Jamaican, Indian to Vietnamese to support the Massachusetts Affordable Housing Alliance. Many restaurants feature their signature seafood dishes.

Taste of South Boston, tasteofsouthboston.com. The easiest way to get a taste of the dining renaissance along the waterfront in South Boston is by attending this event at the Seaport World Trade Center. Many restaurants feature their signature seafood dishes.

July
Boston Chowderfest, bostonharborfest.com. Chowderfest is one of the highlights of Boston Harborfest, a weeklong celebration leading up to Independence Day.

August
Fisherman's Feast, fishermansfeast.com. Founded in 1910, the Fisherman's Feast is the oldest of the North End's religious festivals. Vendors sell all kinds of Italian foods. For a full list of summer feasts, see northend boston.com.

Restaurant Week Boston, restaurantweekboston.com. The economically priced lunches and dinners at many Boston restaurants are so popular that Restaurant Week is held twice a year (see March). Many restaurants feature their signature seafood dishes.

OUTSIDE OF BOSTON
From Westport to Springfield, from the North Shore to the South Shore, this section of *Seafood Lover's New England* explores the entire state of Massachusetts outside of Boston, Cape Cod, and the Islands. For this is how most people view Massachusetts, in general terms. Of course there's central Massachusetts and the Berkshires. But for the purposes of this book, we have categorized the seafood restaurants, clam shacks, and specialty and seafood markets as coming from Boston, Outside of Boston, and Cape Cod and the Islands (the Islands being Martha's Vineyard and Nantucket).

Seafood Restaurants

Bayside Restaurant, 1253 Horseneck Rd., Westport; (508) 636-5882; thebaysiderestaurant.com. For decades this funky family restaurant has been pleasing sun-worshippers who can dine on the lively terrace or in the shade of the bright blue and yellow grass umbrellas. The dog-friendly patio offers a view of a wildlife sanctuary with Buzzard's Bay in the distance. Environmentally conscious, this was the first restaurant in Massachusetts to be granted a "green" certification. Fresh seafood, local produce, and all-natural free-range chicken and beef, that's what sets this place apart. The quahog chowder and coleslaw are made from scratch, using old family recipes. The salmon and asparagus wrap with dill mayo, spinach, and tomato is very tempting. And if you like old-fashioned pies, this is the

place for you. Johnny-cakes and Indian pudding round out the menu, a real slice of Americana. Open for lunch and dinner daily from Memorial Day to Labor Day, lunch and dinner Thurs through Sun from Labor Day to Memorial Day, breakfast Sat and Sun year-round.

The Back Eddy, 1 Bridge Rd., Westport; (508) 636-6500; the backeddy.com. Aptly named, the Back Eddy (a current that runs counterclockwise to the mainstream) is a seafood restaurant that does everything just a little differently. This was one of the first restaurants to invest in local ingredients, especially produce and fish. The menu offers old-fashioned dishes, some with a Portuguese accent, all with a modern touch. Their raw bar is one of the best. The signature clam chowder is flavored with roasted corn and apple wood bacon. The oven-roasted native cod comes with local littlenecks and chorizo. The colorful outdoor patio/bar/grill area leads to a pier where you can tie up your boat, with views of Westport Harbor, spectacular at sunset. It can get noisy, and the wait for a table can be long. Beware of the "wicked" mosquitoes, so notorious that the Back Eddy website gives updated reports on the summer pests. This is a seasonal operation, open late Mar through Jan 1, with hours that vary. Check the website for hours.

Chef Wayne's Big Mamou, 63 Liberty St., Springfield; (413) 732-1011; chefwaynes-bigmamou.com. If you like your seafood to have a Cajun kick, this is the little place for you, thanks to Chef Wayne Hooker. His busy Louisiana-style restaurant also offers Creole dishes. Some of the most popular items on the extensive menu are the fried oysters with remoulade, crab cakes with Creole spices, spicy fried catfish with jambalaya rice, crawfish quesadillas, blackened shrimp, seafood jambalaya, and the signature dish on the dinner menu—a spicy combination of crawfish tail meat, shrimp, and vegetables in a lobster brandy cream sauce served over puff pastry. This is a BYOB establishment, so bring a cooler packed with cold beer and wine. Open for lunch and dinner Mon through Sat, for private parties only Sun.

Duckworth's Bistrot, 197 E. Main St., Gloucester; (978) 282-4426; duckworthsbistrot.com. Ask anyone in the beautiful coastal town of Gloucester where to eat, and chances are you'll hear an enthusiastic one-word response: Duckworth's. This is fine dining that marries the bounty of local waters with local, seasonal ingredients. What makes this restaurant unique is that you are able to choose any entree in a full or half portion, and that includes seared sea scallops with honey grapefruit beurre blanc, seafood stew, lobster risotto, line-caught cod, and pan-roasted monkfish. Open for dinner in winter Tues through Sat in winter, Tues through Sun in summer.

Essex Seafood, 143 Eastern Ave. (Rte. 133), Essex; (978) 768-7233; essexseafood.com. All the standard seafood fare is on the simple menu, and then there are the intriguing dishes: the popcorn haddock boat, the cod cheek boat, and fried lobster plate. They even offer clam cakes, something rarely seen north of Rhode Island. This Cape Ann restaurant offers generous portions in the dining area or for takeout. The fish market and lobster pool on the premises can provide almost any kind of seafood you desire with 24 hours notice. This is a great place to stop at after a day at the beach. Open for lunch and dinner daily.

FINZ, 76 Wharf St., Pickering Wharf, Salem; (978) 744-8485; hipfinz.com. Three sides of this waterfront restaurant are huge windows overlooking Salem Harbor. In warm weather the huge deck gives you an up close view of boats in the marina. In the off-season the fireside lounge is the place to be. Not surprisingly, seafood is the main attraction here, from the truly impressive raw bar to the most popular menu selections: buffalo calamari, wasabi oysters, and lobster ravioli. A children's menu is available. Open for lunch and dinner daily.

The Lobster Pool, 329 Granite St. (Rte. 127), Cape Ann, Rockport; (978) 546-7808. You won't be disappointed here—big portions of delicious fresh seafood at outdoor tables by the rocky shore with incredible views of Folly Cove, especially at sunset. It's an unpretentious seafood shack that serves boiled lobsters, seafood plates with fries and coleslaw, and chowders. The catch of the day, often bought right off the boats that come into the harbor, can be broiled or grilled. The fried fish on a toasted roll comes highly recommended. Bring your own alcoholic beverages, because this is a BYOB establishment. You can dine inside this seasonal fish house or out back where it's dog friendly. Tipping the waitstaff is not allowed. Open Apr through Oct—it's recommended that you call for hours of operation. During spring and fall, The Lobster Pool can be booked for private parties, including clambakes.

The Lobster Shanty, 25 Front St. at Artist's Row, Salem; (978) 745-5449; lobstershantysalem.com. A local dive bar with class—that's how the folks at The Lobster Shanty feel about their seasonal operation. For more than 30 years, great food and great service in a very casual setting have been their formula for success. Popular menu items include wicked spicy crab cakes, hot and cold lobster rolls, lobster risotto, lobster mac and cheese, and the catch of the day, baked or fried. For a real treat while waiting for your food, have a Lobstertini, a cocktail of vodka and lobster essence garnished with a chilled lobster claw. The patio is dog friendly— they even have a doggie menu. Open from Apr 1 to Jan 15 with seasonal hours. In summer open for lunch and dinner daily; in the off-season for lunch Thurs through Sun and for dinner nightly.

Red Rock Bistro, 141 Humphrey St., Swampscott; (781) 595-1414; redrockbistro.com. What a setting! Indoors, almost every table has a water view of the Boston skyline, ideal at sunset. In nice weather there are 2 outdoor patios overlooking the waves crashing below. Mostly sea-food is on the menu, from spicy tuna tartare and colossal shrimp cocktail for starters to shrimp and lobster pizzas. Entrees include pan-seared scal-lops, bouillabaisse, salmon with vegetable fritters, and sushi-grade tuna with jasmine rice. The swordfish chop is slathered with peach barbecue sauce. Open for lunch and dinner daily, for brunch Sun from 10:30 a.m. to 3 p.m.

Riva, 116 Front St., Scituate; (781) 545-5881; rivarestaurant.net. Rated as one of the top restaurants on the South Shore, Riva is a casual Italian trattoria in the scenic downtown of a quaint fishing village. With a view of Scituate Harbor, you can dine on Chef Michael Tondorf's scal-lop risotto or pancetta-wrapped day boat cod. The calamari is served with garlic butter sauce. The shrimp carbonara is to die for. The nightly specials

Sensational Seafood in a Strange Setting

The North Shore of Massachusetts has some of the state's strangest restaurant architecture and signage. The strangest of all just might be the Clam Box, which looks like a giant clam box, in historic Ipswich. The local landmark was built in 1938 by Dick Greenleaf to resemble the open-flapped carton in which fried clams are served. Plates overflow with fresh fried seafood, and mini meals are also on the menu. You can dine in the comfortable dining room or out on the deck. A seasonal operation, they urge everyone to call ahead for their hours, which vary and are subject to change without notice. Open for lunch and dinner daily in the summer.

Clam Box of Ipswich, 246 High St. (Rte. 1A), Ipswich; (978) 356-9707; ipswichma.com/clambox

showcase what was landed in local waters that day. Open for dinner nightly, for brunch Sun from 8 a.m. to 1 p.m.

Turner's Seafood Grill & Market, 506 Main St., Melrose; (781) 662-0700; turners-seafood.com. You can't go wrong when a restaurant has a seafood market on its premises. Turner's does everything right with a turn-of-the-twentieth-century oyster bar and an open kitchen. Classic New England fare—clam chowder, lobster bisque, oyster stew, baked stuffed shrimp, fish-and-chips, and so much more—is on the menu. But there's also plenty of exotic food to tempt you: Szechuan shrimp and scallops, hake almondine, orange ginger salmon, and mussels and calamari fra diavolo. The big menu's most intriguing dish? Blackened wild jumbo shrimp with orange marmalade vinaigrette and a fried blue cheese risotto cake. A children's menu is also available. Open for lunch and dinner Tues through Sun.

Clam Shacks

Handy Hill Creamery, 55 Hixbridge Rd., Westport; (508) 636-8888. Starting out in 1975 as a simple ice cream stand, Handy Hill added food to its menu over the years. Folks look forward every summer to seeing the bright blue and white awning open up for the season, signaling it's time for the long lines to form at the take-out window. The beach food, especially the clam fritters, is worth the wait. The lobster roll also gets a thumbs-up, as does the ice cream. So many flavors! Picnic tables are scattered throughout the shady property. In the summer this place is often packed with sunburnt people on their way home from nearby Horseneck Beach. Open daily in the summer. In the off-season, open Fri from 3 to 8 p.m., Sat and Sun from 11 a.m. to 8 p.m.

Kelly's Roast Beef, 410 Revere Beach Blvd., Revere; (781) 284-9129. Rte. 1 South at Lynn Fells Parkway, Saugus; (781) 233-5000. Rte. 9 East (inside Jordan's Furniture), Natick; (508) 872-4900. 165 Endicott St. (Liberty Tree Mall), Danvers; (978) 777-1290. 35 Revere Beach Pkwy./Rte. 16 East, Medford; (781) 393-4899. kellysroastbeef.com. It all started in 1951 in Revere, right across from the beach, and it seems to get more popular with each passing year. Yes, it says roast beef, but the seafood is sensational. Kelly's is really a modern-day clam shack that also serves fabulous roast beef sandwiches. The freshest available seafood is fried in pure vegetable oil, from the basic North Atlantic fish plate to the tender, whole-belly clams. Scallops and shrimp are other

An Authentic Clambake at Francis Farm

Since 1890, traditional New England clambakes have been held at Francis Farm in Rehoboth. It used to be that you had to be part of a family reunion or company picnic to dine in the open-air pavilion, but this landmark facility now offers public dining Fri through Sun in the summer. A full menu is offered to diners under a large tent. Public clambakes are also scheduled on certain dates in July and Aug. You can play horseshoes or bocce while the clams, potatoes, sausage, fish, and sweet corn bake in 4 inches of rockweed layered over hot cast-iron rocks, all under a heavy canvas. Make sure you try some lemonade from the Sweet Shop as you explore the 60-acre farm. Watch out for the mosquitoes.

Francis Farm, 27 Francis Farm Rd., Rehoboth; (508) 252-3212; francisfarm.net options. The fish sandwich can't be beat. The lobster roll is made with the meat from two whole lobsters. You can dine in or take out at each location. Hours vary; generally open for lunch and dinner daily.

Kent's Restaurant, 1675 GAR Hwy., Swansea; (508) 672-9293; kentsrestaurant.com. Kent's may be short on ambiance, with just three picnic tables on a grassy area next to the parking lot, but that doesn't stop the crowds from forming at the take-out window, especially on Friday and Saturday nights. Chances are, many of them are craving the creamy New England clam chowder. Try dunking one of their golden clam cakes into the chowder. You can buy the clam cakes individually, which is great when you're craving just 1 or 2 instead of the usual dozen. Another plus—they offer a full clam boil, a local fave. That includes steamers, potatoes, corn on the cob, 2 hot dogs, 2 sausages, 2 chorizo links, and a cup of that excellent chowder. Open for lunch and dinner daily.

Woodman's of Essex, 121 Main St. (Rte. 133), Essex; (978) 768-6057; woodmans.com. If you are a lover of fried clams, you have to make a pilgrimage here, where the fried clam was invented by Lawrence "Chubby" Woodman. With that, Chubby's tiny seafood shack prospered and grew into an award-winning, nationally known eatery. All the usual fried seafood is

offered along with steamed clams and boiled lobsters. A spacious, sunny dining room is open year-round. Picnic tables are on the grounds. Woodman's also offers authentic clambakes and ships live lobsters and clams anywhere in the country. A gluten-free menu is available. Children eat free with the purchase of a dinner plate Sept through Apr. Insider tip: Lines can be long, so go in the off-season, if you can. Open for lunch and dinner daily.

Seafood & Specialty Markets

Amaral's Market, 488 Belleville Ave., New Bedford; (508) 996-1222; amaralsmarket.com. An excellent market that specializes in fresh and frozen fish with strong ties to the local Portuguese community. Here you'll find fish rarely found in mainstream markets, as well as the more common sea bass, haddock, hake, and squid. Proximity to the local catch enables Amaral's to carry the freshest cold-water seafood every day of the year. Frozen octopus and salt cod are always available. Online shopping is offered. Open daily at 8 a.m.

Brant Rock Fish Market, 267 Ocean St., Marshfield; (781) 834-6231. For more than 50 years, this market has been pleasing customers with nothing but the highest-quality seafood. Fans rave about the sweet scallops and the fairly priced "lobstahs." Owner Henry Dunbar relies on local fishermen for most of his inventory and travels to the Boston Fish Market as needed. The old-time fishmonger buys whole fish and custom cuts the fillets and steaks. Bay scallops from Nantucket are available in season from Apr to Nov. Open daily from 9 a.m. to 6 p.m. in summer; closed on Mon in the off-season.

Cape Quality Seafood, 657 Dartmouth St., Dartmouth; (508) 996-6724; capequalityseafood.com. A seafood market with a restaurant on the premises—you can't go wrong here. The market carries some of the largest lobsters you'll ever see, as well as local fish rather than from overseas. The restaurant has a huge menu and relies on family recipes from past generations in making everything from Portuguese littlenecks to stuffed fillet of sole. They also claim to have the best coconut shrimp from here to the Caribbean. A children's menu is available. The much shorter lunch menu even offers a clam boil—very unusual. The restaurant is open for lunch and dinner Wed through Sun. The market is open Mon through Sat from 9 a.m. to 6 p.m., Sun from 9 a.m. to 2 p.m.

Fisherman's Fleet, 689 Salem St., Malden; (781) 322-5200; fresh fish.net. This quality seafood purveyor is *the* source for lobsters, shellfish, seafood, chowder and bisques, caviar, and clambake packages. Online shopping is available on the website. This is a fourth-generation family operation. Open Mon through Fri from 9 a.m. to 5:30 p.m.

Hingham Lobster Pound, 4 Broad Cove Rd., Rte. 3A, Hingham; (781) 749-1984; hinghamlobster.com. Since 1958 this no-frills take-out joint has had folks lining up for its fried and grilled seafood, especially for its generous lobster roll. A children's menu is available. A fish market is also located inside the red building with white trim. With 2 hours advance notice, they can also provide you with steamed lobsters. In the summer open Tues through Sun from 11 a.m. to 8:30 p.m. In the off-season open Wed through Sun from 11 a.m. to 8 p.m.

Ipswich Shellfish Fish Market, 8 Hayward St., Ipswich; (978) 356-6941; ipswichfishmarket.com. This giant wholesale distributor of seafood has a modern fish market next door where owner Chrissi Pappas oversees the full line of the freshest daily catch on the North Shore. In addition the market has a gourmet chef who prepares a hot lunch every day, as well as seafood that is cooked while you wait and fully prepared food for you to take home and cook. That includes marinated mussels, jumbo crab cakes, fish cakes, salmon cakes, traditional and lobster stuffed clams, lobster salad, panko-crusted fried haddock, grilled salmon, and grilled shrimp with a Greek accent. You also can arrange to have seafood shipped anywhere in the country. Open Tues through Sat from 10 a.m. to 6 p.m.

Mullaney's Harborside Fish Market, 8 Allen Place, Scituate; (781) 545-5000. 754 Chief Justice Cushing Hwy., Cohasset; (781) 383-1181; mullaneysfish.com. This wholesale fish purveyor has two retail stores in Scituate and Cohasset. Seafood lovers describe Mullaney's as "excellent" with lots of praise for them getting their cod, haddock, sole, and shellfish from local day boats, so it's always super-fresh. Prepared seafood dishes are also available. Open daily from 10 a.m. to 6 p.m.

Nautical Mile Market, 406 Columbia Rd., Rte. 53, Hanover; (781) 826-2001; nauticalmilemarket.com. In search of a jumbo lobster? This is the place for you. Lobsters weighing as much as 6 pounds are available, as well as fresh and frozen fish, shellfish, prepared food items (clam chowder, lobster bisque, stuffed quahogs), and heat-and-eat dishes (lobster mac and cheese, seafood Alfredo, baked haddock). The live lobsters can be cooked upon request for an additional charge. A short menu of cooked seafood for takeout is also offered—a family fish feed, appetizers, sandwiches, and fried seafood. Open Mon through Sat from 10 a.m. to 7 p.m., Sun from 9 a.m. to 6 p.m.

Roy Moore Lobster Company, 39 Bearskin Neck, Rockport; (978) 546-6696; no website. Location, location, location. This authentic seafood shack is on quaint Bearskin Neck. Around back on the deck you have a perfect view of Rockport's famous Motif No. 1 as you sit on an old lobster crate to eat a pretty good lobster roll. It's BYOB, so bring your own alcoholic beverages in a cooler. And then you can use that cooler when you stop inside to buy impeccably fresh fish, clams, and live crabs and lobsters at the small retail fish market. This is a seasonal operation. Open from late Mar through Oct daily from 8 a.m. to 6 p.m.

Sid Wainer & Sons Specialty Produce and Specialty Foods, 2301 Purchase St., New Bedford; (800) 249-0447; sidwainer.com. A bit hard to find, but worth the trip, especially if you are a foodie. This company supplies the best restaurants in New England with gourmet ingredients, and now The Gourmet Outlet is also open for home cooks who might be looking for smoked seafood, imported anchovies, and caviar. The best day to visit is Saturday, when a remarkable number of taste samples are offered by the corporate chef, everything from Spanish olive oils to aged balsamic vinegar and other specialty foods. Open Mon through Sat from 9 a.m. to 5 p.m.

Snug Harbor Fish Company, 459 Washington St., Duxbury; (781) 934-8167; snugharborfishcompany.com. This family-owned business has an excellent reputation for the freshest seafood, and that includes lobsters, halibut, codfish, haddock, shrimp, salmon, sole, scallops, oysters, littlenecks, mussels, squid, and tuna. Popular prepared foods are the housemade Portuguese stuffed quahogs, crab cakes, and salmon burgers. Hours change with the seasons. In the fall and winter, open Thurs through Sun from noon to 6 p.m. In the spring and summer, open daily at 11 a.m.

Tony's Seafood, 1365 Fall River Ave., Seekonk; (508) 336-6800; tonysfreshseafood.com. For more than 30 years, this spotless market has been satisfying the local need for the finest in seafood. Freshly caught fish is delivered daily via the company's wholesale operation. Tony's also has a sterling reputation when it comes to ready-to-cook meals, appetizers such as stuffed quahogs, and "hot to go" lobsters, shrimp, clams, and oysters. This is one of the few fish markets to carry select wines and craft beers. Open Mon through Sat from 9 a.m. to 6 p.m.

Turner's Seafood Grill & Market, 506 Main St., Melrose; (781) 662-0700; turners-seafood.com. This combination restaurant and fish market is part of an impressive operation that includes the Gloucester Seafood Market (4 Smith St., Gloucester; 978-281-7172) and the Turner Fish Plant in Gloucester. With a history that dates back to 1920, the Turner family knows seafood. The online store offers fresh fish, appetizers, main dish specialties such as baked stuffed shrimp, live lobsters, and party packages that are delivered dock to door. The Gloucester site is open Mon through Sat from 10 a.m. to 6:30 p.m.; in summer it's also open on Sun from 10 a.m. to 2 p.m. The Melrose location is open Tues through Thurs from 9 a.m. to 9 p.m., Fri and Sat from 9 a.m. to 10 p.m., Sun from 1 to 8 p.m.

Westport Lobster Company, 915 Main Rd., Westport; (508) 636-8500. Located in a brown-shingled former stable, this unassuming market is the go-to place for locals in search of deep-sea fish such as tuna and swordfish and the more coastal haddock, flounder, and cod. Fresh shellfish glistens on crushed ice. Lobster is the main attraction, but there's also great interest in the seafood that is smoked on the premises. The service is friendly and knowledgeable. Open Tues through Sun from 10 a.m. to 6 p.m.

Wood's Seafood Market & Restaurant, 15 Town Pier, Plymouth; (508) 746-0261. Here's another one of those wonderful seafood market/restaurant collaborations, right on the Town Pier. A throwback to the fish shacks of yesteryear along the New England coast, Wood's gets mixed reviews—folks seem to either love or hate this place. The market carries everything you'd expect, from cod and haddock to tuna and swordfish, with plenty of lobsters always on hand. The market is open daily from 9 a.m. to 7 p.m. The restaurant is open daily from 11 a.m. to 8 p.m.

Outside of Boston Events

May
Taste of Essex, Essex Room, Woodman's, 121 Main St. (Rte. 133), Essex; (978) 768-7335. A gala food and wine reception, with plenty of

seafood being served, features specialties from Essex restaurants as a benefit for local scholarships.

June
New Fish Festival, Gloucester House Restaurant, 63 Rogers St., Gloucester; (978) 283-1601. Chefs from restaurants all over Cape Ann participate in a cooking contest to highlight the appeal of underutilized species.

Mid-July
Annual Clambake, sponsored by the Lloyd Center for the Environment and held at Demarest Lloyd State Park, 430 Potomska Rd., Dartmouth; (508) 990-0505, ext. 13. This environmental research and education organization serves up an old-fashioned clambake with all the fixings to raise funds to support its programs.

Mid-August
Gloucester Waterfront Festival, Western Avenue and Stacey Boulevard, Gloucester; (978) 283-1601. A pancake breakfast on Saturday and a gala lobster bake on Sunday anchor this celebration of Gloucester.

September
Fall Festival, various locations, Marblehead; (781) 631-2868. The main event: tastings of chili and chowders from local restaurants.

Early September
Bourne Scallop Fest, Buzzards Bay Park, Main Street, Buzzards Bay; (508) 759-6000. Buzzards Bay is renowned for its scallops, and this long-standing annual celebration of the harvest features grilled, fried, and baked scallop dishes.

Late September
Essex Clamfest, Memorial Park, Essex; (978) 283-1601. Essex has been famous for its clams for more than three centuries, and a chowder-tasting competition is at the heart of this annual celebration.

CAPE COD & THE ISLANDS

To appreciate this part of Massachusetts, you must look at a map so you can see how Cape Cod extends like a curled arm out into the Atlantic Ocean with Martha's Vineyard about 7 miles off its coast and the slightly more exclusive Nantucket about 30 miles south. The amount of coastline, all told, is staggering. Sport fishermen rave about the striped bass and bluefish in these waters; halibut and tuna can be found around the Nantucket shoals. Wellfleet oysters and mussels from Chatham are just some of the local delicacies available to home cooks in local fish markets. If you prefer to eat out, you can chow down at a shabby clam shack or dine in an elegant old inn. If you're really lucky on your visit to this region, you'll get to experience an authentic Cape Cod clambake.

Seafood Restaurants

Black Dog Tavern, Coastwise Wharf, Beach Street Extension, Vineyard Haven, Martha's Vineyard; (508) 693-9223. Black Dog Cafe, 509 State Rd., Vineyard Haven; (508) 696-8190; theblackdog .com. This is not a seafood restaurant per se, but no trip to this island would be complete without a stop at the iconic Black Dog. A true landmark, the tavern is a good place for quahog chowder and hearty sandwiches such as the coconut-crusted tuna on brioche or the crab cake on focaccia. The entrees include fish-and-chips, steamed lobster, pan-seared salmon, and white clam linguine. The cafe serves lighter fare. Open daily from 7 a.m. to 10 p.m. June through Sept. In the off-season, they recommend that you call ahead for their hours.

Nantucket Harbor

Bookstore & Restaurant, 50 Kendrick Ave., Wellfleet; (508) 349-3154; wellfleetoyster.com. This restaurant offers waterfront dining overlooking Wellfleet Harbor. Family owned and operated since 1964, the restaurant is open daily from Valentine's Day through New Year's Day. The shellfish on the menu comes from nearby beds. All the seafood comes from local fishermen—key ingredients in the buttery fish pot, fruits of the sea over linguine, Portuguese stew, shrimp scampi, and other dishes on the modern American menu. A real bookstore can be found in the back, and the downstairs pub is called The Bomb Shelter. Open mid-Feb through Dec for breakfast, lunch, and dinner.

Brant Point Grill at the White Elephant, 50 Easton St., Nantucket; (508) 228-2500; whitelephanthotel.com. BPG, as it is called by the locals, offers unbeatable harbor views and a menu anchored by fresh seafood. Dinner might begin with white sturgeon caviar or a Nantucket crab cake. Entrees could be arctic char, fluke, cod, or a grilled 2-pound lobster. At lunch you can graze on fried calamari with zucchini chips, a lobster roll with lemon chervil mayo, or fried clams with seasoned fries. This is a seasonal restaurant that reopens every year for the island's famous Daffodil Weekend in April. In season BPG is open for breakfast, lunch, and dinner daily, for brunch Sun from 10 a.m. to 3 p.m.

Brewster Fish House, 2208 Main St., Rte. 6A, Brewster; (508) 896-7867; brewsterfish.com. Arguably the best restaurant on Cape Cod, Brewster's is respected for its fresh, artful food. At this former fish market, that means all the usual fare is beautifully presented. On the more unusual side of things, the oyster po' boy gets kicked up a notch with a spicy red pepper aioli. The sesame-crusted flounder is served with bok choy salad. The grilled Atlantic salmon is garnished with an Asian pear salad. The no-reservations policy makes for long waits—try to arrive early. Open for lunch and dinner daily in summer; in the off-season, open for lunch and dinner Wed through Sat.

Cape Sea Grille, 31 Sea St., Harwich Port; (508) 432-4745; capesea grille.com. Housed in a 19th-century sea captain's home near the water's edge, this creative American restaurant marries fresh local ingredients and native seafood under the watchful eye of Chef-Owner Douglas Ramler. His calamari is dusted with cornmeal, the grilled yellow fin tuna is rubbed with coriander and fennel. Other entrees of seared sea scallops, oven-roasted

local cod, and a whole lobster are paired with exceptional accompaniments, often with a Mediterranean touch. Hours of operation change with the seasons, so it's wise to call ahead. Open for dinner Apr through mid-Dec.

Captain Parker's Pub, 668 Rte. 28, West Yarmouth; (508) 771-4266; captainparkers.com. This family restaurant with outdoor seating overlooking Parker's River has been pleasing people for more than three decades. Mostly it's the award-winning chowder that folks come for, thick and creamy, loaded with clams. It's so popular that they now sell their clam chowder "to go" starting every day at 8 a.m., and it's also available through their website. Parker's is open year round, serving lunch and dinner every day of the week.

Chillingsworth, 2449 Rte. 6A, Brewster; (508) 896-3640; chillingsworth.com. Another contender for the title of best restaurant on Cape Cod, Chillingsworth has an elegant menu that changes daily. Typical dishes are basil-crusted Atlantic salmon, seared scallops with corn risotto, and native flounder with Israeli couscous. A relatively new bistro in the greenhouse area is more casual with a New American bill of fare: crab cakes with corn relish, panko-crusted oysters, and angel hair pasta with fresh lobster in a cognac cream sauce. Hours of operation change with the seasons, so it's wise to call ahead. Open from Mother's Day through late Nov. The bistro is open for dinner nightly. Brunch is offered on Sun beginning at noon.

Cooke's Seafood, 7 Ryan's Way, Mashpee; (508) 477-9595; 1120 Rte. 132, Hyannis; (508) 775-045 cookesseafood.com. Cooke's has been serving award-winning broiled and fried seafood since 1977 and is known for their excellent seafood platters. Their fried clams consistently rank with the best on Cape Cod. Both the Hyannis and Mashpee locations are open seasonally at 11:30 daily.

Home Port Restaurant, 512 North Rd., Menemsha, Martha's Vineyard; (508) 645-2679; homeportmv.com. A few years ago, when word got out that the Home Port might be closing, locals went into a panic. How could they survive without this Menemsha institution that had been in business since 1930? Fortunately the quaint restaurant remained open, serving "old school" full meals—that's salad, appetizer, entree, and dessert for one price. That might mean quahog chowder or lobster bisque with a boiled lobster or broiled fish plus blueberry or pecan pie. A children's menu is available. When the Home Port closes for the winter, they invite their customers to dine at their sister operation, the Beach Plum Restaurant (12 Menemsha Inn Rd., 508 645-9454). Open for dinner nightly from late May through mid-Oct.

Hooked, 15 Island Inn Rd., Oak Bluffs, Martha's Vineyard; (508) 693-6093; hookedmv.com. With a real beach house vibe, this island fish house offers not just lots of lobster but also lawn games on their beautiful grounds, something the kids will appreciate. Chef Christian Thornton has crafted a seafood-centric menu that's easy to fall in love with—for starters,

BYOB Translated

First, the bad news: Like most of Martha's Vineyard, **Menemsha** is a dry town, which means restaurants cannot serve alcoholic beverages. The good news is that you can bring any wine, beer, or spirits you choose to complement your meal. Most people bring their alcoholic beverages to the restaurant in a small cooler.

Many restaurants provide glassware and ice buckets for your wine, should it need to be chilled. They will even open your bottles of wine for you. Often there is a small charge for this. It's called a corkage fee.

crispy crab and summer corn fritters, lobster tacos, and wok-fired calamari with sambal aioli. The catch of the day is served with a choice of sauces, from caper vinaigrette to Cajun cream. Every Friday it's all-you-can-eat catfish. House specialties include the fisherman's stew, blackened swordfish, and flounder stuffed with lobster, prawns, and crab. Hooked is a seasonal operation. Open for dinner Wed through Sun in season.

Impudent Oyster, 15 Chatham Bars Ave., Chatham; (508) 945-3545. It's a big thumbs up for this comfortable restaurant and bar where you can have a relaxing meal with cozy ambiance. Online reviews are overwhelmingly positive for the delicious seafood and huge portions. The famous Wellfleet oysters on the half shell are hard to beat, and people rave about the chowder ("the best on the Cape"), the seafood medley with vodka sauce ("spicy and complex"), and "the killer lobster roll." Open for lunch and dinner daily.

Lobster Pot, 321 Commercial St., Provincetown; (508) 487-0842; ptlobsterpot.com. This is an institution in P-town, overlooking the harbor, with its trademark neon signage. Award-winning food is served in 2 waterfront dining rooms. The huge menu has it all, the basics and then some: house-made salmon gravlax, Russian oysters, sea clam cake with béarnaise sauce, soft-shell crab, paella, Cajun bouillabaisse, seafood crepes, and Portuguese specialties. A children's menu is available. This is a seasonal operation, which reopens in April. It's recommended that you call ahead for hours of operation.

Mac's Seafood, Mac's Shack, 91 Commercial St., Wellfleet; (508) 349-6333. Mac's on the Pier, 265 Commercial St., Wellfleet; (508) 349-9611. Mac's Market, 265 Commercial St., Wellfleet; (508) 349-0404. Mac's Market, 14D Truro Center Rd., Truro; (508) 349-9409. Mac's Market, Route 6 near Brackett Road, North Eastham; (508) 255-6900; macsseafood.com. This family operation got its start in 1995, and over the years it grew into a group of seafood restaurants and fish markets, most of them open on a seasonal basis. Mac's Market in Eastham is open year-round, and it is well stocked with fresh seafood, house-smoked favorites, and their popular clambake in a box. Mac's Shack is anything but that—it's a sit-down, cloth-napkin establishment, open spring through fall and serving sea scallops with green curry, skate in browned butter, and sushi. Mac's on the Pier is more casual but just as creative, with grilled tuna and fish tacos on the menu. Mac's Parties & Provisions caters all kinds of events, from cocktail parties to clambakes. Chefs and home cooks in the continental United States can shop online via the website. Hours vary with the seasons. The year-round market in Eastham is open daily from 10 a.m. to 6 p.m.

Ocean House, Depot Street, Dennisport; (508) 394-0700; ocean houserestaurant.com. With a formal dining room on the water's edge, Chef Anthony Silvestri creates seasonal menus of fusion cuisine with a local influence: seafood bruschetta starring mussels, clams, shrimp, and lobster; yellow fin tuna tartare "ice cream cones" with wasabi foam; and Cape Cod potato chip–encrusted codfish with hand-cut fries. Right next door is The Beaches Cafe, where you can have a more casual lunch. Open for dinner Tues through Sun in summer; for dinner Wed through Sun in the off-season; closed Jan through Mar.

The Red Inn, 15 Commercial St., Provincetown; (508) 487-7334; theredinn.com. The award-winning restaurant at this waterfront inn offers views of P-town's harbor, Cape Cod Bay, the lighthouse at Long Point, and the sandy cliffs along the shores of the outer cape. Chef-Owner Philip Mossy gives lobster a prominent place on his New American menu: lobster and artichoke fondue, lobster sliders, spicy lobster corn chowder, and grilled (yes, grilled) local lobster with lemon butter sauce. Also worth trying is the seafood pasta in a light sherry Creole tomato cream. This is a seasonal operation—it's wise to call ahead for their hours.

The Regatta, Route 28, Cotuit; (508) 428-5715; regattarestaurant .com. You have a choice here—fine dining off the a la carte dinner menu or lighter fare on the Tap Room menu. If you're living large, order the baked Cotuit oysters over sautéed baby spinach and the house-made lobster ravioli. In a more casual mood? Try the crispy scallops or the shrimp pad Thai at the warm and friendly bar. The Regatta is housed in a cranberry red building that dates back to 1790, when it was a stagecoach inn. Open for dinner Tues through Sun in the off-season; nightly in the summer.

Sea Grille, 45 Sparks Ave., Nantucket; (508) 325 5700; thesea grille.com. A favorite with locals and seasonal visitors for more than 20 years, this mid-island restaurant specializes in seafood, local and regional. Chef-Owners EJ and Robin Harvey are well-known for their Nantucket quahog chowder, lobster bisque, bouillabaisse, and day boat cod. (Insider

Lobster boats docked in Sandwich, Cape Cod

tip: The chowder is so good, it's now sold frozen in quart containers. Visit the Nantucket Chowder Company website to make a purchase.) Pastas and breads are made daily on the premises. It's not surprising that the Sea Grille has won so many awards and accolades. Open nightly for dinner; Mon through Fri for lunch.

The Sea Shanty, 31 Dock St., Edgartown, Martha's Vineyard; (508) 627-8622; theseafoodshanty.com. Start off with a refreshing beverage while you take in the harbor view, perhaps with some sushi or shellfish from the raw bar. For lunch the lobster quesadilla is highly recommended. At dinner live the island life with the Mahi Madness, a fillet of wild mahi with mango fruit salsa. In warm weather request a table on the deck with a dark blue market umbrella for shade. A children's menu is available. Open for lunch and dinner daily from mid-May to mid-Oct.

Straight Wharf Restaurant, 6 Harbor Sq., Nantucket; (508) 228-4499; straightwharfrestaurant.com. This is the place if you're craving

Nantucket Bay Scallops: Less Is More

Scallop enthusiasts know that the most revered scallop is the Nantucket bay scallop. Their season commences in October, and these delicate mollusks can be found in fish markets and on restaurant menus from fall into early spring. Clearly a case of "less is more," these small bay scallops are mild, sweet, and buttery. They caramelize beautifully when cooked. They can be sautéed, baked, and broiled, but many Nantucket natives prefer to eat them raw with a simple squirt of fresh lemon.

While Nantucket bay scallops are a bit costly in mainland restaurants and markets, you can harvest them yourself if you're willing to get a scalloping permit and don a pair of waders. Die-hard fans know the best spots for scalloping on the shores of Nantucket: Coatue, Madaket Harbor, Monomoy, and Shawkemo. From October 3 on, you can spot scallopers in the eelgrass with their push rakes and floating baskets, collecting their beloved bivalves for that night's dinner.

Nantucket bay scallops are easy to recognize in their natural habitat. Their small corrugated shells are beautiful in an array of colors. Smaller than sea scallops, bay scallops are about the size of the tip of your thumb once shucked. That amounts to between 60 and 100 scallops per pound.

Scalloping permits are available at the Nantucket Public Safety Facility, 4 Fairgrounds Rd. Permits are $25 for residents, and free if you are over 60 years old. Non-residents may obtain a $50 weekly permit or a $100 annual permit.

Fear not, landlubbers. If scalloping in cold Northern Atlantic waters is not your thing, you have your choice of bay scallop specials offered at local restaurants throughout the season.

The quintessential commercial source for this delicacy is the Nantucket Bay Scallop Trading Company, a division of the Nantucket Lobster Trap restaurant, located at 23 Washington St. in Nantucket. Fresh bay scallops can be ordered on their website, nantucketbayscalloptradingcompany.com, with overnight delivery.

high-end seafood. Consider the possibilities: Island Creek oysters with lemon granité, poached Chatham mussels, wood-grilled local swordfish, day boat scallops, and the SWR clambake with buttered lobster, sweet corn, spicy chorizo, potatoes, and littleneck clams. A separate bar menu offers smoked bluefish pâté and grilled Apalachicola shrimp. This is a seasonal operation that reopens in May. It's recommended that you call ahead for hours of operation.

TOPPER'S, The Wauwinet, 120 Wauwinet Rd., Nantucket; (508) 228-8768; wauwinet.com. One of the finest restaurants on the island, TOPPER'S is known for its elegant New American menu with an emphasis on seafood. Stunning views of Nantucket Bay make it an ideal place for lunch, especially on TOPPER'S Deck, a seasonal operation with more causal fare. TOPPER'S offers a water shuttle in season—with cocktail service on board—that cruises across the harbor picking up guests at other hotels who wish to experience TOPPER'S at The Wauwinet. Insider's tip: The west-facing terrace is an ideal spot at sunset. Open from early May through late Oct for breakfast, lunch, and dinner daily, for Sunday brunch from 11:30 a.m. to 2 p.m.

Clam Shacks

Arnold's Lobster & Clam Bar, 3580 Rte. 6, Eastham; (508) 696-8190; arnoldsrestaurant.com. Cape Cod's award-winning clam shack, Arnold's has grown into a family dining destination over the past 30 years. At night it's a popular watering hole with "shucked-as-you-watch" oysters at the raw bar. Folks come from far and wide for the whole-belly fried clams, lobster rolls, baked scallops, and steamed clambake. They accept cash only. This is a seasonal operation, open mid-May through Oct for lunch and dinner.

Baxter's, 177 Pleasant St., Hyannis; (508) 775-4490; baxterscapecod.com. One of the oldest clam shacks on Cape Cod, perched right on the water so some customers arrive by boat. Especially known for their fish-and-chips made with haddock. A favorite of the Kennedy clan who summer in Hyannis. Open daily from mid-Apr to mid-Oct from 11 a.m. to 10 p.m.

The Bite, 29 Basin Rd., Menemsha, Martha's Vineyard; (508) 645-9239. Let's get a bite to eat at The Bite, the island's favorite clam shack with its bright blue picnic tables and market umbrellas. Close to the beach with a view of the beautiful Menemsha sunsets. So tiny, you just might speed right by it. Be prepared to wait in line for the excellent fish-and-chips made with local flounder. This is a seasonal operation, and they accept cash only. It's recommended that you call ahead for hours.

Cap'n Frosty's, 219 Rte. 6A, Dennis Village; (508) 385-8548; captainfrosty.com. A barn-like seafood shack, very popular with the locals, which is always a good sign. When it comes to clams, they do it all, from clam chowder to clam cakes with soft-serve ice cream for dessert. Seating inside as well as on the shaded brick patio. Open daily for lunch and dinner from mid-Apr to late Sept.

Cap't Cass Rock Harbor Seafood, 117 Rock Harbor, Orleans; no phone; no website. Step back in time at this charming clam shack for a taste of "old Cape Cod." All the usual fried seafood is on the menu as well as an outstanding lobster roll. Cash only; no credit cards. Open late June to mid-Oct, Tues to Sun from 11 a.m. to 2 p.m., 4 to 9 p.m.

The Clam Shack, 227 Clinton Ave., Falmouth; (508) 540-7758; no website. A true rustic shack overlooking Falmouth Harbor. Fried seafood done to perfection plus marvelous lobster rolls. If you're lucky, you'll dine at one of the picnic tables. Open daily from Memorial Day to Labor Day from 11:30 a.m. to 7:30 p.m.

Cobie's Clam Shack, 3260 Main St., Brewster; (508) 896-7021; cobies.com. A Cape Cod institution, Cobie's has been serving excellent fried clams and so much more since 1948. Clam pie is one of their specialties. Known for their "squeaky clean" dark green picnic tables. For dessert, there's hard ice cream as well as soft serve. Open daily for lunch and dinner from Memorial Day through Columbus Day.

Kream 'N Kone, 961 Route 28, West Dennis; (508) 394-0808; kreamnkone.com. This award-winning classic clam shack has been around since 1953 and has become the go-to place for great fried seafood. They also offer 27 flavors of soft-serve ice cream. Indoor seating is available as well as a patio with views of Swan River. Open daily for lunch and dinner from mid-Feb to late Oct.

Lobster Trap Fish Market & Restaurant, 290 Shore Rd., Bourne; (508) 759-7600; lobstertrap.net. This just might be the best clam shack on Cape Cod. At least that's what food writers and fans of the golden whole belly fried clams say. The overflowing lobster roll is served on buttery brioche. The full menu also offers yellow fin tuna pad Thai, lobster mac 'n cheese, and pan-roasted seafood pasta as well as all your fried favorites. The views of Buzzards Bay from the deck make it just about perfect. Open year round every day for lunch and dinner.

Menemsha Galley, 515 North Rd., Menemsha, Martha's Vineyard; (508) 645-9819; menemshagalley.com. A local favorite for more than half a century, this little take-out shack has been winning the hearts of seafood lovers with old-fashioned comfort food. That includes chowder, crab cakes, and a lobster roll that people will gladly stand in line for, even in the rain. With luck you can snag a seat on the cozy back porch with its sunset views of the harbor. Hours of operation change with the seasons, so it's wise to call ahead. Open with limited hours from mid-May to mid-Oct; late June to early Sept, open for lunch and dinner daily.

Seafood Sam's, 6 Coast Guard Rd., Sandwich; (508) 888-4629; 356 Palmer Ave., Falmouth; (508) 540-7877; seafoodsams.com. With more than 100 items on the menu, there's surely something for everyone in your party. Generous portions, friendly service, and scenic locations make this shack a winner. Open daily from 11 a.m. to 9 p.m.

The Seafood Shanty, 803 Scenic Hwy., Route 6, Bournedale; (508) 888-0040; theseafoodshanty.net. Located almost at the midpoint between the Sagamore and Bourne Bridges, the Seafood Shanty is one of the Cape's best-kept secrets. A standout on the menu is a delicious lobster roll filled with tender chunks of lobster and just enough mayonnaise and served on a toasted hot dog roll with a side of french fries and coleslaw. Order your food, sit in one of the Adirondack chairs, and take in the view of the boats passing by on the Canal. The portions are generous, and the service is fast and efficient. They don't serve alcohol, but you're welcome to bring your own beer or wine. You won't find a more perfect setting! Open daily May through Labor Day and on weekends in Apr and Sept–Nov.

Cape Cod Clambakes

Like many areas along the New England coast, Cape Cod claims to be the birthplace of the clambake, but the Cape's claim is said to be the strongest, because this is the first part of North America that the Pilgrims set foot on.

Today the clambake is a big social event for native New Englanders and vacationers. It ranks up there with other all-American eating institutions, such as the backyard barbeque, the Saturday night church supper, and the family picnic.

Places for Summer Clambakes—Pit Style and Steamed

Chatham Bars Inn
297 Shore Rd., Chatham
(508) 593-4978
chathambarsinn.com

Call well in advance.

The inn has pit-style clambakes from Memorial Day to Labor Day. They are family-friendly events that start at six o'clock every evening, Mon through Fri. There are games for the children and live entertainment. The evening ends with toasting s'mores by the fire pit.

Clambakes Etc.

2952 Falmouth Rd. (Route 28), Osterville
Jason Maguire, Sales
(508) 420-0500
clambakesetc.net
If you are in the Upper Cape and decide you want a pit-style clambake, contact Jason. He will help you with the planning for a minimum of 50 people.

Backside Bakes

Nick Moto and Michael Silvester, Owners
nutonic@aol.com
(508) 527-9538
Facebook: backside bakes
Twitter: @BakesideBakes
Nick and Michael do family-style, customized clambakes for as few as 7 and as many as 60 people. They can do a complete party, including everything from a raw bar to desserts.

The Lobster Trap Fish Market and Restaurant

290 Shore Rd., Bourne
(508) 759-7600
lobstertrap.net
The Lobster Trap has been catering events for 20 years—everything from weddings and rehearsal dinners to company events and birthday parties—and clambakes are their specialty. They cover Cape Cod as well as Southeastern Massachusetts.

Spanky's, 138 Ocean St., Hyannis; (508) 771-2770; spankysclam-shack.com. This "seaside saloon" is one of the few restaurants right on the water in Hyannis. The menu is huge, from oysters on the half shell to steamers, plus a "wicked good" seafood stew. Table service is offered, a rarity with clam shacks. You can dine inside or out under the navy blue market umbrellas. Open daily for lunch and dinner from mid-Apr to late Oct.

Seafood Markets

Catch of the Day Seafood Market & Grill, 975 Rte. 6, Wellfleet; (508) 349-9090; wellfleetcatch.com. A seasonal operation, this combination fish market/restaurant carries lobsters of all sizes, the famous shellfish of Wellfleet, steamers from Chatham, mussels from Eastham, and much more, always as local as possible. In the restaurant part, they serve lots of that seafood in the form of lobster rolls, fried clams, and steamed lobsters to their lunch and dinner customers. Both businesses are open Apr through Oct.

Chatham Fish & Lobster, 1291 Main St., Chatham; (508) 945-1178. 485 Rte. 134, South Dennis; chathamfishandlobster.com. Now with two locations on Cape Cod, this seafood market has it all, including lobsters weighing more than 6 pounds. In addition to all the fresh fish and shellfish, they also carry specialty items such as seafood pâté, seafood marinades, house-made chowders, and cocktail sauces. Three clambake packages are also on their menu. Live lobsters for an authentic Cape Cod dinner can be shipped overnight to your door or anywhere in the United States. Open daily.

Cuttyhunk Shellfish Farms, Town Wharf, Gosnold; (508) 990-1317; cuttyhunkshellfish.com. For a unique Cape Cod experience, purchase fresh oysters, clams, shrimp cocktail, crab spread, chowder, and stuffed quahogs off the floating raw bar on Cuttyhunk Pond on summer afternoons. It's all from this aquaculture operation that usually sells its oysters and clams to restaurants and wholesalers. Hail the raw bar boat on VHF Channel 72. On into the evening they will deliver whatever seafood you desire right to your boat. Check the website for prices and hours of operation.

Hatch's Fish Market, 310 Main St., Wellfleet; (508) 349-2810; hatchsfishmarket.com. Over the years the family-owned Hatch's has

Fisherman's shack in Menemsha

evolved from a simple stand behind the town hall into a quaint enclosed building. Whatever the local fishermen are catching or digging, Hatch's is selling. This seasonal operation also smokes fish and mussels and makes pâté. The lobster pool is always full, and they will steam them upon request. The biggest selection, however, is shellfish, including local blue-point oysters, prized as some of the finest in the Northeast. During July and August a produce stand almost obscures the fish market as it over-flows with local tomatoes, peppers, summer squash, and corn. Open late May through mid-Sept.

Larsen's Fish Market, Menemsha Harbor, Menemsha (Martha's Vineyard); (508) 645-2680; larsensfishmarket.com. Ask anyone who has spent time on Martha's Vineyard about local fish markets, and odds are excellent they will mention Larsen's. This seasonal operation in the fishing village of Menemsha offers a full array of fish and shellfish as well as pre-pared foods, including lobsters cooked to order, chowder, lobster bisque, crab cakes, and more. In their cooler they always have lobster rolls, shrimp cocktail, and various seafood spreads. All these products are also available at the Edgartown Seafood Market (138 Cooke St., Edgartown; 508-627-3791). In the summer Larsen's is open daily from 9 a.m. to 7 p.m. They close for the year in mid-Oct.

Nauset Fish Market & Lobster Pool, 38 Rte. 6A, Orleans; (508) 255-1019. Sir Cricket Fish & Chips, (508) 255-4453. Home of the King-Size Lobster—that's this market's claim to fame, along with a fine reputation for fresh finfish, shellfish, frozen chowders and dinners, and other prepared seafood. The attached take-out fish shack, Sir Cricket Fish & Chips, is a definite destination for fans of English-style fish-and-chips. Other fried food is also available. It's open for lunch and dinner daily. The market is open from 9 a.m. to 8 p.m. in summer, 9 a.m. to 6 p.m. in winter.

Net Result, 79 Beach Rd., Vineyard Haven (Martha's Vineyard); (508) 693-6071 or (800) 394-6071; mvseafood.com. This operation is the largest distributor of seafood on Martha's Vineyard. Operated by the Larsen family, Net Result expanded recently with an on-premises cafe for steamed lobster, clams, sushi, and other briny delights. The cafe also packs up cooked fish for takeout and will ship fresh fish and shellfish overnight

to anywhere in the continental United States. Open daily in summer. In the off-season, open Mon and Wed through Saturday at 9 a.m., Sun from 11 a.m. to 4 p.m.; closed Tues,

Sayle's Seafood, 99 Washington St. Extension, Nantucket; (508) 228-4599; saylesseafood.com. A complete retail fish market, Sayle's specializes in Nantucket Bay scallops, native lobsters, Atlantic sea scallops, and the house-made Nantucket clam chowder. Three clambake packages are available. All their products can be purchased online and shipped to your door. Sayle's also serves lunch and dinner daily. For a wonderful Nantucket experience, sunset clambake cruises on a 1938 sailing sloop can be arranged. The market is open Mon through Sat from 10 a.m. to 8 p.m., Sun from noon to 8 p.m.

Straight Wharf Fish Store, Straight Wharf, 4 Harbor Sq., Nantucket; (508) 228-1095; straightwharfrestaurant.com. Located right on the docks of Nantucket, this fish market carries all varieties of finfish, shellfish, and specialty foods, including the house-made bluefish pâté. Take-out seafood is also available for lunch and dinner. Cash only. In season, open daily from 9:30 a.m. to 7 p.m.

Swan River Fish Market, 5 Lower County Rd., Dennisport; (508) 398-2340; bestcapecodlobster.com. More than 50 years ago this fish market opened on marshlands at the mouth of the Swan River, and to this day it is where local fishermen unload their catch. A complete line of seafood is available, including local lobsters that they will steam at no additional cost. The market also offers clambakes for 2 to 200 people. A take out menu features chowder, lobster bisque, stuffies, fish-and-chips, and more. The market provides their fresh products to a sister operation, the landmark Swan River Restaurant, open for lunch and dinner daily from late May to mid-Sept. The market is open daily from 10 a.m. to 7 p.m.

Cape Cod & the Islands Events

Spring and Fall
Nantucket Restaurant Week, nantucketrestaurantweek.com. A great way to experience the island's dining scene. More than 30 top restaurants will offer special three-course menus with reduced prices.

Dig Your Own

Shellfish don't come any fresher than those you've just plucked from the sand. Each coastal town has its own regulations and licensing procedure (always more expensive for visitors than residents), but with a little care and a copy of the tide tables, especially for Cape Cod Bay, you can assemble your own feast. Note that Wellfleet, in particular, has set aside specially seeded oyster and clam beds for recreational shellfishing. If you just want to give clam digging a try, Harwich is one of the few towns offering a one-day license for nonresident families. The following are the main shellfish taken on Cape Cod.

Bay scallop: Also called the Cape scallop, most people eat only the hinge muscle of this shellfish, saving the body for bait. Scallops live about two years and develop a pronounced growth line the second year. Only second-year scallops can be legally harvested. They are found on the bottom in shallow flats and protected bays, often in eelgrass beds. Harvest with a dip net from a boat or wearing waders.

Blue mussel: This mussel with a dark blue shell grows in clumps on rocks, pilings, and flats. Gather by hand or with a rake. Scrub well to remove external mud and tiny anchor threads. They open when steamed. (Mussels that don't open should not be eaten.)

Oyster: Oysters live on hard, sandy bottoms or attach themselves to rocks and piers. They must be at least 3 inches long for legal harvest.

Quahog: Also known as the hard clam or round clam, quahogs are harvested by digging just below the surface between low and high tide. Clams less than an inch thick at the hinge must be carefully replanted. Small quahogs are often called littlenecks; medium-size ones are cherrystones. Those larger than 3 inches are good for chowder, clam pie, or fritters.

Razor clam: Sometimes called the jacknife clam, this strong digger is usually found near the low-water mark. Dig as for soft-shell clams, but deeper and faster.

Barnstable Oyster (barnstableoyster.com) supplies many upscale restaurants with product harvested on their oyster farm.

Sea clam: Also known as surf or bar clams, these are the biggest clams found in Massachusetts waters. At 5 to 9 inches, they're good for clam pie or chowder. They're easily dug by hand, as they sit just below the surface of flats exposed at low tide.

Soft-shell clam: Found 4 to 12 inches below the surface between tide lines, these clams must be dug carefully to avoid breaking their fragile shells. Clams under 2 inches long are seed clams and must be replanted quickly with necks up under a very thin sand layer. Served steamed, fried, or stewed, they are also called steamer, longneck, or long clams.

FRIED OYSTERS
FRIED CLAMS
CLAM CHOWDER
FRIED CALAMARI
EAT THIS SHELLFISH

September
Scallop Fest, Cape Cod Fairgrounds, 1220 Nathan Ellis Hwy., Route 151, East Falmouth; 508-759-6000, ext. 10; scallopfest.org. Each year over 50,000 people show up to feast on scallops and other foods. The festival includes an arts and

craft show, rides and games for the kids, and live entertainment by local musicians in the main tent.

Mid-June
A Taste of the Vineyard, Martha's Vineyard Preservation Trust, 99 Main St., Edgartown; (508) 627-4440. The top restaurants and caterers of Martha's Vineyard turn out to offer samples of their cuisine, much of it seafood, and beverages to benefit the Preservation Trust.

Mid-October
Wellfleet Oysterfest, various locations in Wellfleet; wellfleet oyster.org. The Atlantic bluepoint oysters of Wellfleet are famed throughout the Northeast as some of the finest cold-water oysters of the region. This festival brings out restaurateurs to show off their oyster dishes, lets champion shuckers compete against one another to separate the bivalves from their shells, and even pits local restaurants against one another.

◀ Wellfleet Oysterfest is traditionally held the weekend after Columbus Day.

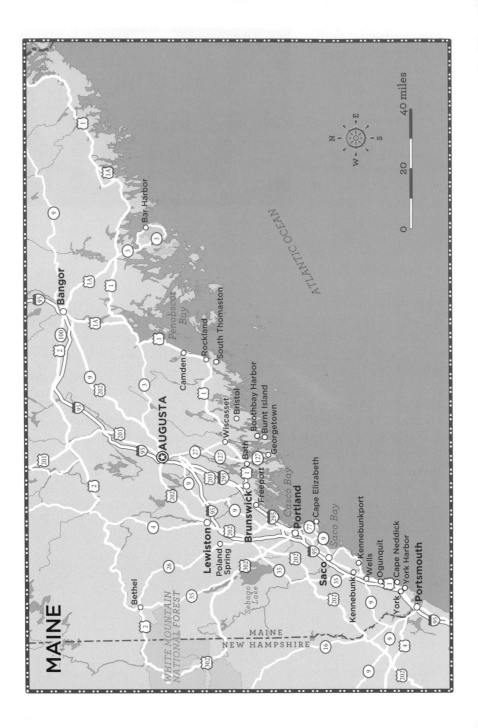

Maine

When most people think of Maine, they almost immediately picture a magnificent bright red lobster ready to be devoured. And they also remember how the man who sold them that lobster talked. People who live outside of Maine would call that man a "Mainiac," but residents are more respectful and call themselves "Mainers." To be precise, they would say "Mainahs" much like Bostonians would say "pahk the cah."

So the first rule in how to talk like an authentic Mainah is to pronounce all words ending in *er* as if they ended in *ah*. There is no end to this distinct accent: "Mothah is cookin' chowdah and a lobstah dinnah."

That's another rule in how to talk like a true Mainah—always drop the *g* in words ending in *ing* as in: "Fathah is goin' fishin'." You must also broaden your *a* sounds so that *market* becomes *mahket*.

Likewise, babies are *cunnin'* ("cute"), certain people are *numb* ("dumb and stupid"), and everything that is very good or very bad is *wicked* good and *wicked* bad. If you hear two old fishermen talking about "pot," it's not marijuana they're referring to but their lobster pots or buoys that mark where a lobster trap can be found.

Mainahs also turn one-syllable words into two—a country fair becomes a country *fa-uh* and the number four becomes *foh-ah*. The most famous example of this unusual way to talk is the true Mainah's positive response to any question: *Ayuh*. And if you're "from away" (that is, not from Maine), and you ask for directions, you'll likely be told: "You can't get they-uh from hee-ah."

Hopefully you won't hear those words in your travels through Maine, the Pine Tree State, aka Vacationland, according to Maine license plates. Maine is an incredibly special part of the United States, totally unlike any other region, and synonymous with seafood. Traveling from Kittery in the south to Bar Harbor in the north, along the 3,500-mile-long coastline, and inland through the more remote lakes region and vast farmland, you will come upon many a true Mainah as well as some of the most honest food you could ever imagine.

PORTLAND

One of the hottest food cities in the nation, Portland is the cultural and culinary heart of Maine. This historic city by the sea is alive with thriving independent businesses, an impressive arts and music scene, and an energetic food community. A seaport and railway hub through the early 19th century, much of the city was destroyed in the Great Fire of 1866, though one institution has remained constant—the Portland Farmers' Market, founded in 1768, is the country's oldest continually operating market of its kind.

As in many cities, the 20th century marked a gradual migration out of Portland's downtown, but an urban revitalization movement began in the 1990s, which has energized the city and turned the Old Port into a tourist destination, known especially for its restaurants and small markets. The Arts District on Congress Street, named for the Maine College of Art at its center, is home to galleries and storefront art spaces, as well as coffee shops, ethnic markets, and funky restaurants. The Portland Museum of Art, also on Congress, was designed by I. M. Pei and houses an extraordinary collection, including the works of many Maine artists. Portland is considered one of the safest cities in the nation, according to *Travel + Leisure* magazine. It's the ideal place to stay in Maine if you are planning several day trips to explore the Pine Tree State.

Portland is widely considered to have one of the country's most vibrant food scenes, and in 2009 it was named "America's Foodiest Small Town" by *Bon Appetit* magazine. Restaurants range from Chef Sam Hayward's pioneering farm-to-table mecca, Fore Street, to divey holes-in-the-wall, and include everything in between. Wander the streets for just a few blocks and you'll find an Eritrean cafe, a beer garden with more than 300 brews, a Japanese noodle bar, a restored club-car diner, and a gelateria run by a family from Milan. An active Slow Food convivium (chapter) holds potlucks,

Foodie Tours

The best way to explore Portland's food scene is through **Maine Foodie Tours,** which offers a guided culinary walking tour, a trolley tour, and progressive dinner tours via boat. The tours start at the Old Port Wine Shop, 223 Commercial St. in Portland (207-233-7685; mainfoodietours.com). Similar tours are now also offered in Kennebunkport.

Portland Head Light, Cape Elizabeth

lectures, and events, including the annual Writer's Night, in which food writers read from their works, and a winter CSA fair, at which participants can sign up for a summer farm share.

It's impossible to sample all of Portland's kaleidoscopic culinary offerings in just one visit, but with enthusiasm and an adventurous palate, you'll have fun trying.

Seafood Restaurants

Caiola's, 58 Pine St., Portland; (207) 772-1110; caiolas.com. This cozy neighborhood restaurant in the historic West End combines a warm atmosphere with a well-considered menu. Chef Abby Harmon's variations

Portland's Food News

Food scenes are fluid, and restaurants emerge and disappear more quickly than books can be written. If you're planning a visit to somewhere off the beaten path, make sure to call ahead so you're not disappointed. For the most up-to-date listings, check out the following online sources:

downeast.com: *DownEast* magazine's website includes a food section with all the state's dish—from kitchen gossip to restaurant guides.

eatmainefoods.org: The Eat Local Foods Coalition of Maine has developed an online map to find farmers' markets, farm stands, restaurants serving local foods, and more.

portlandfoodmap.com: A comprehensive map of local eateries, with links to reviews and foodie news.

themainemag.com: In print and online, *Maine* magazine focuses on culture, people, destinations, art, and food in the state. Their "eat" section visits a specific region each month and reports back with the best bets. For candid opinions about the Maine food scene, visit their Facebook page. With more than 10,000 fans contributing to the conversation, you're sure to find a recommendation: facebook.com/ EatMaine.

Portland Harbor

on American comfort foods are peppered with upscale surprises—the Caesar salad is topped with spicy fried oysters, lobster pudding with corn salad is an appetizer, the swordfish is served with chorizo—and local ingredients are showcased. The Sunday brunch menu is extensive and satisfying, ranging from Cajun fish tacos to a fried oyster po' boy. Open for dinner Mon through Sat, for brunch Sun from 9 a.m. to 2 p.m.

DiMillo's Floating Restaurant, 25 Long Wharf, Portland; (207) 772-2216; dimillos.com. With seating for more than 600, this former ferry turned restaurant offers a menu of classic New England and Italian-style seafood dishes from its dockside dining room. Family owned and operated since 1954, it's the only floating restaurant on the upper East Coast and offers beautiful views of the harbor, generous portions, and a full bar. Early dinner specials include fresh Atlantic haddock, salmon glazed with honey and mustard, and Maine shrimp fried until golden. A children's menu is available. Open for lunch and dinner daily year-round.

El Rayo, 101 York St., Portland; (207) 780-8226; elrayotaqueria
.com. Housed in a renovated gas station at the edge of the working waterfront, this cheerful restaurant brings the flavors of Oaxaca to Maine. Bright
colors, Latin music, communal tables, and a sprinkle of kitsch make every
meal festive. Citrus and seafood figure prominently in the lively menu—
don't miss the fish tacos and seviche. In warmer months, sit outdoors and
watch the world go by with a glass of potent house sangria, a margarita, or
a refreshing hibiscus cooler. Open for lunch and dinner daily.

Fore Street, 288 Fore St., Portland; (207) 775-2717; forestreet.biz.
Since 1996 this Old Port restaurant has blazed the trail for dining that
celebrates Maine's local, sustainably grown and harvested ingredients.
Pioneering Chef Sam Hayward, recipient of the James Beard Foundation's
Best Chef: Northeast 2004 Award, has been at the forefront of the city's
food renaissance. He changes the menu daily to reflect what's in season,
and he puts into practice his belief that "good food travels the shortest
distance between the farm and the table." His menu includes oven-roasted
mussels and hand-harvested diver scallops. The kitchen and its wood-
burning oven, grill, and turnspit are visible to diners. Reservations are
recommended. Open nightly for dinner.

Hi Bombay, 1 Pleasant St., Portland; (207) 772-8767; hibombay
.com. With Bollywood on the television, this family-owned north Indian
restaurant offers a taste of south Asia in downtown Portland. Their Bay of
Bengal seafood specialties use local fish, and the menu includes shrimp
vindaloo, saag, and tandoori masala as well as fish curry, vindaloo, and
labadar. Open for lunch and dinner every day of the year.

Hot Suppa, 703 Congress St., Portland; (207) 871-5005; hotsuppa
.com. This West End favorite, run by brothers Moses and Alec Sabina,
aims to provide "simple, affordable food done right." The Victorian building with high ceilings and original moldings nicely complements the
classic American fare. The menu includes Southern favorites and soul
food—corn meal–crusted catfish, gumbo, chicken and waffles—as well as
quirky takes on regional dishes, such as calamari with pesto aioli and fried
oysters on baby spinach. Open for breakfast and lunch daily, for dinner
Tues through Sat.

The Daily Catch

Perched at the edge of Casco Bay, Portland's working water-front has for centuries been an integral part of the city's life. In the briny morning mist, boats come in along the pilings of each wharf, unloading their haul of the Gulf of Maine's best, from haddock and cod to monkfish, eel, pollack, and the ubiquitous lobster. Since 1986 the nonprofit Portland Fish Exchange has run a daily auction, organized to ensure fair prices and provide impartial grading and weighing of seafood, and fishmongers from Portland and beyond can be found bidding on the daily catch.

For the public, a stroll down Commercial Street and the adjacent wharves will bring the clean whiff of fresh fish and stops at the famed **Browne Trading Company** (Merrill's Wharf; 800-944-7848), known for the custom-cured seafood from its boutique smokehouse and its extensive selection of caviar, and **Harbor Fish Market** (9 Custom House Wharf; 800-370-1790), owned and operated by the Alfiero family since 1969, with a storefront so iconic it's been featured in countless advertisements, paintings, and postcards.

J's Oysters, 5 Portland Pier, Portland; (207) 772-4828; no website. Opened in 1977 by Janice "J" Noyes, this unpretentious waterfront raw bar was the first of its kind in Maine. Raw oysters are served by the baker's dozen from beds of ice and seaweed in the center of the bar. Raw scallops, steamed mussels, and shrimp and lobster-claw cocktails can be washed down with the local beers on tap, while baked oysters, oyster stew, chowders, and seafood entrees make a hearty meal. Seasonal outdoor seating has a view of the docks, and the indoor bar is popular with regulars slurping oysters and spinning yarns. Open daily for lunch and dinner.

Miss Portland Diner, 140 Marginal Way, Portland; (207) 210-6673; missportlanddiner.com. Housed in a dining car built in 1949 by the famed Worcester Lunch Car Company, this classic diner has moved several times in its 60-odd years, most recently in 2007 after a total restoration. Now reopened, the diner offers plenty of comfort food and a full line of

classic seafood platters, from fish-and-chips to broiled scallops. The warm atmosphere is kid friendly. Open for breakfast, lunch, and dinner daily.

Miyake Restaurant, 468 Fore St., Portland; (207) 871-9170. **Pai Men Miyake,** 188 State St., Portland; (207) 541-9204; miyake restaurants.com. Chef Masa Miyake's first restaurant, an acknowledged hole-in-the-wall with limited seating and a BYOB policy, raised the bar for Portland's sushi. A la carte dishes are jewels of fresh seafood—some of it harvested by the chef—and the *omakase* (chef's tasting) is a carefully assembled progression of up to seven delicate dishes. Pai Men Miyake, a noodle and sake bar, is a more casual experience with heartier food, but the attention to detail is equally meticulous. It's a great restorative if you've over-indulged the night before. Both are open for lunch and dinner daily.

Old Port Sea Grill, 93 Commercial St., Portland; (207) 879-6100; theoldportseagrill.com. The main event at this upscale Old Port eatery is an expansive marble raw bar, offering the city's largest selection of

Lobster Doughnuts? Only in Maine

Chances are, if you're reading this book, you love lobster. And for many of us, a simple doughnut is a guilty pleasure. But a lobster doughnut? Yes, thanks to The Holy Donut in Portland, known for their wildly popular potato-based doughnuts made with local, healthy ingredients. On any given day, a dozen unusual flavors are available, from ginger and sweet potato to dark chocolate sea salt and pomegranate. And now they've added the savory lobster doughnut to the menu.

Leigh Kellis is the creative baker who owns The Holy Donut. Two years ago she was struggling, selling a dozen doughnuts a day. Now, with a growing fan base and two locations, she's selling 10,000 a week.

Kellis was inspired to make her first lobster doughnut using "the best of Maine"—potatoes, fresh lobster, and herbs. The fresh lobster meat is coated with butter and herbs, wrapped in Maine potato doughnut pastry, and then deep fried. Her many fans say it's incredible—imagine a traditional doughnut with a big chunk of lobster in the middle. The lobster doughnut costs $9 while a dozen assorted doughnuts is $16.50.

Kellis reports that the best selection of flavors can be had before noon. "We often sell out and close early," she says. "Feel free to call first."

The Holy Donut (two locations), 194 Park Ave. and 7 Exchange St., Portland; (207) 874-7774; theholydonut.com.

oysters on the half shell coming in from 10 locations, mostly in Maine. Also on the menu are clams, crabs, mussels, and calamari and entrees of local meat and fish. Wood-grilled seafood provides a flavorful, light alternative to fried, which is also available. Open for lunch and dinner daily.

Street and Company, 33 Wharf St., Portland; (207) 775-0887; streetandcompany.net. For more than two decades, this upscale seafood restaurant in the Old Port has set the standard for fresh, beautifully prepared fish. The open kitchen, rustic brick walls, and copper-topped tables provide an engaging backdrop for the main event: strictly seafood served broiled, grilled, in the pan, or with linguine. The menu leans to the Mediterranean, with "tastes" and appetizers that bring in the flavors of Spain and Italy. Seating is limited, and reservations are recommended. One third of the restaurant is always available for walk-in seating. Open for dinner nightly.

Vignola-Cinque Terra, 10 Dana St., Portland; (207) 772-1330; vignolamaine.com. Tucked down a narrow cobbled street in a historic ship chandlery in the Old Port, chef Lee Skawinski's crisp, upscale restaurant incorporates local flavors into traditional Italian cuisine, offering a regularly changing high-end dinner menu. Highlights include hand-cut pasta and local seafood—if grilled octopus is on the menu, it's not to be missed. Entrees include basil-crusted sole fillet, broiled Atlantic swordfish with shaved fennel, and Maine lobster ravioli. (Note: These used to be two separate restaurants next door to one another that have merged into one entity.) Produce for both restaurants is supplied by Grand View Farm, in Greene, Maine, which is owned by restaurant proprietors Dan and Michelle Kary. Open for dinner daily, also for lunch on Fri and Sat, and brunch on Sun starting at 10 a.m.

Lobster Shacks & Clam Shacks

Benny's Famous Fried Clams and Lobster Pound, 199 West Commercial St., Portland; (207) 774-2084; bennysfamousfriedclams .weebly.com. This seasonal clam shack, near the highway on an empty stretch of outer Commercial Street, is beloved by locals for its ample baskets of fried clams, scallops, and Maine shrimp; unadorned lobster rolls; and hand-cut fries. Drinks are self-serve from the cooler, and seating is at outdoor picnic tables by the busy road, but the reasonable prices for fresh seafood more than make up for the stripped-down atmosphere. Open for lunch and dinner daily from May to Nov.

The Lobster Shack at Two Lights, 225 Two Lights Rd., Cape Elizabeth; (207) 799-1677; lobstershacktwolights.com. The sweeping view from this landmark lobster shack perched above the sea is renowned throughout the state and beyond. Drawing crowds since the 1920s, the quaint dining room and picnic tables overlook two lighthouses on the rugged coast and Portland Harbor. Boiled lobster dinners, hearty lobster rolls, and fried local seafood are on the menu, as well as really good clam chowder and lobster stew. Open for lunch and dinner daily from late Mar through late Oct.

Portland Lobster Co., 180 Commercial St., Portland; (207) 775-2112; portlandlobstercompany.com. Serving tasty lobster rolls, boiled lobster dinners, and fried fish, this seasonal waterfront restaurant is a great stop on a day of sightseeing in the Old Port. Basic clam shack fare is available and then some—try the peekytoe crab and avocado wrap for a refreshing change from the usual fried food. The atmosphere is a little kitschy—a plastic lobster vibrates when your order's up—and can be boisterous when there's live music (daily during the summer). A tented bar with local beers on tap is convenient to plenty of outdoor seating on the pier. Open May through Oct.

Seafood Markets

Browne Trading Company, Merrill's Wharf, Portland; (207) 775-7560 or (800) 944-7848; brownetrading.com. Known to chefs

throughout the country for wholesale fresh and smoked seafood and fine caviars, Browne Trading Company's retail market in the Old Port District adds an extensive selection of wines and lunch service to its exquisite seafood offerings. Chowders, stews, and wonderful sandwiches—try the house-smoked trout salad—are available for takeout. Seafood is processed on-site, and shellfish and salmon (among other fish) are cured in a boutique smokehouse adjacent to the market. They ship their products overnight to anywhere in the United States. Open Mon through Sat from 10 a.m. to 6 p.m.

The Challenge of the Perfect Boiled Lobster

Maine native Colin Woodard is the author of *The Lobster Coast,* a cultural and environmental history of coastal Maine and its lobstering communities. He's spent a great deal of time on the coast and can now be found in Portland or at colin woodard.com. His thoughts on the perfect lobster:

"There's nothing technically challenging about cooking the perfect boiled lobster. It's not that much different from cooking pasta: You have to boil water, put your prey in it, keep an eye on the time, and know how to test it for readiness to avoid having it overcooked or underdone. The challenge for some is that the lobster, unlike pasta, is tossed into the pot alive. Cooking lobster at home is fundamentally a test of one's commitment and mettle, not their culinary skills."

"Some reassure themselves that lobsters, as lowly decapodous crustaceans, don't really mind being boiled alive. I'm certain this isn't the case. Their brains may be a simple bundle of nerves, but they're still nerves. Death comes quickly in the pot, but I doubt it's painless. A better way to look at it is that (a) it's a lot better way to die than the lobster would likely experience on the seafloor, where they're often swallowed whole by codfish, to be slowly digested, or simply dismantled by a larger lobster or other predator, and (b) it's a better fate than the chicken, cow, and pig in your refrigerator probably experienced. Here's one of the few times many people actually kill their food and eat it, and I think it honors the animal more than outsourcing the task. Revel in the ritual and be proud your meal lived its life in its natural environment and, particularly if sourced from Maine, was harvested by one of the world's few truly sustainable fisheries."

"Apart from that, boiling a lobster is really easy. Make sure you have a pot big enough to completely submerge all the lobsters you plan to cook. Add a tablespoon or so of salt per

quart of water and bring to a full-on boil. Put the lobster in, claws first, immediately cover, and set the timer. A 1¼-pound lobster takes 8 or 9 minutes, a 1½- to 2-pounder, 8 to 11. Test it at the early end of the time frame by trying to lift one by its antenna. If it pulls out, the lobster is ready. Serve with melted butter and enjoy!"

Free Range Fish & Lobster, 450 Commercial St., Portland; (207) 774-8469; freerangefish.com. Look for the enormous mounted lobster, and you'll know you're there. The briny smell promises good things will come from this no-frills fish shop, steps from the docks of Portland's waterfront. Friendly, knowledgeable fishmongers crack jokes with patrons while helping navigate mountains of mollusks and whole and filleted fish. Large tanks hold lobsters of all sizes, and the staff is happy to give instructions on preparation. They have a sister operation in New Hampshire (see page 256). Open Sun through Thurs from 9 a.m. to 6 p.m., Fri and Sat from 8 a.m. to 6 p.m.

Harbor Fish Market, 9 Custom House Wharf, Portland; (207) 775-0251 or (800) 370-1790; harborfish.com. Since 1969 the Alfiero family—father Ben Sr. and sons Nick, Ben Jr., and Mike—have sold live lobster, fish, and shellfish from this waterfront market, located above the pilings on one of the Old Port's wharves. Fresh seafood glistens in the long glass cases that line the shop (more than 50 feet of linear display), and the charming historic storefront has been used as the backdrop for myriad advertisements. Customer service is a priority, and the staff operates by the motto: "If it's not fresh enough for us to take home and prepare, then we're not going to sell it. Period." They also ship live lobsters and fresh seafood to your door. Open Mon to Sat from 8:30 a.m. to 5:30 p.m., Sun from 9 a.m. to 3 p.m.

Portland Events

October
Harvest on the Harbor, (207) 772-4994; harvestontheharbor.com.
This annual celebration of the flavors of Maine features 3 days of food and
wine tastings, cooking demonstrations, culinary-themed tours, and more.
Held on a waterfront pier in the Oceanside Pavilion tent, the festivities
include the Maine Lobster Chef of the Year Competition, a meal crafted by
local James Beard Award–winning chefs, and a daily marketplace featuring
more than 140 Maine-made products. Tickets available in advance; must be
21 to attend.

SOUTHERN MAINE
The most accessible region in the state, southern Maine is also the most
visited, with tourists from near and far flocking to its sandy beaches,
sparkling waters, and festive boardwalks. Daytrippers from Boston meet
Quebecois in search of relatively warm southern waters at Old Orchard
Beach, and shoppers hunting for bargains scour the outlets in Kittery and
Freeport.

Since the late 1800s, southern Maine has been a region of tourism,
and many of the area's lobster shacks, saltwater-taffy shops, and ice cream
stands date from the first half of the 20th century. Here, you're in the heart of
"Vacationland," a moniker officially added to Maine's license plates in 1936.

But southern Maine is also a region of elegance, and affluent summer
communities in Kennebunkport—home of the presidential Bush family compound—and Prouts Neck, among others, have inspired exquisite
restaurants, like the White Barn Inn, arguably the finest restaurant in the
state. Surrounded by lush gardens, Arrows in Ogunquit is a foodie destination, serving meals that come almost entirely from produce grown on the
restaurant's property. And Stonewall Kitchens in York operates a cooking
school and cafe in addition to creating its famed jams and sauces.

Away from the coast, the land is agricultural, and roughly painted
signs point you to farm stands and pick-your-own strawberry fields.
Cheese makers tend herds of goats, young families pick up their winter
CSA shares, and beekeepers check on the hives that edge their fields.
Offering a microcosm of Maine's food culture, the southern region has it
all, from fried clams and ice-cream sundaes to peekytoe crab cakes and
crème brûlée.

Old-fashioned lobster pounds, clam shacks, seafood markets, and even a clam festival are waiting to be explored.

Seafood Restaurants

50 Local Restaurant, 50 Main St., Kennebunk; (207) 985-0850; localkennebunk.com. This hip neighborhood restaurant offers an ever-changing menu of French bistro foods with an American twist served in an elegant yet comfortable atmosphere. Chef-Owners Merrilee Paul and David Ross are committed to using local ingredients in their modern-day comfort food fare: lobster carbonara, fish stew, arctic char with lemon risotto, and butter-poached lobster. Open for dinner Tues through Sat, for brunch Sun from spring through fall.

Azure Cafe, 123 Main St., Freeport; (207) 865-1237; azurecafe.com. The seasonally changing menu is Italian inspired, and each plate meticulously arranged, at this elegant restaurant in the heart of Freeport. Creative entrees include Maine white fish with crab, salmon, and shrimp stuffing; Scottish salmon with wild Maine blueberry barbecue sauce; and the house specialty, Sicilian-style cioppino, a plethora of seafood in spicy tomato broth. A less-formal lunch menu is available, as well as seasonal outdoor seating. Open for lunch and dinner daily.

Barnacle Billy's, Perkins Cove, Ogunquit; (207) 646-5575; barnbilly.com. For more than 50 years, the original Barnacle Billy's has been charming guests with its picture-postcard view of sailboats passing under a hand-cranked drawbridge. They wait for the counter girl to call out their number, signifying their order for steamers, a lobster dinner, or an overflowing lobster roll is ready. The no-nonsense goes so well with the oversize rum punch cocktail. In the summer, grab a table on the wraparound sundeck. In the fall, sit by the window or near the roaring fireplace—perfect with a steaming bowl of the paprika-laced clam chowder. And now Barnacle Billy's Etc., right next door, is an upscale full-service restaurant. Both are seasonal operations. Open for lunch and dinner daily from spring through late Oct.

Blue Sky on York Beach, 2 Beach St., York Beach; (207) 363-0050; blueskyonyorkbeach.com. Located above Clara's Cupcake Cafe on the second floor of the renovated Atlantic House Hotel, this restaurant has

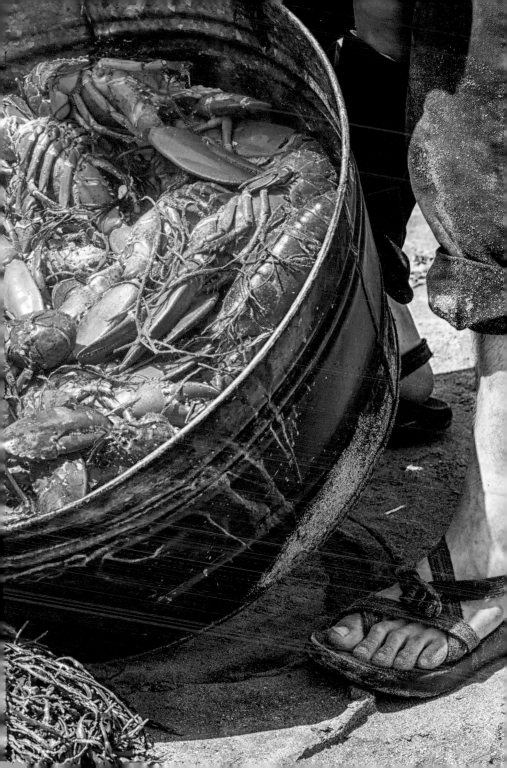

a warm, modern design as inviting as the seafood-laden menu. Sit at the food bar and start the evening with a signature cocktail. The sophisticated menu includes oysters Rockefeller, lobster Bolognese, baked haddock over fettuccine, and wood-fired lobster pizza. Blue Sky is owned by Lydia Shire, the well-respected Boston restaurateur. Open for dinner daily, jazz brunch Sun from 11 a.m. to 3 p.m.

The Captain's Restaurant, 1 Pier Rd., Cape Porpoise; (207) 967-2341; thewrightgallery.com/captains; cash only. Plain and simple comfort food is on the menu at this ultracasual seasonal restaurant, which has been in business for more than half a century. White wooden booths with turquoise cushions and knotty pine paneling set the scene. Loyal fans return year after year, craving the twin lobsters and the "amazing" blueberry pie made by owner Ruth Persson, also famous for her soft oatmeal rolls hot from the oven. This is a BYOB establishment, so feel free to bring your own wine or beer to go with dinner. Open for dinner nightly from mid-June through Labor Day, weekends only in spring and fall.

Chebeague Island Inn Restaurant, 61 South Rd., Chebeague Island; (207) 846-5155; chebeagueislandinn.com. With a diverse and changing menu that celebrates the flavors of the region, the restaurant of this celebrated 1880s inn is as much a destination as the island itself, which is located a leisurely ferry ride 15 minutes from Portland. Entrees include lobster risotto, pan-seared halibut or flounder, and butter-poached lobster. At the more casual lunchtime, try the oyster po' boy sandwich or the house-smoked salmon salad. Reservations are recommended, especially in the busy summer season, even if you're a guest of the inn. Jackets are not required, but dress is generally smart. Open for dinner nightly, with lunch offered Fri and Sat and brunch Sun.

Cole Farms Restaurant, 64 Lewiston Rd., Gray; (207) 657-4714; colefarms.com. Serving honest food for more than 50 years, this homey diner offers seafood entrees, mostly fried, including Maine clam cakes (which are totally different than the clam cake of Rhode Island and Connecticut). Everything is made in-house, from the salad dressing (available bottled) to the rolls to the perfectly battered onion rings. Save room for one of the more than 40 desserts made on the premises. A children's menu is available. Open for breakfast, lunch, and dinner daily.

The Harraseeket Inn, 162 Main St., Freeport; (207) 865-9377;
harraseeketinn.com. There are two dining options at this historic inn:
the elegant Maine Dining Room and the more casual Broad Arrow Tavern.
Crafting their menus with a commitment to supporting local agriculture,
both kitchens serve a seasonally changing menu. In the dining room try
jumbo scallops with celery root, sliced almonds, golden raisins, and parsley
foam. In the tavern snack on wood-fired, oven-roasted Maine mussels, the
award-winning lobster stew, or panko-crusted haddock. The tavern serves
lunch and dinner. The dining room is open for dinner nightly and hosts a
spectacular Sunday lobster brunch (reservations are highly recommended).

Hurricane Restaurant, 29 Dock Sq., Kennebunkport; (207) 967-
9111; hurricanerestaurant.com. This romantic restaurant, perched
over the water and mentioned in the travel guide *The Best Places to Kiss in
New England*, features an intimate atmosphere with river views from every
table, thanks to owners Brooks and Luanne MacDonald. The menu is eclectic, with offerings that range from garlic shrimp over freshly made fettuccine to a Maine lobster cobb salad. All desserts on the changing menu are
made in-house. Open for lunch and dinner daily "almost year-round."

Jameson Tavern, 115 Main St., Freeport; (207) 865-4196; jameson tavern.com. This historic tavern, founded in 1801, can be considered the birthplace of Maine, as the papers giving Maine independence from Massachusetts were signed in a meeting room on its second floor. The town of Freeport has grown up around it, and the tavern is now next door to the L.L. Bean flagship store, making it popular with tourists looking for a place to rest after a day of shopping. The restaurant includes a casual tavern, with a menu of well-executed pub fare and seafood standards, and a more formal dining room, with a cozy working fireplace and a menu of local meats and seafood, including several lobster preparations. There is seasonal outdoor seating on two patios. Open for lunch and dinner daily.

Johnson's Seafood & Steak, 18 Elm St., North Berwick; (207) 676-7900; eatatjohnsons.com. It started in Northwood, New Hampshire, where the Johnson family opened their first restaurant (see page 245). They quickly became a welcome stop along the back roads of New England. Today they still promise home-cooked food and warm hospitality. A wide variety of seafood, baked and fried, is offered. From the kettle comes clam chowder, fish chowder, and lobster stew. At lunch you can't go wrong with the clam, shrimp, or lobster roll or the baked salmon salad. Twin lobsters are also available for those with heartier appetites. Open for lunch and dinner daily.

Maine Diner, 2265 Post Rd. (Rte. 1), Wells; (207) 646-4441; maine diner.com. This landmark diner, first opened in 1953 to serve locals in the off-season, is now a major summer attraction, serving more than 1,000 patrons daily in the high season in its two cheerful blue-and-white dining rooms. Since brothers Miles and Dick Henry bought the diner in the 1980s, the menu has been expanded to include new specialties as well as old standbys. Try the lobster pie—their justly famed specialty of fresh lobster meat baked with stuffing—or the Clam-O-Rama: clam chowder, fried clams, clam strips, and a clam cake. A hearty breakfast, from lobster quiche to crab Benedict, is served from 7 a.m. Open daily year-round for breakfast, lunch, and dinner.

MC Perkins Cove, 111 Perkins Cove Rd., Ogunquit; (207) 646-6263; mcperkinscove.com. This upscale American bistro was created by Mark Gaier and Clark Frasier, the team behind nearby Arrows, and the kitchen at this beachfront spot uses produce from the same gardens. The menu and atmosphere are more casual, with offerings such as Maine peekytoe crab cakes, but there are still elegant touches: lemon fennel salad with the fried haddock, house-cured gravlax with watercress, and the Grand Shellfish Tower to start any meal. In the off-season, a reasonably priced midweek Date Night menu includes 3 courses and a bottle of wine. Open for lunch and dinner Wed through Mon; closed Jan.

On the Marsh Bistro, 46 Western Ave., Lower Village, Kennebunk; (207) 967-2299; onthemarsh.com. With a romantic atmosphere of cozy tables, rich drapery, and—in warm weather—French doors that open onto lush gardens, this elegant restaurant serves the extraordinary food of Chef Jeffery Savage. The menu verges on decadent, offering oysters with cucumber mignonette and sea scallops with lobster-truffle risotto on the savory side, and desserts like chèvre cheesecake with port-fig syrup. Open for dinner nightly.

The White Barn Inn, 37 Beach Ave., Kennebunk Beach; (207) 967-2321; whitebarninn.com. Housed in two restored 19th-century barns, the atmosphere of this acclaimed restaurant is at once rustic and crisp. Table settings are immaculate, as is the service, and the menu is a changing, 4-course prix fixe in the French tradition. Main courses might include pistachio-crusted halibut with sweet potato custard, sole and lobster on seafood potato mousseline, and pan-roasted salmon with crab succotash. Chef Jonathan Cartwright combines local flavors with his own European culinary roots and features seafood and local game paired with creamy sauces, truffles, and caviar. This is arguably the finest restaurant in the state, a sister property of Vanderbilt Grace in Newport, Rhode Island (see Muse on page 90). Reservations are essential, and dining is formal; for men, a jacket is required, though tie is optional. Open for dinner nightly.

Lobster Pounds

Bayley's Lobster Pound, Pine Point, 9 Ave. 6, Scarborough; (207) 883-4571 or (800) 932-6456; bayleys.com. Family owned and operated since 1915, this year-round lobster pound sells whole lobsters (live and cooked), fresh fish and shellfish, and take-out sandwiches, seafood salads, chowders, and stews. Open daily from 9 a.m. to 6 p.m.

Cape Neddick Lobster Pound-Harborside Restaurant, 60 Shore Rd., Cape Neddick; (207) 363-5471; capeneddick.com. What started

What Is a Lobster Pound?

Someone once said a lobster pound is similar to a dog pound—people who don't want their lobsters drop them off there where they are cared for and fed, and people looking to adopt a lobster, come by and pick one up. Nice try, but not true.

The official definition is "a large commercial enclosure filled with circulating water in which lobsters are kept alive pending sale." It is something that is found only in the North Atlantic region of America, especially in the states of Maine and New Hampshire. The first lobster pound appeared on Vinalhaven, a small island off the coast of Rockland, Maine, in 1875, and others quickly followed. The first one was in a deep tidal creek, but today they are more common on docks floating in the harbor. By keeping their lobsters in a pound, dealers can take advantage of price fluctuations or allow a newly molted lobster time to harden its shell.

Lobster pounds are found mostly in Maine and New Hampshire. Ask anyone in Rhode Island to recommend a good lobster pound, and he or she won't know what you're talking about. Many lobster pounds are seasonal operations, open from late spring to early fall, and many do not serve alcohol (so bring your own in a cooler), nor do they take credit cards—so be prepared.

Lobster aficionados claim the best place to purchase a lobster is a pound because it is the closest thing to the crustacean's natural environment. Often you can pick out the exact lobster you desire, while other pounds simply want to know what size lobster you would like. The size is gauged by how much a lobster weighs, starting with a small chicken lobster (a young lobster weighing 1 pound or less). The standard serving is between 1 and 1½ pounds. There is much debate on whether a small lobster is more tender than a very large lobster. One important thing to remember is: If you're planning on taking the live lobster to cook at home, make sure you have a stockpot large enough to cook the creature.

Some pounds are nothing more than a shack on a dock where you can buy live lobsters to take home and cook. Other pounds will boil or steam the lobster for you, and you eat it

"in the rough." That can mean you're sitting on a lobster trap on the dock or at nearby picnic tables. Still another type of pound is part of a full-service restaurant that serves fresh lobsters and other seafood dishes that you dine on either indoors or out, with all the refinements of a full dinner.

Insider tip: Cull lobsters have only one claw and are always cheaper than regular lobsters. Their tail meat is always intact, so by purchasing cull lobsters, you will get more for your money.

Eating a cooked lobster is messy and takes a bit of work and the right utensils. Many lobster pounds offer their guests plastic bibs to wear when eating. You'll rarely see a Maine resident wearing that bib, the sign of a novice. Some lobsters have soft shells, making it easy to break open and get every bit of meat. The meat can be sweeter, but there is usually less meat to eat. Hard-shell lobsters are tougher to crack open, but there is always more meat. Prepare to get dirty with lobster juices running down your arms as you crack open both claws and rip the tail section off the body of the lobster.

The witty author Calvin Trillin once noted: "It is apparent to serious shellfish eaters that in the great evolutionary scheme of things crustaceans developed shells to protect them from knives and forks."

out as a lobster pound more than 50 years ago has evolved into a seasonal restaurant that is very busy in the summer. Consistency is their strong suit. The attentive staff is very good with children. The baked stuffed lobster gets rave reviews, as does the lobster stew and lightly battered fried seafood. A seat by the window gets you a view of the nearby marsh and Cape Neddick River. Be prepared to wait for a table in July and August. This is a fun spot with a very casual atmosphere. Closed in winter, reopens in mid-Mar.

Chauncey Creek Lobster Pier, 16 Chauncey Creek Rd., Kittery Point; (207) 439-1030; chaunceycreek.com. One of the best-kept secrets amid the madness of nearby outlet malls on Route 1, this authentic riverside shack has been quietly providing lobsters and a raw bar to guests who bring everything else, including coolers of wine and beer, since the early 1950s. Select the lobster you want cooked and grab a brightly painted picnic table on the dock. If the bugs are out, head for the screened-in deck. A quiet tidal river and a scenic pine forest provide a serene view. Live lobsters are also available to take home. Open daily from 11 a.m. to 8 p.m. from Mother's Day to Labor Day, Tues through Sun from 11 a.m. to 7 p.m. Labor Day to Columbus Day.

Day's Crabmeat and Lobster, 1269 Rte. 1, Yarmouth; (207) 846-3436; dayscrabmeatandlobster.com. This seasonal marsh-side lobster pound has been in business since the 1920s, when founders John and Charles Hilton began selling crabmeat and crabmeat rolls (lobster came later). The tradition continues with the handpicked crabmeat salad, lobster rolls, and steamed clams. Orders are picked up at a take-out window, and seating is outdoors at picnic tables. Inside, pick your own live lobsters at the pound. Open daily May to Oct, Mon through Sat from 8 a.m. to 5 p.m., Sun from 8 a.m. to 2 p.m. The take-out window opens at 11 a.m.

Estes Lobster House, 1906 Harpswell Neck Rd., South Harpswell; (207) 833-6340; esteslobsterhouse.com. Well off the beaten path but well worth the trip, this lobster house is on "the reaches," those long, narrow peninsulas that stretch like fingers southward into Casco Bay. Celebrating its 50th year in business, this seasonal restaurant is surrounded by water with outdoor seating and a fire pit and torches lit every night. The Crooker family and crew serve up a fun menu that includes lobster dip served in a bread bowl and their famous lobster mac and cheese. Seafood selections feature a Maine shore dinner starting with chowder and ending with strawberry shortcake. A special menu is available for children and senior citizens. This is a seasonal operation that reopens every year on Memorial Day weekend in May. Open for lunch and dinner daily in summer.

Fox's Lobster House, 8 Sohier Park Rd., York Beach; (207) 363-2643; foxslobster.com. No visit to York is complete without a stop at the famous Nubble Lighthouse. Nearby is this charming restaurant where lobsters are prepared the old-fashioned way—they are boiled in a lobster pound that dates back to 1936. Locals say: "One nibble on the Nubble, and you're hooked." A seasonal operation, this oceanfront restaurant offers all you expect and then some surprises, such as baked maple salmon and golden fried lobster tails. The dessert menu is almost as long as the dinner menu. A children's menu is also available. Open from late Apr through Oct.

Harraseeket Lunch & Lobster, 36 Main St., South Freeport; (207) 865-4888 (lunch) or (207) 865-3535 (lobster); harraseeketlunch andlobster.com. No trip to L.L. Bean would be complete without a stop here, especially after dark when this "shack" is lit up like a carnival. Owned and operated by the Coffin family for more than 40 years, this waterfront spot offers fried seafood by the pint, lobster rolls, and homemade desserts

Ordering Lobsters Online

Craving the ultimate indulgence but you're far from Maine? Fresh live lobsters can be ordered from a number of websites.

Lobsteranywhere.com ships Maine lobsters and fresh seafood to just about anywhere in the United States, even as far as Hawaii and the North Pole. Lobster tails are a specialty, ranging in size from 7 ounces to giant tails coming from 6-pound lobsters. Dinner packages are also available. Order by noon Eastern Standard Time, and your live Maine lobsters will be delivered within 24 hours.

Lobsters-online.com offers traditional lobster clambakes for two and four persons. The basic package includes 2 lobsters and steamer clams. Other packages add lobster bisque, clam chowder, mussels, and even the pot to steam them in, if desired. Order any combination by 2:30 p.m. Eastern Standard Time, and enjoy your lobster feast the next day.

MaineLobsterDirect.com is one of the oldest Internet-based suppliers of fresh Maine lobster and seafood. It has a very wide variety of complete dinner packages, from the popular CanBake to the Downeast Feast. Order as late as 4:30 p.m. Eastern Standard Time, and your order will be delivered within 24 hours.

from family recipes. By day the outdoor seating offers views of fishing boats on the harbor—you can watch the day's catch come in as you eat. The lunch counter is open for lunch and dinner. The lobster pound, open every day at 7 a.m., sells live and freshly cooked lobsters, clams, crabs, and more, including packing boxes and ice packs for traveling. They accept cash only. Open daily from May 1 through Columbus Day.

Nunan's Lobster Hut, 9 Mills Rd., Kennebunkport; (207) 967-4362; nunanslobsterhut.com. The menu is pretty simple—lobster, lobster, and more lobster, plus a steak dinner for landlubbers, lighter fare for children, and wonderful desserts made on the premises. Richard and Keith Nunan serve their daily catch at the restaurant, while Keith's wife Kim bakes dessert pies according to her mother-in-law's famed recipes. Steamed lobsters in various sizes are served with melted butter, clam chowder, potato chips, and rolls. If you want extra melted butter, that'll cost you 25 cents. Founded in 1932, Nunan's is considered by many to be the ultimate lobster pound with its long tables, bench seats, and communal seating. Just look for the brightly painted building in the fishing village of Cape Porpoise. A seasonal operation, they open in early May with limited hours Thurs through Sun. Open for dinner nightly from Memorial Day through Columbus Day.

Ogunquit Lobster Pound, 504 Main St., Ogunquit; (207) 646-2516; ogunquitlobsterpound.com. Since 1931 this authentic lobster pound has been serving hot boiled lobsters and steamed clams "in the rough" to happy customers from near and far. A full menu is available, as well as a children's menu. Save room for the individual deep-dish dessert pies. Generations of families believe this is life in Maine as it should be. Open for dinner from mid-Mar to Thanksgiving, nightly in the summer, and only on weekends in spring and fall.

Clam Shacks

Billy's Chowder House, 216 Mile Rd., Wells; (207) 646-7558; billys chowderhouse.com. With views of the Rachel Carson Wildlife Refuge and Tidal Marsh, this seaside restaurant has a classic menu: large portions of fried seafood, baked and broiled fish, boiled lobster, and rich seafood chowders. The lobster rolls must be good—they sell about 20,000 of them a year. A children's menu is available. Open for lunch and dinner daily Feb through Nov; closed Dec and Jan.

Bob's Clam Hut, 315 Rte. 1, Kittery; (207) 439-4233; bobsclamhut .com. Since 1956 this landmark clam shack has been serving fried seafood via basket, sandwich, roll, and dinner. Fried clams are the specialty, but oysters, bay scallops, shrimp, and haddock are also on the menu. Originally just for takeout, but indoor and seasonal outdoor seating at bright blue picnic tables is now available. In the heart of busy Kittery's outlet country, just look for the white picket fence surrounding this incredibly busy clam shack. Make sure you say hi to Miss Lillian when you place your order. She's been at that window for more than 25 years. Tues is senior appreciation day—customers 60 years and older get 15 percent off their total check. Open for lunch and dinner daily year-round.

The Clam Shack, 2 Western Ave., Kennebunk; (207) 967-2560; theclamshack.net. Nothing spells summer as much as a sturdy white paper carton overflowing with fried clams. At this genuine clam shack, you'll feast on such goodies as you sit on wooden benches and lobster crates. Make sure to try the lobster roll served on a grilled, locally made bun with both a touch of mayo and a drizzle of butter. And bring a cooler so you can shop at their on-premise seafood market (see page 184). Cash only. Hours change with the seasons—always call ahead is their advice.

Fisherman's Catch, 134 Harbor Rd., Wells; (207) 646-8780; fishermanscatchwells.com. One of the best little seafood dives in New England, serving simple Maine food for more than 25 years, the Catch, as it is called, may be off the beaten path, but fans flock there every summer, hungry for the chowders and stews, seafood dinners, and the South Shore Bake—a complete lobster feast. This is an award-winning seasonal operation with a children's menu. Open for lunch and dinner daily from early May to mid-Oct.

Ken's Place, 207 Pine Point Rd., Scarborough; (207) 883-6611. This seasonal seafood restaurant with its extensive menu is famous for meaty clam cakes (also available as burgers), plump fried scallops, crispy onion rings, and generous baskets of fried seafood. An institution since 1927, it's popular with locals—be prepared for long lines in the summer. This is the perfect place to stop on your way to Old Orchard Beach. You can sit at indoor and outdoor tables with colorful umbrellas. A children's menu is available. Open for lunch and dinner daily from late Mar through Oct.

Linda Bean's Maine Lobster, 88 Main St., Freeport; (207) 865-9835; Portland Jetport, South Portland; (207) 773-2469; linda beansperfectmaine.com. Opened by Linda Bean, granddaughter of L.L. Bean, these casual restaurants are an extension of her efforts to conserve the working waterfront of the fishing villages of Downeast Maine. Serving Maine-caught seafood from the Port Clyde Lobster Company, also owned by Bean, the menu's signature offering is its lobster roll, made with ¼ pound of claw meat and dressed with Bean's secret recipe of herbs, served on a buttered white or whole wheat roll. Also on the menu are a variety of other seafood specialties, including a lobster panini sandwich. Linda Bean's Maine Kitchen & Topside Tavern, across from the L.L. Bean flagship store, is open daily from 6:30 a.m. to late night. The take-out window in Freeport is open from Apr to Jan. The Dip Net is an additional seasonal location in Port Clyde next to the Monhegan Ferry terminal (207-372-1112). And watch for the Lobstermobile at country fairs and festivals. They also ship live lobsters anywhere in the United States.

Mabel's Lobster Claw, 124 Ocean Ave., Kennebunkport; (207) 967-2562; mabelslobster.com. This homey restaurant, beloved by the presidential Bush family who are summer regulars, serves classic seafood in a relaxed atmosphere. A local landmark since 1953, Mabel's has paper placemats that illustrate the proper way to eat a lobster. The menu includes creamy chowder, rolls full of sweet lobster meat, and the shore dinner—boiled lobster over steamers with clam broth and drawn butter. Finish it off with a slice of the blueberry or raspberry pie baked every morning on the premises. Open for lunch and dinner daily Apr through Oct.

Seafood Markets

Bob's Seafood, 901 Roosevelt Trail, Windham; (207) 893-2882; lobsters-shipped.com. A "total seafood store" near Sebago Lake, Bob's sells fresh fish, live lobsters and shellfish, precooked steamahs (steamed clams) and mussels, along with a menu of fried seafood, chowders, and lobster stew available by the pint and quart. They will ship whatever you are craving anywhere in the continental United States. Bob's Restaurant, a BYOB establishment on the premises, is open for lunch and dinner daily, with a special menu for children and senior citizens and patio seating in the summer. Open Tues to Thurs from 10 a.m. to 7:30 p.m., Fri and Sat from 10 a.m. to 8 p.m., Sun from 10 a.m. to 7 p.m.

Clam Shack Seafoods, 2 Western Ave., Kennebunk; (207) 967-2560; theclamshack.net. Right next door to The Clam Shack restaurant (see page 182) is Clam Shack Seafoods, a market propped up on pilings directly over a river. The gurgling lobster tanks are next to an iced case for freshly caught fish. What isn't sold at the market is fried up at the restaurant that night, so the limited selection is always fresh. The daily catch usually includes Maine shrimp, lobster, haddock, salmon, and steamers (and swordfish is always on hand for the presidential Bush family, who spend summers in Kennebunkport). Lobsters are boiled in fresh seawater for you to take home and eat. The "striper cam" is an underwater camera rigged on a piling beneath the shack, which gives visitors a view of the local striped bass feeding on the customers' dropped snacks. Live lobsters are shipped anywhere overnight. Hours change with the seasons—always call ahead is their advice.

Fishermen's Net, 59c Portland Rd., Gray; (207) 657-3474. 849 Forest Ave., Portland; (207) 772-3565. 93 State St., Presque Isle; (207) 762-3782; fishermensnet-gray.com. This simple, unpretentious fishmonger sells fresh, locally caught fish, live lobster, and a small take-out menu of fried seafood, sandwiches, lobster rolls, and homemade chowder. This place comes highly recommended by local fishing guides. Stuffed lobsters and prepared seafood can be ordered ahead to cook at home. Open Mon from 2 to 6 p.m., Tues through Sat from 10 a.m. to 6 p.m., Sun from 11 a.m. to 5 p.m.

Southern Maine Events

July
Yarmouth Clam Festival, downtown Yarmouth; clamfestival.com. This annual weekend-long celebration of all things clam has been a Yarmouth tradition since 1965. Beginning with the kickoff parade down Main Street, the festival includes an arts and crafts fair, a kayak and canoe race, a firefighters' muster competition, the official Maine State Clam Shucking Contest, and, of course, plenty of clams to eat. A midway offers carnival rides. Always begins on the third Friday in July.

MID-COAST MAINE

With quaint fishing villages nestled among its harbors and inlets, the Mid Coast presents Maine at its most picturesque. Restored 18th- and 19th-century homes, built by sea captains and marked with historical plaques, are tucked down seaside lanes, their gardens teeming with flowers from spring to fall. Yachts and schooners dock in the marinas, bobbing in the glinting water through the summer; beyond them, wooded and rocky islands dot the bays. The area is known for its seafood—lobsters are caught in the waters of Muscongus Bay, oysters are cultivated in the mouth of the deep Damariscotta River, and haddock, cod, and other fin fish are brought in with every day's catch. Fishing families have been here for centuries, and many mailboxes sport the same names as the coves they're on.

European settlers recognized the region's beauty, abundant seafood, and perfect situation for maritime pursuits. Beginning in the 18th century, tall ships were crafted at shipyards throughout the region, and the Bath Iron Works continues to build vessels for the US Navy to this day.

The bucolic beauty of the Mid Coast has drawn artists—from painters to poets—to the region for more than a century, and cultural highlights include the Farnsworth Art Museum and Wyeth Center in Rockland, the historic Camden Opera House, and the Boothbay Opera House in Boothbay Harbor.

The town of Brunswick, since 1794 the home of Bowdoin College, is in many ways the intellectual hub of the Mid Coast. The alma mater of President Franklin Pierce, Henry Wadsworth Longfellow, Nathaniel Hawthorne, and Arctic explorer Admiral Robert Peary, Bowdoin hosts lectures and cultural events throughout the academic year.

While the Mid Coast is known primarily for its seafaring and aquaculture—the majority of Maine's oysters are gathered here—it is also a region of avid gardening and some of the earliest farm-to-table restaurants in the state. All along the coast, a growing number of restaurants are receiving national recognition for their commitments to farm-to-table dining, and chefs change their menus daily to reflect what's in season. The Mid Coast was the site of Maine's first Slow Food convivium, and that movement's philosophy of slowing down to savor life is a good fit with the region.

The seafood here is stupendous, and seasonal lobster shacks can be found in every town, serving up lobsters boiled in seawater and heaping plates of steamed clams. This is Maine at its most iconic, and its most delicious.

Seafood Restaurants

Anchor Inn, Anchor Inn Road, Round Pond; (207) 529-5584; anchorinnrestaurant.com. See the sister operation Damariscotta River Grill below.

Brunswick Diner, 101½ Pleasant St., Brunswick; (207) 721-1134; no website. This tiny red train car has been serving diner delights to locals and Bowdoin students since 1946. Yes, it can be cramped at peak hours—weekend breakfasts are especially so—and yes, the food is classic diner fare with a few Maine embellishments (the generous lobster roll is outstanding). Still, a seat at the counter with a bottomless cup of coffee and a wisecracking waitress can be just the thing. Open for breakfast, lunch, and dinner daily, with 24-hour service on Fri and Sat.

Cappy's Chowder House, 1 Main St., Camden; (207) 236-2254; cappsychowder.com. In the heart of the Maine coast, Cappy's is a family-owned business, the kind of fun place where everyone shows up eventually. Locals rave about the creamy, thick, peppery, clam-filled chowder and the nightly lobster specials. The food is so good, you'll want to shop online to get a case of that chowder shipped to your door. The seasonal menu changes monthly, so there's always something new to try. A children's menu is available. Open daily for lunch and dinner.

Conte's 1894 Restaurant, 148 South Main St., Rockland; no phone; no website. There's no signage or menu at this local landmark, nearly hidden beneath piled nets and dangling lobster crates, but for the hardy souls who duck in, there's unique seafood to be had. The reviews are mixed—people either are madly in love with the funky decor and food, or they hate it. Chef John Conte's servings are gigantic: garlicky lobster and shrimp on a bed of fresh linguine or sausage and whole lobster napped with spicy tomato sauce. In the winter the dining room is heated by a single pot-bellied stove, so plan to bundle up. Cash only. Open for dinner nightly; hours vary according to the quirky chef's mood.

Damariscotta River Grill, 155 Main St., Damariscotta; (207) 563-2992; damariscottarivergrill.com; **Anchor Inn,** Anchor Inn Road, Round Pond; (207) 529-5584; anchorinnrestaurant.com. At the year-round Damariscotta River Grill, the husband-and-wife team of Chef

Rick Hirsch and Jean Kerrigan serve upscale comfort food, from Steak & Cakes—grilled rib eye paired with lobster cakes—to lobster strudel, a combination of fresh-picked lobster meat and mascarpone wrapped in phyllo. Sister restaurant, the seasonal Anchor Inn, has a more casual menu of traditional broiled and baked seafood with a few twists, like the yellow fin tuna with curried coconut-peanut sauce. At both restaurants the food is fresh and the service welcoming. Damariscotta River Grill is open for lunch and dinner daily, for brunch on Sun.

Dolphin Marina and Restaurant, 515 Basin Point Rd., Harpswell; (207) 833-6000; dolphinmarinaandrestaurant.com. Perched over Pott's Harbor at the tip of Basin Point, this seasonal restaurant and marina have offered home-style meals and unrivaled views of Casco Bay to travelers since 1966. Recently this family-owned business undertook a major redesign of the marina to make it environmentally friendly, and it's been certified a "Clean Marina" by the Maine Marine Trades Association. The food is fresh from the sea, and entrees come with a big, warm blueberry muffin. Open from Apr to Nov. They recommend calling ahead for hours of operation.

King Eider's Pub, 2 Elm St., Damariscotta; (207) 563-6008; kingeiderspub.com. This place is known for their luscious crab cakes— fresh-picked lumps of crabmeat sautéed and dressed with freshly made tartar sauce—and the plump Damariscotta River oysters they get daily from Dodge Cove Marine Farm. With brick walls and low wooden beams, this comfy pub serves local and imported beers on tap, as well as a wide range of bottled brews. A children's menu is available. Open for lunch and dinner daily.

Larson's Lunch Box, 430 Upper Main St., Damariscotta; (207) 653-5755; larsonslunchbox.com. Since 1962 this seasonal lunch stand has served up grilled burgers and sandwiches, soups and chowders, and local comfort foods. Crab, shrimp, and lobster rolls are among the most generous, and everything is reasonably priced. Sit at an outdoor table, or take a picnic to Pemaquid Point. Cash only. Open for lunch and dinner from May 1 to late Oct; closed Wed.

The Lobster Pound Restaurant, Rte. 1, Lincolnville Beach; (207) 789-5550; lobsterpoundmaine.com. It all started way back in the 1920s, a humble seasonal restaurant with 60 seats. After a flood caused severe damage, renovations increased the seating to 260 and included a new nautical gift shop. In the 1980s a fire nearly destroyed the building, and it was rebuilt once again. Now owned by Richard and Patricia McLaughlin, this is a restaurant that perseveres! This full-service family restaurant now has a patio, picnic area, and 70 open-air seats overlooking Penobscot Bay. A fairly extensive menu is offered, featuring seafood specialty dishes such as baked stuffed haddock and, of course, lobster in every preparation imaginable. A children's menu and senior citizen's menu are available. Open for lunch and dinner daily from May to Oct.

Montsweag Roadhouse, 942 Rte. 1, Woolwich; (207) 443-6563; montsweagroadhouse.com. Combine live music, home-style bar food, and a few pool tables, and you get this lively roadhouse. Popular among locals, there are dartboards, foosball, and Thursday open-mic nights. Food is solidly good, with fresh seafood, creamy chowder, and dressings made on the premises, plus plenty of offerings for non-seafood lovers. A children's menu is available. Open for lunch and dinner daily.

Pemaquid Point Restaurant at the Bradley Inn, 3063 Bristol Rd., New Harbor; (207) 677-3749; bradleyinn.com. The elegant dining room at this charming inn has received national acclaim for its warm atmosphere and finely prepared meals. Open to the public as well as guests, the inn is at the tip of the Pemaquid peninsula. The luxurious menu features local Pemaquid oysters, house-cured charcuterie, locally foraged mushrooms, and pasture-raised meats. Pairings are inventive, and plates are composed with a delicate hand. Entrees include soft-shell crabs, grilled black sea bass, pan-seared wild salmon, olive oil-poached sturgeon, and herb-basted Atlantic salmon. The more casual Chartroom Tavern has a full bar and is frequented by hotel guests, restaurant patrons, and locals. Open for dinner nightly.

Suzuki's Sushi Bar, 419 Main St., Rockland; (207) 596-7447; suzukisushi.com. The calm that radiates through this stylish sushi restaurant is mirrored by the menu of fresh seafood, brought in hours before and arranged with precision on each plate. Chef-Owner Keiko Suzuki Steinberger commands the kitchen, which is entirely staffed by women and is considered by many to turn out the best sushi in the region. Dishes are made with predominately local ingredients—including unusual by-catch such as mini octopus and whelk that the chef buys off fishermen on her way to work—and the kitchen has neither a grill nor a fryer, preferring to poach, steam, or serve food raw. Open for dinner Tues through Sat.

Three Tides/Marshall Wharf Brewing Company 2 Pinchy Ln., Belfast; (207) 338-1707; marshallwharf.com. Above the water on Marshall Wharf, this brewery and bar serves its own craft beers, many with funky names—Doktor Dunklesweizen and Chaos Chaos Russian Imperial Stout—as well as a dozen or so other brews and a small menu of tapas. Pair Pemaquid Oyster Stout with half a dozen, or snack on Maine crabmeat quesadillas with a pale ale. Open nightly Tues through Sat in the off-season, Tues through Sun in summer.

Lobster Shacks & Lobster Pounds

Boothbay Lobster Wharf, 97 Atlantic Ave., Boothbay Harbor; (207) 633-4900 or (800) 996-1740; boothbaylobsterwharf.com. At this working lobster pound and seafood wholesaler, you can watch the workings of the waterfront while enjoying lunch at a picnic table on the deck. The seasonal restaurant (open for lunch and dinner daily from mid-May to mid-Oct) is no frills—order your chowder, fried seafood, or lobster under one striped awning, pick it up from the window under another—but the food is as fresh as can be. The year-round fish market sells the daily catch, as well as mussels, cherrystones, clams, oysters, and cooked lobster, crab, and shrimp. They ship live lobsters overnight to your door. Open daily from 7 a.m. to 5 p.m.

Cameron's, 18 Bath Rd., Brunswick; (207) 725-2886. Follow the yellow chaser lights to this classic drive-in, pull your car under the flat-roofed canopy, and enjoy lobster dinners and rolls, grilled crab and cheese, or fish-and-chips at the counter or delivered by car-side service. The menu includes all the favorites, plus a few extras like the fried oyster roll, heaped with crunchy nuggets of sweet meat. Live lobsters, steamers, and fresh haddock can also be picked up to make at home. Open daily from 8 a.m. to 7 p.m.

Cook's Lobster House, 68 Garrison Cove Rd., Bailey Island; (207) 833-2818; cookslobster.com. Come for the island view, stay for the lobster dishes and steamed mussels. Lobster is prepared 10 different ways, including steamed in seawater. Sit inside in a rustic pine booth or out on the deck at round tables made from old cable spools and let the view of Casco Bay sink in, truly beautiful at sunset. Since 1955 this award-winning landmark lobster house has attracted seafood lovers by car and boat. Lobster bakes on the beach can be scheduled in warm weather, and they ship live lobsters anywhere in the continental United States. If you have the time, take a cruise through local islands, which is available in the summer; details are on the website. Open for lunch and dinner daily.

Five Islands Lobster Company, 1447 Five Islands Rd., Georgetown; (207) 371-2990; fiveislandslobster.com. First, look for the red building marked LOBSTERS. That's where you select a live lobster to be cooked while you head next door to the fry shack for the best fried clams in the state, according to *DownEast* magazine. Then grab a weathered blue table on the dock with a 360-degree view of the five pine-covered islands. This BYOB establishment offers a quintessential Maine dining experience, especially at sunset. The hours change seasonally. Open daily in summer.

Hawkes' Lobster, Cundy's Harbor, Harpswell; (207) 721-0472; hawkeslobster.com. Selling live lobsters and nautical-themed gifts and antiques, this tiny lobster pound sits in a sea-weathered shop above the harbor. It's a family business, and Gary and Sue Hawkes sell lobsters caught by their two sons and two brothers. Sue's family has lived and fished in the area since the 1700s. They ship live lobsters year-round. Open daily from 10 a.m. to 6:30 p.m. from May to Oct, and by appointment.

Red's Eats, 41 Water St., Wiscasset; (207) 882-6128; no website. With a name like Red's Eats, you just have to check out this place, and you

won't be sorry. Every lobster roll contains the meat from a whole 1-pound lobster, stuffed into a toasted bun with mayo and melted butter on the side, so you can have it your way. It definitely helps you endure the tedious traffic on Wiscasset Bridge. A summer institution here since 1954 (and dating back to 1938 in Boothbay), the tiny red and white building that houses Red's overlooks the water. This is a seasonal operation with shaded outdoor seating. Open for lunch and dinner daily from mid-Apr to mid-Oct.

Sea Basket, 303 Bath Rd., Rte. 1, Wiscasset; (207) 882-6581; sea basket.com. With a legendary lobster stew and fried seafood by the basket, this classic roadside cafe is just what it seems: tidy and friendly with good, fresh food. The chowders are creamy and full of meat without being too heavy, fried seafood is crisp and not overly greasy, and homemade cole-slaw has a refreshing bite. Open Wed through Sun from 11 a.m. to 8 p.m.; closed Jan and Feb.

Shaw's Fish and Lobster, Wharf, 129 Rte. 32, New Harbor; (207) 677-2200. An authentic fishing village, this is where the Kevin Costner/ Paul Newman film *Message in a Bottle* was filmed. This wharf-side restaurant has seating in the indoor dining room and on the open deck with a wonderful view of the working waterfront. Inside it's no frills—place your order at one end of the wooden counter and pick it up at the other—but there's a full bar, a rarity at lobster shacks. On a beautiful midsummer day, expect a wait, but the food is fresh and portions are generous—the lightly buttered lobster rolls virtually explode with meat; Shaw's serves about 10,000 of them every year. Open for lunch and dinner daily from mid-May to mid-Oct.

Waterman's Beach Lobster, 343 Waterman's Beach Rd., South Thomaston; (207) 596-7819 or (207) 594-7518; watermansbeach lobster.com. This beautifully situated lobster shack was the winner of a James Beard Foundation America's Regional Classics Award in 2001, and it's easy to see why: Peacock-blue picnic tables sit above the ocean on a tented deck, each table bearing blue mason jars filled with fresh flowers. The lobsters and clams are steamed in salt water, seafood rolls are made with freshly picked meat from that day's catch, and luscious rhubarb, berry, and lemon sponge pies are baked from family recipes. The view of Muscle Ridge Channel is filled with working fishing boats, shorebirds, and seals. This is the only BYOB restaurant in the area, so bring your own wine and beer. Cash only. Open for lunch and dinner Wed through Sun from mid-June to Sept, with seasonal hours.

Young's Lobster Pound, 4 Mitchell St., Belfast; (207) 338-1160; no website. Look for the big barn-red building right on the dock in Belfast Harbor. Here everyone's got one thing on the mind: lobsters. Choose hard-shell or soft-shell (in season) from the large tanks. The staff will weigh them, and, if you'd like, cook them in seawater at no extra charge. Crabs, clams, and mussels are also available by the pound, and they'll steam them, too. Pick up your order at the long stainless steel counter, and you're good to go. They offer seasonal outdoor seating at picnic tables by the water's edge. If you prefer, the staff will pack your fresh seafood order to go, or they'll ship it overnight to your door. Hours change with the seasons. Open from 7:30 a.m. to 4 p.m. in winter, from 7:30 a.m. to 8 p.m. in summer.

Seafood Markets

Gilmore's Seafoods, 129 Court St., Bath; (207) 443-5231 or (800) 849-9667; gilmoreseafood.com. Serving Bath since it was founded by Lefty Gilmore in 1958, this unpretentious wholesale and retail fish market is a local institution. Selling everything from Maine rock crabs and fresh cusk to finnan haddie and sun-dried pollack, the market is full service—mongers know their fish and are likely to throw in a cooking suggestion with your order. Live lobsters are brought in by the shop's boat, *Rebel,* and can be shipped overnight to your door. The shop also operates a small take-out business of prepared seafood. Open daily from 11 a.m. to 6 p.m.

Glidden Point Oyster Co., 707 River Rd., Edgecomb; (207) 633-3599; oysterfarm.com. If no one's around, you choose your own oysters and put money into an honor-system cashbox at this family-owned sea farm. The diver-harvested oysters are plump and firm, briny yet sweet, with deep shell cup. And they are harvested sustainably. The Sea Farm Store stocks oyster essentials like shucking tools, as well as oysters, steamers, and littleneck clams. Open daily from 8 a.m. to 5:30 p.m.

Megunticook Market, 2 Gould St., Camden; (207) 236-3537; megunticookmarket.com. For more than 100 years, this country market has been known for its custom-cut meats. Current owner Lani Temple has expanded the offerings to include local and imported cheeses, organic produce, an impressive wine section, freshly caught seafood, locally roasted coffee, and made-from-scratch baked pastries and pies. The seafood is from Port Clyde Fresh Catch. Open Mon through Sat from 7 a.m. to 7 p.m., Sun from 9 a.m. to 6 p.m.

Mid-Coast Maine Events

April
Fishermen's Festival, Boothbay Harbor; (207) 633-6280; boothbay harbor.com. This weekend of festivities begins with the Miss Shrimp Pageant and ends with a traditional blessing of the fleet. Events include a codfish relay, lobster-trap hauling, dory bailing, and lobster-crate running. A fish fry and plenty of chowder feed the crowd.

A Brief Guide to Maine Oysters

Maine's mid-coast provides ideal conditions for the cultivation of plump, briny oysters. A few are exported down the coast, but many are from small producers who make just enough to satisfy the state. Below is a brief guide to the oysters of the region.

Bagaduce: from the Bagaduce River; lovely alabaster shells, plump, meaty oysters

Belon: from the Damariscotta River; large flat shell, crisp, coppery oyster that almost fizzes in the mouth

Flying Point: from the waters near Yarmouth; large, with a mild, light flavor

Gay Island: from the deep open waters near Cushing Harbor; briny and intense

Glidden Point: from the deep waters of the Damariscotta; rich, dense, briny

Little Bay: technically from the Little Bay, New Hampshire waters near Eliot, Maine; small, full meat, salty, with a crisp, sweet finish

North Haven: from North Haven; large, high salinity; available year-round

Oak Point: from Harrington; briny, exceptionally uniform size

Pemaquid: from the Damariscotta River; briny, firm, even a little tart

Taunton Bay Oyster: from waters near Acadia National Park; deep cupped, salty, with a metallic finish

Wawenauk: from Hog Island in the Damariscotta River; plump, deep cupped, briny

Wiley Point: from Damariscotta River Estuary; clean, smooth shell, large and light

Winter Point: from Mill Cove, West Bath; thick shell, meaty, almost a hint of sweetness

June

Taste of Brunswick, Town Green, Maine Street, Brunswick; (207) 729-4439; tasteofbrunswick.com. Sample the flavors of the best restaurants in town while cheering on their waitstaff in the waiter's race at this daylong benefit for the Mid-Coast Hunger Prevention Program. More than 20 area restaurants donate their time and talent, and live bluegrass, jazz, and rockabilly music keeps everyone moving.

August

Maine Lobster Festival, Harbor Park, Rockland; mainelobster festival.com. For more than 60 years, this 5-day crustacean celebration has drawn crowds to the seaside town of Rockland. Festivities range from a children's lobster-eating contest to the coronation of the Maine Sea Goddess. Tents display arts and crafts, live music fills the air, and more than 20,000 pounds of lobster are pulled from the sea, cooked on the shore, and served with drawn butter.

September

Annual Pemaquid Oyster Festival, Schooner Landing, Damariscotta; (207) 380-9912. More than 10,000 oysters are consumed during this free 1-day celebration on the working waterfront where Pemaquid oysters are cultivated. Festivities include a shucking contest, oyster poetry, live music, and, of course, oysters by the dozen, still glistening with brine as they're harvested from the Damariscotta River.

October

Beer and Pemaquid Mussel Festival, Three Tides, Belfast; (207) 338-1707. More than 30 beers are on tap for tasting along with the famous mussels of Pemaquid at Three Tides, part of the Marshall Wharf Brewing Company. Rain or shine under heated tents. Must be 21 to attend.

DOWNEAST MAINE

With its craggy granite cliffs and piney, windswept islands, Downeast Maine's distinctive image is hard to resist. In the briny water, brightly colored buoys mark the lobster traps deep below, and the cold spray of the Atlantic is alluring and wild. Acadia National Park, with its rocky outcroppings and panoramic ocean views, draws thousands each year, and midsummer brings the island communities to life, their populations tripling and their lobster shacks boiling for another season. The charming towns of Bar Harbor, Blue Hill, and Ellsworth bustle with tourists all season.

Lobster Boat in Bar Harbour

Farther along the coast, the pace slows and communities are centered around the water and, in Machias, the University of Maine satellite campus.

Originally the home of the Wabanaki Indians—whose oyster middens, discovered by archeologists digging at sites of Native American encampments in Acadia, date back more than 6,000 years—the region was settled by French Jesuits, who arrived and founded a mission under the authority of Father Pierre Biard, in the early 1600s. Over the next 200 years, the area passed back and forth between the French and the English until the Revolutionary War, when it became a part of the United States.

By the mid-1800s, artists were drawn to the powerful beauty of Mount Desert Island, and painters of the Hudson River School put the region's iconic imagery on canvas. Later in the century, industrialists like the Rockefellers, Vanderbilts, Carnegies, and Morgans began to vacation here, building elegant wooden "cottages"—rather grand estates—to serve as rustic summer retreats.

A large seasonal community continues to vacation Downeast—including foodie Martha Stewart, who has a home near Bar Harbor on Mount Desert Island. Sea life is a great attraction, and whales swim in the cold waters, while puffins inhabit small, rocky islands off the coast. Salmon, which run upstream from Passamaquoddy Bay, are celebrated each year in the Eastport Salmon Festival.

Year-round the island communities are distinct, but all depend on fishing and lobstering. Though it's based inland in Orono, the University of Maine's Lobster Institute, created in 1987, is devoted to the region's most recognizable export and promotes research and education on lobsters, the lobstering industry, and the lobstering way of life. Buy a bottle of Big Claw Wine, crafted from California grapes to pair perfectly with lobster and available from wine sellers throughout the state, and a portion of the proceeds benefits the institute.

Away from the coast, Downeast is blueberry country. Home to Maine's blueberry industry, more than 60,000 acres of wild blueberry bushes stretch along the region. Raked clean in summer, the barrens are aflame with color in fall. Blueberries weren't cultivated commercially here until the 1840s, but now they are the state's most beloved berry. The University of Maine's wild blueberry research center, Blueberry Hill Farm, is the only facility of its kind in the country and can be found in Jonesboro.

In Harborside, the homestead of pioneering Helen and Scott Nearing is now an educational back-to-the-land retreat, and pilgrims visit the Good Life Center and the nearby Four Season Farm, home of gardening gurus Eliot Coleman and Barbara Damrosch.

Like the Mid Coast, Downeast is home to an array of farm-to-table restaurants, and inventive chefs such as Rich Hanson of Cleonice in Ellsworth are found as often in their fields as they are in the kitchen. Combine freshly picked produce with sweet berries, succulent lobster, and the myriad fruits of the sea, and the region's culinary delights are as exciting as its coast.

Seafood Restaurants

The Brooklin Inn, Rte. 175, Brooklin; (207) 359-2777; brooklininn .com. The tiny coastal village of Brooklin on Eggemoggin Reach is famed for its wooden boat building school. The inn has been a fixture for generations, and its dining room and Irish pub are popular with locals and visitors alike. The dining room menu changes daily to reflect what's seasonally available, but it always includes elegant preparations of local seafood; if it's on the menu, don't miss the bouillabaisse. The pub features more casual fare and freshly caught fish from the Gulf of Maine. Open for dinner year-round, nightly in summer, Wed through Sun in winter.

Brown's Coal Wharf, 5 Boatyard Rd., North Haven; (207) 867-4739. This casual, relaxed restaurant sits in the marina, perched over the water, with spectacular ocean views. The menu includes dishes from the island of North Haven and "from away." The former includes seafood risotto, fried battered fish and Maine shrimp, and locally caught lobster; the latter includes barbecued ribs smothered in blueberry bourbon sauce, pan-seared chicken, and a variety of sandwiches and burgers. Open for lunch and dinner daily in summer.

Burning Tree, Rte. 3, Otter Creek; (207) 288-9331; no website. Since 1987, Chef-Owners Allison Beal and Elmer Beal Jr. have served fresh, healthy meals created from regionally sourced ingredients in this bucolic island restaurant. The daily catch from local fishermen is paired with vegetables from the restaurant's gardens, mushrooms foraged in nearby woods, and cheese from local producers to create dishes that emphasize the flavors of the region. The changing menu features at least 10 seafood and 3 vegetarian entrees daily, and offerings can range from pan-fried sage-and-almond flounder to crispy kale and oven-roasted littleneck clams. Open for dinner nightly; closed Tues.

Cleonice Mediterranean Bistro, 112 Main St., Ellsworth; (207) 664-7554; cleonice.com. Chef-Owner Rich Hanson's elegant bistro brings the flavors of the Mediterranean to Downeast Maine, serving tapas, paella, and Italian *timpano*, as well as entrees of freshly caught seafood and locally raised meats and poultry. Much of the restaurant's produce comes from Hanson's farm in Bucksport, and the menu changes regularly to reflect the harvest. The raw bar and seafood tapas are particularly fine, with *opah crudo* (sometimes referred to as Sicilian sushi), fluke seviche, spice-rubbed tuna carpaccio, and grilled baby octopus joining the classic oysters and clams. Open for lunch and dinner daily.

Galyn's, 17 Main St., Bar Harbor; (207) 288-9706; galynsbarharbor .com. Since 1986 this casually upscale restaurant near the waterfront has served local seafood, steaks, and pastas. Lobster comes several ways—boiled in the shell, sautéed with butter and sherry, baked in enchiladas—and local crabs, scallops, and fish are offered grilled, baked, and sautéed. Open for lunch and dinner daily from mid-Mar to Nov.

Georgetown

The Harbor Gawker, 26 Main St., Vinalhaven; (207) 863-9365; no website. Owned by the Morton family since it opened in 1975, the Gawker—as it's called—is a local landmark, named for the island term for people living on the inlet to Carver's Harbor. With an extensive menu—close to 100 options—its most popular offerings are still the classics: chowder, lobster and crab rolls, and assorted seafood specialties. Soft-serve ice cream is a cornerstone of the business, and the first Saturday in May marks the annual Free Ice Cream Day, begun decades ago on the first day of the summer season. Open seasonally.

Helen's Restaurant, 111 Main St., Machias; (207) 255-8423; no website. The sign on this converted house sports an *H* designed from a knife, fork, and spoon, and locals have been dining under the flatware since 1950. Though it's changed ownership in recent years, the kitchen still turns out heaping mounds of whole-belly clams, perfectly fried haddock, and deconstructed lobster rolls—a bowl of freshly picked lobster, bathed in melted butter, with soft buttered bread tucked beneath.

Maine Lobsterbakes

In Rhode Island they are called clambakes. But in Maine you'll also hear them called lobsterbakes, that time-honored New England tradition of gathering for a seafood feast optimally done right on the beach.

The clambake/lobsterbake can be traced back to Native Americans, who taught the early settlers along the New England coast the art of steaming fresh seafood in a rock-lined pit dug in the ground in close proximity to the ocean. Fresh seaweed, seawater, and driftwood are the key ingredients for an authentic pit-dug bake. The dry wood is placed over the rocks in the pit, and a fire is lit that heats the stones. When the stones are red hot and glowing, it's time to add a layer of seaweed and then the ingredients: potatoes, corn on the cob, onions, clams, and live lobsters. Top all this with another layer of seaweed, and then cover it with a canvas tarp or potato sacks that have been soaked in seawater. After 2 hours, the food should be cooked to perfection. A good way to check is with the potatoes—if they are soft, the entire clambake/lobsterbake is ready. The great food writer Craig Claiborne described this uniquely New England tradition as "the most colorful, joyous and festive of American events." True, and it's also a great deal of work. Thankfully there are a number of companies that will do all the work for you. Here's a sampling of such businesses:

Coastal Critters Clambakes and Catering, 551 Atlantic Hwy., Northport; (207) 338-3384; coastalcrittersclambakes.com. Since 1978 this catering company has been doing events for groups as small as 25 and as large as 1,500—everything from family gatherings to company picnics.

Cook's Lobster House, Rte. 24, Bailey Island; (207) 833-2818; cookslobster.com. Located at the tip of a peninsula, this restaurant offers lobsterbakes on its premises.

Crustacean Creations, (207) 239-0038; crustaceancreations .net. With more than 50 years of experience, this company takes its lobsterbake on the road for all occasions and groups of 50 to 500.

Foster's Downeast Clambake, 5 Axholme Rd., York; (800) 552-0242; fostersclambake.com. For six decades, Foster's has been transporting seafood lovers back in time when families and friends would gather for good food and fun at an old-fashioned clambake. This happens in the Pavilion, which accommodates up to 450 people, or at a location of your choice.

Gilmore's Maine Lobster and Fresh Seafood, 129 Court St., Bath; (207) 443-5231; gilmoreslobster.com. Gilmore's offers lobsterbakes for parties of any size or occasion. All their ingredients are from local farms and fishermen. The bake master wraps the live Maine lobsters in seaweed and steams them in salt water over an open fire.

The Maine Lobsterbake, PO Box 15412, Portland; (207) 828-6374; cascobaylobsterbake.com. One of the best lobsterbake experiences you can have, this one is an all-day affair that begins with a voyage by schooner to Peaks Island in Casco Bay. After exploring the island in a variety of ways, you are treated to a traditional Maine lobsterbake.

Migis Lodge, 30 Migis Lodge Rd., South Casco; (207) 655-4524; migis.com. Every Friday night, June through August, a lakeside lobsterbake takes place at this exclusive resort, and it's open to nonguests by reservation. Migis Lodge is located on Sebago Lake in southern Maine.

Sam's Great Northern Lobsterbakes, 1281 Forest Ave., Portland; (207) 797-6719; samslobsterbakes.com. A full-service catering company, Sam's will set up a lobsterbake at the beach, at a park, almost anywhere. They offer various packages. They can supply everything, from tents and canopies to tables and chairs.

If you don't have a sufficient number of people for a full-blown clambake/lobsterbake, you can always go to **The Clambake Restaurant** in Scarborough (207-883-4871, theclambake.com). This seasonal establishment near Old Orchard Beach seats more than 700 seafood lovers, and folks can custom design their dining experience and dine in air-conditioned comfort. A children's menu is available.

The Jordan Pond House, Acadia National Park; (207) 276-3316; jordanpondhouse.com. This venerable teahouse and restaurant has been serving summer visitors to Acadia National Park since 1870. Situated on an overlook with views of Jordan Pond, Penobscot Mountain, and "the Bubbles" (North and South Bubble Mountains), the seasonal Jordan Pond House offers visitors a refreshing glass of just-squeezed lemonade on the lawn or a full meal in the garden-side dining room. The menu includes famed popovers, served warm from the oven; rich lobster stews and rolls; seafood entrees; and house-made ice cream. Open for lunch, tea, and dinner daily from mid May to late Oct.

Maggie's Restaurant, 6 Summer St., Bar Harbor; (207) 288-9007; maggiesbarharbor .com. With an elegant atmosphere—white table linens, muted terra-cotta walls, French doors opening onto the outdoor patio—this seasonal restaurant is known for its inventive seafood and attentive service. The lobster crepes, filled with succulent meat in a creamy sherry sauce, are a signature dish, and other favorites include garlicky mussels and mixed seafood stew. Reservations are essential. Open for dinner nightly June through Oct; closed Sun.

Nebo Lodge, 11 Mullins Ln., North Haven; (207) 867-2007; nebolodge.com. Owned by the Pingree family, this beautifully appointed inn holds the island's only year-round restaurant. Chef Amanda Hallowell's menu emphasizes local ingredients, from a smoked fish Caesar salad to a dinner entree of seared Vinalhaven halibut with oregano stuffing, pancetta, locally foraged fiddleheads, and spring parsnip *frites*. Small bites, including nuggets of fried cod, can be ordered at the bar. Open for dinner nightly.

Nostrano, Bar Harbor; (207) 288-0269; nostrano.com. Chef-Owner Frank Pendola came to Maine in 1992 as a molecular biologist working with the Jackson Laboratories; he gardened and cooked as a passionate weekend hobby. Today Pendola cooks full-time, making delectable country Italian meals, smoking Atlantic salmon and barbecue in-house, and running the annual Mount Desert Island Garlic Festival. (The smoked salmon is done with your choice of herb and spice rubs and may be purchased to go, or they will ship it to you.) Housed in the lower level of his home, the restaurant is family style, with an open kitchen and multiple courses. By reservation only. Open year-round.

Red Sky, 14 Clark Point Rd., Southwest Harbor; (207) 244-0476; redskyrestaurant.com. Something in this unpretentiously elegant restaurant—the wood-paneled ceilings, the row of small porthole-like windows—gives an impression of the snug belly of a ship. The menu of Chef-Owners James and Elizabeth Geffen Lindquist changes to reflect what's seasonally available, but includes a variety of seafood dishes, from peeky-toe crab salad with citrus to lobster paired with risotto, as well as sustainably raised meats and house-made pastas. Fresh bread is baked on-site, as are rich desserts, often paired with Mount Desert Island Ice Cream. Dinner hours vary with each season.

Rupununi: An American Bar and Grill, 119 Main St., Bar Harbor; (207) 288-2886; rupununi.com. This casual bar and grill, named for a South American river, has an aquatic feel to it, with stylized fish adorning one wall, an immense freshwater aquarium stocked with the fish of the Rupununi River, and a menu that features Maine's best seafood: charbroiled Atlantic salmon, pan-seared tuna, baked stuffed haddock, grilled swordfish, lobster, and more. Open for lunch and dinner daily.

Lobster Shacks & Lobster Pounds

Abel's Lobster Pound, Route 98, Mount Desert Island; (207) 276-5827; abelslobsterpound.com. When visiting Acadia National Park, eating at local lobster pound is a must, and Abel's gets the nod for having the best setting—in a pine grove overlooking majestic Somes Sound. You can sit at a picnic table or inside the rustic knotty pine dining room. Abel's opened in 1939 and was taken over by the Stanley family in 1985, remaining very much a family business. There are 7 boiled lobster dinners from

How to Eat (or Deal with) a Cooked Lobster

1. Twist off the claws.

2. Crack each claw with a nutcracker.

3. Separate the tailpiece from the body by arching its back until it cracks.

4. Remove the meat from the tail by holding it in your hand and squeezing to break the shell. Grasping both sides of the tail, use thumbs to separate the tail and remove the meat.

5. Unhinge the back from the body. The body contains the "tomalley" or liver of the lobster. This turns green when cooked. Many people consider this one of the best parts of the lobster. If it is a female lobster, you might find the bright red "coral," or eggs, a real delicacy.

6. Open the remaining part of the body by cracking it apart sideways. There is some good meat in this section of the body.

which to choose, including twin lobsters, and a great deal more, including excellent service. Open late June to Sept with varying hours; in July and Aug daily from noon to 9 p.m.

Bagaduce Lunch, 19 Bridge Rd., Brooksville; (207) 326-4729. An American Classic, according to the James Beard Foundation, and it's easy to see why. This no-frills take-out spot is on the banks of the rushing Bagaduce River, where the rapids change direction with the tides. Family owned and run, the Bagaduce, in local parlance, has been there since 1946 and became popular for its view of the falls and its house specialties—half-pound fried haddock sandwiches, generous seafood baskets, and rolls overflowing with lobster. Owner Judy Astbury's brother is the lobsterman who hauls in the local crustaceans. As you dine at a waterside picnic table, watch for eagles and osprey swooping overhead. A seasonal operation, open for lunch and dinner daily from Mother's Day to mid-Sept.

Lunt & Lunt; Lobsters and Lunt's Dockside Deli, Lunt Harbor, Frenchboro; (207) 334-2902 (July and Aug) and (207) 334-2922 (Sept through June); luntlobsters.com. The Lunt family has operated fishing businesses in Lunt Harbor since the 1820s, and this year-round lobster pound and seasonal restaurant continue the family tradition. A wholesale and retail business, Lunt & Lunt sells live lobsters year-round from its dock. The seasonal deli serves homey sandwiches, steamed lobsters and clams, seafood rolls, ice cream, and freshly made desserts—as well as a limited breakfast menu and Wicked Joe Coffee (brewed in Brunswick). The deli is open July 6 through Labor Day from 7 a.m. to 7 p.m.

Lunt's Gateway Lobster Pound, 1133 Bar Harbor Rd., Trenton; (207) 667-2620; luntsgatewaylobster.com. The walls are lined with kitschy collectibles, and the tables are covered with simple oilcloth at this lobster pound and casual seafood restaurant, family owned for more than 40 years. Located across the road from the Bar Harbor Airport, it's often the first place hungry visitors see, and the restaurant's quality matches its convenience. Seafood is fresh, desserts are homemade, and service is friendly and attentive. You can eat in the dining room, on the screened-in porch, or at picnic tables in a shaded area. A challenge for the daring: Successfully conquer a 3 pound (or larger) steamed lobster and your photo will grace the Wall of Fame. The lobster pound will ship Maine lobsters to your door. Open for lunch and dinner daily May through Oct.

Thurston's Lobster Pound, 1 Thurston Rd., Bernard; (207) 244-7600; thurstonslobster.com. Perched high above the working waterfront on Mount Desert Island, this seasonal lobster pound offers a tableau of coastal life. Watch lobster boats rumble in and unload their traps as you dine on lobster and seafood "in the rough." Dinner comes with corn on the cob, coleslaw, and blueberry cake for dessert. A full selection of beers and wine is available, unusual for a lobster pound. Open for lunch and dinner daily from Memorial Day to Columbus Day.

Trenton Bridge Lobster Pound, 1237 Bar Harbor Rd. (Rte. 3), Trenton; (207) 667-2977; trentonbridgelobster.com. With a long row of open pots boiling seawater over smoking wood fires, you can't miss this authentic lobster pound, just before the bridge to Mount Desert Island. Family owned for four generations, the pound has been boiling lobster the old-fashioned way since 1956, evolving with the times to offer mail-order seafood, from live lobsters to local scallops and steamer clams. But don't come here for fried food—they are proudly grease free. The lobster pound is open year-round, and they ship live lobsters packed in seaweed with cooking instructions and bibs for diners. Serving lobsters "in the rough" from Memorial Day to Columbus Day.

Trenton Bridge Lobster Pound

Seafood Lover's New England

Union River Lobster Pot, 8 South St., Ellsworth; (207) 667-5077; lobsterpot.com. On the banks of the Union River, the tanks of this seasonal restaurant hold nearly 1,000 pounds of live lobsters, the makings of classic shore dinners piled high with a boiled crustacean, steamed clams, and native mussels from Blue Hill Bay Mussel Company. The menu ranges from cedar-planked salmon, swordfish, and snapper to fried seafood platters. Entrees are served with warm, freshly made bread, and the home-style desserts will tempt you, especially the summer berry crisp. A children's menu is available. Open for dinner nightly June through Oct.

Clam Shacks

Jordan's Snack Bar, 200 Downeast Hwy., Ellsworth; (207) 667-2174; jordanssnackbar.com. This local landmark has been a seasonal favorite for three decades, thanks to Jimmy and Carol Jordan and their two sons, Shawn and Michael. Their fresh crab rolls are never made from frozen meat—they're only offered when a hand-lettered sign in the window reads FRESH CRABMEAT TODAY. The menu also includes perfectly battered onion rings and addictive fried clams that you can enjoy in the dining room or at picnic tables under the trees. There's even a playground for children, and Gifford's of Maine ice cream is available. Stop in on Wednesday night and watch all the classic cars cruise in. Open for lunch and dinner daily from mid-Mar to mid-Oct.

Seafood Markets

Sawyer's Market, 353 Main St., Southwest Harbor; (207) 244-3317; mdiwine.com. In a lovely recessed storefront, this family-owned market has been a local landmark since 1946, selling organically grown produce; custom-butchered meats; fresh seafood; warm baked goods; an extensive list of wines, beers, and spirits; and a variety of prepared foods, deli meats, and cheeses. The market specializes in boat provisioning—pick up a form or fill it out online and they'll deliver to the town dock or Great Harbor Marina. At the checkout take note of the mounted photo: loyal customer Julia Child with the market's previous owner—an endorsement if ever there was one. Open daily year-round.

Downeast Maine Events

August
Frenchboro Lobster Festival, Frenchboro; frenchboroonline.com.
After more than 50 years, this annual crustacean celebration still offers
scenic boat rides through the picturesque harbor and a dinner featuring
boiled lobster, coleslaw, potato chips, soda, and homemade pie.

Maine Lobster Festival in Winter Harbor, acadia-schoodic.org/
lobsterfestival. Held for more than four decades at various points on the
western side of the Gouldsboro Peninsula, this 1-day festival features the
famed Maine Lobster Boat Races, a lobster dinner, a parade down Winter
Harbor's Main Street, and much more. Always held on the second Saturday
in August.

September
Eastport Salmon Festival, downtown Eastport; eastportsalmon-
festival.com. For more than 20 years, this 3-day festival has celebrated
the salmon of Passamaquoddy Bay. Popular events include a guided walking tour, boat tours of the salmon pens, and the highlight: a grilled salmon
lunch.

North Haven Oyster Festival, Nebo Lodge, nebolodge.com. This
annual event is a celebration of all things oyster, kicking off on Labor Day
weekend.

October
Foliage, Food, and Wine Festival, Blue Hill; (207) 374-3242; blue
hillpeninsula.org. A weekend of leaf peeping, tastings, tours, and more,
this 4-day festival features panel discussions of local farming, guided walks,
tastings of local products—from regional apples to smoked seafood—as
well as themed dinners, cooking workshops, and more.

CENTRAL MAINE
Away from the tourist destinations of Maine's coastal waters and wooded
mountains, the central part of the state is a quiet region with a rich history
of agriculture and industry. The landscape is a tapestry of sparkling lakes
and rolling emerald pasturage, dotted by family farms and orchards con-
tinuing the work of previous generations. This is historically the heart of

Maine's farmland, and commercial dairies, egg farms, and apple orchards are scattered through the area, though on a relatively small scale. These are human-size farms, not industrialized, and many are diversified, filling their old post-and-beam barns with cattle, sheep, goats, and pigs and growing hay and enough produce to sell at farmers' markets and stands along the roadside. An emerging community of artisanal cheese makers has sprung up, and custom butchers specialize in humanely processing organic and pasture-raised animals.

Unity is the home of MOFGA—the Maine Organic Farmers and Gardeners Association—and the site of the annual Common Ground Country Fair, a celebration of sustainability that brings 60,000 visitors to the fairgrounds each year. Nearby Unity College is an "environmental college" that focuses on outdoor learning, community involvement, and issues of environmental responsibility.

At the center of the state is its capital, Augusta, one of the smallest state capitals in the country. It's the site of Old Fort Western, America's oldest wooden fort (circa 1754), a National Historic Landmark on the banks of the Kennebec River and now a museum, store, and interpretive center. By the 19th century, the Kennebec was lined with lumber and fabric mills, as well as paper mills that established a publishing industry in Augusta.

Farther down the river, historic Hallowell was the center of a thriving ice industry, in its heyday shipping massive cubes down the Kennebec and as far as the West Indies. Now the area has a vibrant artistic community, as well as a picturesque antique river port downtown.

A century ago the entire region hummed with industry, and great mill complexes sat at the edges of both the Kennebec and Androscoggin Rivers. Millwork brought an influx of immigrants to towns throughout the 19th and early 20th centuries, and their influences can still be felt on the culture and cuisines, from the French Canadians in Lewiston to the Lebanese in Waterville. More recently, immigrants from troubled spots around the world have sought refuge in central Maine. Augusta is home to a small Cambodian population that arrived in the mid 1980s, while a large number of Somalis settled in Lewiston in the early 2000s.

Those mills are now being reimagined as spaces for offices, restaurants, and small-scale manufacturing, including microbreweries. A creative economy and the fusion of many influences have begun to sweep the region. Young chefs and producers have moved into mill complexes and downtown areas, bringing energy and life to the buildings. College students at Bates in Lewiston and Colby in Waterville are taking part in the renaissance. From cafes to breweries to cinemas, exciting things are happening here.

Seafood Restaurants

Cloud 9 at the Senator Inn and Spa, 284 Western Ave., Augusta; (207) 622-0320; senatorinn.com. The dining room at this elegant hotel and spa is whimsical, with a decor that combines bright accents, contemporary artwork, and comfortable, overstuffed seating. The menu is creative, with an emphasis on locally sourced ingredients, fresh seafood, and light options for the health conscious, which include a variety of entree salads—the lobster cobb salad is a treat. The seafood offerings include spice-crusted salmon, lobster ravioli, and seafood Alfredo over fettuccine. Open for breakfast, lunch, and dinner daily.

Fish Bones American Grill, 70 Lincoln St., Lewiston; (207) 333-3663; fishbonesag.com. Amid weathered masonry and solid wooden beams in the Bates Mill complex, this upscale seafood restaurant specializes in grilled and roasted entrees, arranged beautifully on the plate. The menu influences are varied, and offerings range from seared tuna sashimi on ramen noodles to Cajun sea scallops with lentil ragout. Open for lunch and dinner Tues through Fri, dinner Sat, brunch Sun.

The Last Unicorn Restaurant, 8 Silver St., Waterville; (207) 873-6378; lastunicornrestaurant.com. For more than 30 years, this casual restaurant has been a downtown fixture, drawing patrons for hearty comfort foods, globally inspired specials, and brunch under the umbrellas on the street-side outdoor patio. Now owned by the chef, Fred Ouellette, the popular restaurant has an eclectic menu. You'll find Chesapeake crab cakes next to Thai sizzling catfish. Open for lunch and dinner daily.

Pepper and Spice, 875 Lisbon St., Lewiston; (207) 782-7562; pepperandspice.com. With more than 300 items on the menu, this unassuming Thai restaurant—set back from the road beneath a blue vinyl awning—is as surprising as it is delicious. Noodles and curries are light (especially the popular pad Thai) and can be spiced to taste, and the menu offers an abundance of vegetarian and seafood dishes. Staff is friendly, unobtrusive, and incredibly attentive. Open for lunch and dinner daily.

The Best Sandwich in New England

When the Travel Channel conducted a search for the best sandwich in New England, **The Galley**—a little pub in Naples, Maine—burst onto the national food scene when its Zesty Lemon Lobster Roll was declared the winner. It then went on to be named the best lobster roll in the nation. There are 11 lobster rolls on the huge menu. The Galley is located at 327 Roosevelt Trail, north of Sebago Lake—far from the ocean; (207) 693-1002; thegalleyseafoodpub.com. Open for dinner Mon and Tues, lunch and dinner Wed through Sun.

The Red Barn Drive-In Restaurant, 455 Riverside Dr., Augusta; (207) 623-9485. 50 Bay St., Winslow; (207) 873-9005; theredbarn maine.com. Since 1977 this family-owned business has served fried seafood and chicken, lobster rolls and stew, and legendary onion rings from the original big red barn in Augusta, and now there's a second location in Winslow. Both are fast, casual restaurants—place your order at the outside window or indoor counter, and pick it up a few minutes later, mounded in cardboard boats and disposable cups on a red plastic tray. The food is tasty and fresh, with succulent scallops and sweet Maine shrimp fried to a golden brown, speckled chunks of lobster, and piping hot fries. Outdoor seating is available in warm weather. Open Tues through Sun for lunch and dinner; Mon for lunch only.

Weathervane Restaurant, 1030 Main St., Rte. 17, Readfield; (207) 685-9410; weathervanerestaurant.net. With an outdoor deck overlooking Maranacook Lake, this year-round local favorite serves down-home cooking: baked and fried seafood, plenty of options for landlubbers, housemade soups, and gooey desserts. At night the downstairs hosts live music in the lounge; occasionally the Weathervane House Band—including the owners—gets up to jam. They must be doing something right—they've been in business for more than 50 years. Open for lunch and dinner daily, lunch only on Sun in winter; closed Mon.

Seafood Markets

Ballard Meats & Seafood, 55 Myrtle St., Manchester; (207) 622-9764; lobsterretail.com. For more than 30 years, this family-owned shop near Lake Cobbosseecontee has sold live lobsters, fresh shellfish and seafood, and specialty cuts of beef. Serving both retail and wholesale customers, the shop's not fancy, just solidly good: thick steaks, creamy fresh scallops, and tanks full of large lobsters. Call in advance, and they'll cook your lobsters and steamers for you. They also will ship fresh seafood overnight to your door. Open Tues through Sat from 8 a.m. to 5 p.m.

Central Maine Events

June
Festival Franco Fun, 46 Cedar St., Lewiston; (207) 689-2000. Sponsored by the Franco-American Heritage Center (Le Centre d'Héritage Franco-Américain), this annual festival celebrates the contributions and living legacy of the city's French-speaking Canadian community, who immigrated to the area in droves in the mid-1860s to work in the textile mills. The 3-day festival includes a daily breakfast of traditional foods and delicacies that range from *poutine* to *creton* to salmon pie.

August
Taste of Greater Waterville, Downtown and Castonguay Square; (207) 873-3315. Sample the flavors of local restaurants, from haddock chowder to lobster étouffée, at this 1-day festival. Featuring street-side dining, a beer garden (patrons must be 21 or older), live music, and children's activities.

NORTHERN MAINE & THE COUNTY
The untamed north woods of Maine, with crystalline lakes, wandering moose, and towering pines, are enchantingly beautiful, intensely rugged, and sparsely populated. Here, at the culmination of the Appalachian Trail in Baxter State Park, Mount Katahdin rises from the woods. Farther north, the Allagash Wilderness Waterway challenges intrepid rafters and canoeists.

For more than a century, this was the heart of the state's lumber industry, and throughout the 1800s French-Canadian lumberjacks came south to log the region, sending timber to the shipyards on the coast. They brought with them their own culinary traditions, and in the logging camps they adopted new ones, especially the practice of cooking dried beans in heated holes in the ground ("bean holes"), a technique learned from the local Penobscot Indians.

East of the woods the fertile Saint John River Valley in Aroostook County is the state's largest agricultural region. Commonly referred to simply as The County, this was once considered the breadbasket of New England, and it is still a patchwork of rippling golden grain and vast stretches of potato fields. The region is sparsely populated and relatively remote, dominated by the British and French-Canadian influences of the earliest European settlers. For the last century The County has been known particularly for its potatoes, and tubers are available by the seed, the sack, and in exquisite locally made chips.

Bangor, the cultural and economic seat of the region, has been called the "Queen City of the East" for its beautiful old churches, leafy shade trees, and Greek Revival and Victorian houses, remnants of the lumber barons of the city's heyday. Now the town is noted for its cultural life. The Bangor Symphony Orchestra is the oldest continually operating symphony orchestra in the country, and the city has a variety of public music, theater, and artistic events. The proximity of Orono, home of the University of Maine, adds to the vibrancy of the city. Bangor is also the gateway to Acadia and all points north: I-95 crosses the city before heading straight up to Houlton, and scenic US 1A connects with the interstate to take visitors Downeast.

The traditional foods of northern Maine—potatoes, beans, ployes, freshwater fish—are humble, hearty, and satisfying. In recent years organic farmers have been drawn to The County because of affordable, expansive land, and growers' cooperatives have emerged to sell produce throughout the region. On a large scale Backyard Farms of Madison has begun to grow vine-ripened tomatoes year-round in their immense 42 acres of greenhouses, and their tomatoes are available throughout the Northeast. With nods to the culinary past and the visionary agricultural future, farm-to-table restaurants are emerging, while local landmarks continue to go strong.

Seafood Restaurants

Craig's Clam Shop, 92 Main St., Patten; (207) 528 2784; no website. This beloved clam shack and dairy bar serves fried seafood, grilled burgers, and a range of wraps and salads. But clams are the main event,

and flat clams, whole-belly clams, and clam tenderloins come in baskets and rolls. Craig's is a seasonal operation. Open for lunch and dinner daily in warm weather. A year-round version of this restaurant, Craig's Maine Course, is located in Island Falls at 142 Walker Settlement Rd.; (207) 463-2425.

Elm Tree Diner, 146 Bangor St., Houlton; (207) 532-3777. Since 1947 this local institution has satisfied local seafood cravings with its whole clams, signature Maine shrimp platter, and generous seafood platter. As early as 5:30 a.m. on weekdays, regulars gather for fresh pastry or a loaded omelet before work. After a devastating fire in 2009, the diner relocated to a new, spacious site, but its home-cooked meals have stayed the same. Open for breakfast, lunch, and dinner daily.

The Courtyard Cafe, 61 Main St., Houlton; thecourtyardcafe.biz. Chef-Owner Joyce Transue makes everything from scratch at this casual cafe in the Fishman Mall. The menu has something for all tastes, from comfortable favorites such as baked seafood casserole with crumbled crackers on top, to more sophisticated offerings, including bourbon-glazed Alaskan sockeye salmon. Lunch features salads, quiches, and sandwiches on freshly baked bread. The salad dressing is so popular that it's now available bottled. Open for lunch and dinner Tues through Fri, dinner only Sat.

Grammy's Country Inn, 1687 Bangor Rd., Linneus; (207) 532-7808; no website. This cozy diner promises it's a place "where you get more than you expect," and with heaping platters of home-cooked food at low prices, it delivers. The menu offers diner standards, including the best Maine french fries, and fried anything, including lobster. They are known for their humongous whoopie pies for dessert. Open for breakfast, lunch, and dinner daily.

Nook and Cranny, 575 Airline Rd., Baileyville; (207) 454-3335; nookcrannyrestaurant.com. Though the restaurant may be hard to find—the small town of Baileyville, outside of Calais, is sometimes left off the map—the atmosphere is inviting and the menu is extensive. Owners Steven and Tami Clark serve something for every taste, from lobster bisque to blackened haddock. The majority of the dishes, however, are well-executed Italian and rustic French entrees; baked, broiled, and fried seafood; and classic beef and chicken entrees. Open for lunch and dinner daily; closed Mon.

Thistles Restaurant, 175 Exchange St., Bangor; (207) 945-5480; thistlesrestaurant.com. Owned and operated by the Rave family, this stylish restaurant is infused with the flavors of their native South America. Signature dishes include Spanish paella. Chef Alejandro's menu covers New England ground as well, with crab cakes and clam chowder mixed among the Cuban scallops and tropical grilled salmon. There is live music on Tango Tuesday. Open for lunch and dinner Tues through Sat.

Northern Maine & The County Events

July
Maine Potato Blossom Festival, Fort Fairfield; (207) 472-3802; potatoblossom.org. For more than 60 years, this weekend festival has celebrated the humble heart of Aroostook County's agricultural heritage. Festivities include a potato-picking contest, potato suppers, mashed potato wrestling, and the pageant to crown the Maine Potato Blossom Queen.

Maine Potatoes

Arriving in the early 1800s, the first white settlers to Aroostook County began planting potatoes almost as soon as they'd cleared fields from the forests. The cool climate and fertile soil created ideal conditions for the tubers, and by the middle of the last century, Maine was the country's leader in potato production. Between 1928 and 1958, Aroostook County grew more potatoes than any other state. Over the past 50 years, potato production has declined, and fewer families are farming, but in Maine, The County is still synonymous with potatoes. Schools in the north are closed for late-September Harvest Break so that kids can help their parents dig potatoes; the Maine Potato Blossom Festival is held in Fort Fairfield. Each spring seed potatoes from Aroostook County help gardeners across the country plant their own rows.

August
Ploye Festival, Fort Kent; fortkentchamber.com. On a 12-foot griddle set up under a tent in the heart of downtown, volunteers and members of the Bouchard family pour and smooth 5-gallon buckets of *ploye* batter in this one-day festival, creating their annual "world's largest *ploye*." *Ployes* are buckwheat flatbreads (pancakes) cooked on a griddle. Locals discuss the variations of their family recipes, and everyone digs in while watching the Muskie Derby that follows. Fishermen haul in giant muskellunge pikes—known as "muskies"—from the Saint John River. The muskies, which can weigh as much as 20 pounds, are then cleaned and cooked for a giant community fish fry.

New Hampshire

The New Hampshire you see on TV every presidential election season doesn't begin to depict the wide scope of experiences to be had in the "Live Free or Die" state. It's a great place to be outdoors—swimming, boating, skiing, hiking, and camping—or at a table. From the shore to the mountains—from hardy fishermen to determined farmers—these self-reliant individuals produce some of the freshest and best food that sustains residents and attracts thousands of appreciative, hungry visitors each year.

The foods most representative of the state of New Hampshire include apples from the orchards, maple syrup from the sugar shacks, and fresh seafood from the coastline and beyond.

For those seeking crisp apples and sweet maple syrup, the inland routes are simply charming, especially in the fall. This is a good time for hiking in the White Mountains, canoeing on one of the state's many deep blue lakes, and buying pumpkins at the colorful farmers' markets. In the winter head farther north for skiing, antiquing, and tax-free outlet shopping in the North Conway area. Early spring means one thing in New Hampshire: It's maple-sugaring season, when lodging is most affordable.

One of the most delicious ways to sample local seafood is with a simple car ride starting in historic Portsmouth, a great port city in the 18th and 19th centuries, which still has a working waterfront and a vibrant downtown. There's no shortage of exciting restaurants in Portsmouth—from Jumpin' Jay's Fish Cafe to the Old Ferry Landing. From the city's historic district, head out on Route 1B over the causeway to New Castle. This narrow road winds past the grand Wentworth-by-the-Sea (now a four-diamond Marriott Hotel and Spa) and eventually connects with Route 1A. Heading south along the shoreline, you will pass through a beautiful oceanfront residential area as you head toward Rye, with its busy harbor, onward to North Hampton, Hampton, and a series of state parks with

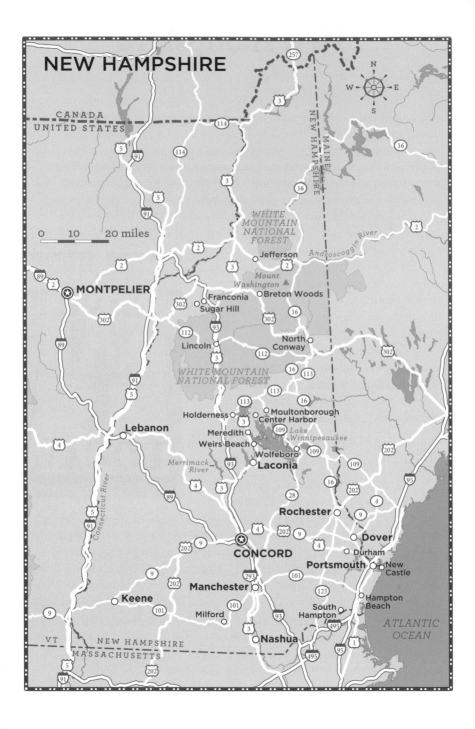

New Hampshire Food News

Thanks to the Internet, we can connect with countless restaurants almost instantly to learn about their location, menu, and hours of operation. Unfortunately not every website is as current as it should be, so we cannot emphasize this enough: Always call ahead to make sure a restaurant is open. Fortunately there are a number of reputable websites that offer the latest information on New Hampshire restaurants, lodging, events, and local products. For up-to-date listings, check out the following online sources:

nh.com: New Hampshire's guide to restaurants, lodging, and activities

nhmade.com: Gourmet gifts and handmade New Hampshire products

nhmagazine.com: The state's hottest new restaurants are listed annually, and reviews are printed in this monthly publication.

northeastflavor.com: A New England–based food, wine, and dining monthly magazine featuring interviews with local chefs, recommendations for the finest restaurants and hidden gems, local recipes, and events

portsmouthnh.com: A diverse list of restaurants listed by location and cuisine in and around Portsmouth

popular beaches. In the summer thousands of sun lovers will be basking by the shore. In the off-season you'll still see beach lovers walking on the miles of sandy beaches with their kids and dogs in tow. Dozens of restaurants known for their exceptional seafood can be found along this oceanfront route, which winds along the coast to Seabrook and eventually the Massachusetts state line.

According to state officials, New Hampshire was made for road trips. From coastal roads that overlook crashing surf to mountain roadways that wind through the Northeast's highest peaks and historic routes that follow Native American trails, New Hampshire's roads are undeniably scenic.

Portsmouth Harbor Lighthouse, New Castle

New Hampshire is bordered on the north by the Canadian province of Quebec, on the east by Maine and the Atlantic Ocean, on the south by Massachusetts, and on the west by Vermont. As you travel through those parts of the state, you'll find local foods influenced by those neighbors, from Downeast Maine lobster to Boston's creamy clam chowder.

There are thousands of restaurants in New Hampshire, and hundreds of them specialize in seafood. This guide includes a little taste of everything, from the classic clam shack to the five-star dining destination at a resort.

PORTSMOUTH

When the early settlers of New Hampshire landed on the west bank of the Piscataqua River in 1630, they were delighted to find the ground covered with wild strawberries. They named their little settlement Strawbery Banke, and it evolved over the years into the seaport of Portsmouth. Even back then fishing was crucial to the survival of the Strawbery Banke residents, and the harbor soon became a shipbuilding center.

Thankfully the city's history is most evident in its many restored buildings and neighborhoods. Wealthy sea captains built finely detailed houses along the narrow, winding streets of historic Portsmouth. In the 1800s, Portsmouth developed a robust summer resort business, which continues to this day. Visitors still dine in former chandleries and warehouses, and overnight travelers have a fine choice of quaint inns. The Old Harbor area at Bow and Ceres Streets is now home to boutiques, quaint shops, and trendy restaurants.

One of the best ways to learn about historic Portsmouth is to take one of the tours offered on land and on the sea. The Portsmouth Harbor Trail (603-436-3988) tours the waterfront and downtown. Portsmouth Harbor Cruises (603-436-8084) sails around the 14 islands of Portsmouth Harbor out to the Isle of Shoals, which beachgoers can see in the distance on clear days. The Isle of Shoals Steamship Company (603-431-5500) cruises by forts and lighthouses via a replica of a 19th-century steamship. Dinner cruises are also available, which are especially nice when fall foliage is at its colorful peak.

Concord may be the capital of New Hampshire, but Portsmouth is the state's largest city and the hub of a metropolitan region that includes the cities of Rochester and Dover. With a population of approximately 21,000 people, Portsmouth is a small city that lands regularly on various "best places to live" lists, notably for its stimulating mix of historic buildings, sidewalk cafes, great restaurants, art galleries, jazz clubs, and artisan boutiques.

The city of Portsmouth's number one attraction is its restaurants. There's not enough time or money to sample every one of them, but hopefully this guide will help you experience at least some of the wonderful restaurants within the city limits.

Seafood Restaurants

Beach Plum #2, 2800 Lafayette Rd. (Rte. 1), Portsmouth; (603) 433-3339; lobsterrolls.com. There are two award-winning Beach Plum restaurants, one by land and one by sea. Beach Plum #1 is a cute little roadside eatery close to the ocean and North Hampton State Park. (A seasonal operation, see page 239 for more information.) Beach Plum #2 is just as cute but open year-round, with beer and wine available. The indoor dining area with polished picnic tables is bright and cheery. The outdoor patio is popular in the summer with colorful umbrellas providing a bit of shade. The expanded menu is sure to please everyone, especially lobster lovers—their pricey lobster roll is a foot long and contains 20 ounces of fresh unadulterated lobster meat. A children's menu is available. And for dessert, they have 78 flavors of ice cream and frozen yogurt waiting to be sampled. Open for lunch and dinner daily.

Black Trumpet Bistro, 28 Ceres St., Portsmouth; (603) 432-0887; blacktrumpetbistro.com. An extraordinary restaurant, the Black Trumpet is perched on the historic waterfront. One small table in particular has a perfect view of the working harbor as well as the kitchen, where you can watch Executive Chef Evan Mallett and his crew craft memorable dishes. This is arguably the most conscientious restaurant in the city when it comes to sustainable seafood. The mostly Mediterranean menu changes every 6 weeks to make the most of seasonal ingredients. Expect dishes such as Atlantic red crab croquettes, fried calamari noodles, day boat sea scallops with bok choy, and pistachio-crusted pollack. Open for dinner nightly.

Blue Mermaid Island Grill, 409 The Hill, Portsmouth; (603) 427-2583; bluemermaid.com. If you like the flavor of the Caribbean, you will love the Blue Mermaid, a beautiful downtown restaurant located in a historic home more than 200 years old. Executive Chef Terrance Remick has made this establishment especially known for its paella and shrimp pad Thai. Small plate offerings include a lobster quesadilla and grilled scallops on crispy wontons. Specialties include a seafood tagine of salmon, cod, and mahimahi. Grilled seafood selections of salmon, shrimp, sea scallops, and mahimahi are simple but delicious. A colorful array of side dishes, such as sweet corn fritters with coconut cream sauce, make for a getaway dinner. You'll really think you're on an island! Outdoor seating on the deck is available in warm weather. Open for lunch and dinner daily, brunch Sun.

The Common Man Family of Restaurants, 60 Main St., Ashland; (603) 968-7030. 96 State St., Portsmouth; (603) 334-6225; thecman.com. This is a wonderful success story. In 1971 Alex Ray opened the first Common Man restaurant in Ashland. With only 35 seats in the dining room, folks would line up outside, even in the winter, to dine there on old-fashioned comfort food. That humble start evolved into a local chain of 18 award-winning restaurants, 2 inns, a company store, and a movie theater. Each establishment has decor that reminds guests of a kinder, gentler time. The company motto is "Doing well by doing good." All locations hold community fundraisers, and employees are given paid time off to volunteer with nonprofit groups. What goes around, comes around, and for the Common Man, that has meant great success. The menus at each establishment are similar. At the Portsmouth Common Man, Executive Chef John Tuttle is in charge of a menu that celebrates local seafood: bacon-wrapped shrimp, rock crab cake, steamed mussels, lobster spring rolls, lobster corn chowder, and lobster macaroni and cheese. House specialties include Portsmouth Pie, a medley of shrimp, scallops, haddock, and lobster meat baked with lobster cream sauce and topped with seasoned cracker crumbs. Open all year except for Christmas Eve and Christmas Day. Open for dinner in Ashland, Lincoln, Windham, Concord, Merrimack, Claremont, and Portsmouth. Also open for lunch in Ashland, Merrimack, Concord, Claremont, Portsmouth, and seasonally in Lincoln. Open for Sunday brunch in Concord, Windham, and Meredith.

Dinnerhorn Seafood Restaurant & Oyster Bar, 980 Lafayette Rd. (Rte. 1), Portsmouth; (603) 436-0717; dinnerhorn.com. Seafood reigns supreme at this family-owned and -operated restaurant in business since 1960. The Kamakas family believes in a well-stocked raw bar, an extensive cocktail menu, friendly service, and a wide variety on the menu. Tried-and-true seafood dishes take center stage, from broiled haddock to

Portsmouth

pan-seared lemon sole. For more exotic taste buds, the sesame-seared ahi tuna comes with a ginger-wasabi sauce. All your fried favorites are here as well. Open for lunch and dinner daily.

Dolphin Striker, 15 Bow St., Portsmouth; (603) 431-5222; dolphin striker.com. New England comfort cuisine is how they describe the food at this harbor-side restaurant surrounded by art galleries and boutique shops. Locally sourced whenever possible, the creatively prepared seafood is elegantly presented. Entrees include fresh sushi grade tuna prepared three different ways, cioppino, paella, jumbo scallops, and fresh local haddock stuffed with lump crabmeat. Basic fish offerings, from lobster to Chilean sea bass, can be paired with a variety of preparations, such as pan braised Mediterranean style in a citrus–white wine broth or blackened with

Cajun seasonings. Open for lunch and dinner Tues through Sun, dinner only Mon.

Harbor's Edge, 250 Market St., Portsmouth; (603) 431-2300; sheratonportsmouth.com. If you're staying at the Sheraton Hotel in Portsmouth, first check out the Riverwatch Lounge with its bay windows that offer a panoramic view of the Port of New Hampshire, and then head over to the hotel's restaurant. The Harbor's Edge offers traditional New England cuisine with a contemporary flair: chilled colossal shrimp in a martini glass, pan-seared diver scallops with an orange chile glaze, lobster and wild mushroom risotto, and lobster crab cakes, for starters. Their lobster and roasted corn chowder is an award winner. Signature entrees include lobster ravioli, chile-rubbed salmon, and lobster and crab stuffed haddock. Open for breakfast, lunch, and dinner daily.

Hebert's, 1500 Lafayette Rd. (Rte. 1), Portsmouth; (603) 431-5882; hebertsrestaurant.com. A 1950s-style diner, complete with Formica and chrome tables and a checkerboard floor, Hebert's is casual dining at its best. This is where locals go to watch the New England Patriots play football on TV, or to play a game of darts in the adjacent pub. Everything you'd expect in the way of seafood is on the menu plus these rather unusual items: seafood-stuffed mushrooms, garlicky broiled fantail shrimp, seafood-stuffed chicken (topped with Swiss cheese), sea scallops over vodka penne pasta, and a haddock wrap. Open for breakfast, lunch, and dinner daily.

Jumpin' Jay's Fish Cafe, 150 Congress St., Portsmouth; (603) 766-FISH; jumpinjays.com. Quite possibly the hottest restaurant in the state, Jumpin' Jay's is known for its exceptional seafood, from local waters and from afar—think New Zealand and Ecuador. At least 4 varieties of fish (from black bass to arctic char) are on the ever-changing "Catch-of-the-Day" menu, each served with a gourmet sauce or marinade (from lobster veloute to pineapple coconut red curry). Begin your meal with the crab grilled cheese sliders served with creamy tomato soup, and move on to one of Jay's specialties like the haddock piccata with white wine–butter sauce. This is one restaurant that seafood lovers should not skip. Open for dinner nightly.

Oar House, 55 Ceres St., Portsmouth; (603) 436-4025; portsmouth nh.com/dining. If we could go back in time, we would watch ships from

Cooking Tips from Sanders Market in Portsmouth

The three most important things to remember when cooking fish are "don't overcook," "don't over-season," and "keep it moist." As a rule of thumb, fish should be cooked 10 minutes per inch in thickness, but this will vary depending on the cooking method. A fish is done when the translucency in the center of the fillet is almost gone. Use a paring knife to test. Also, don't forget that fresh fish should be cooked simply so its flavor stands alone. A touch of butter and lemon may be all you need. Lastly, different types of fish require different cooking techniques. Use the technique that will keep your fillet moist and tender. In general, a leaner fish needs moist heat, while a fattier one does not.

Tips for Grilling Fish
Fish steaks and fillets should be at least ½ inch thick when grilling, and they may or may not need a marinade, depending

yesteryear unload their goods into what is now the dining room at the Oar House, located in the historic Merchant's Row building at the edge of the old harbor. Mementos from that era now decorate this New American restaurant known for its seafood presentations. Fried oysters with a Creole remoulade make a fine start to dinner, followed by the seafood Portofino served in puff pastry. Even the fish-and-chips are a cut above the usual in their tempura batter. The waterfront deck is the place to be in the summer. Open for lunch and dinner Mon through Sat, brunch Sun.

Old Ferry Landing, 10 Ceres St., Portsmouth; (603) 431-5510; old ferrylanding.com. Portsmouth's oldest waterfront restaurant, the Old Ferry Landing is a quaint waterfront eatery with a large outdoor deck and an up close view of the tugboats on the Piscataqua River. They are famous for their fried seafood, including baskets or larger platters of fried clams, shrimp, haddock, scallops, and combo dishes. A seasonal operation, the former ferryboat terminal is owned by the Blalock family, well-known in the golfing world. Open for lunch and dinner daily Apr through Sept.

on the species. A firm-fleshed fish is always a good choice for the grill because it holds together well. Always quickly sear both sides of a fish steak or fillet over the hottest portion of the grill, and then move to the edges to finish the cooking. Again, the hotter and faster the better!

Tips on Baking Fish
Simply stated, fish should be baked in a 425-degree oven for 12 minutes per inch of thickness. Fattier fish, like salmon or black cod, need very little additional fat when cooking, while leaner fish like halibut do need a little oil or butter.

Tips for Pan Searing Fish
Pan frying and pan searing are two of the easiest methods for cooking fish. Simply add oil or butter to a nonstick pan, lightly season the fish, and cook over medium heat. In general, the thinner the fillet, the higher the heat. If a thick fillet is cooked at too high of a heat, the outside will burn and the inside will remain raw.

Pesce Italian Kitchen + Bar, 103 Congress St., Portsmouth; (603) 430-7766; pesceblue.com. Owner Cliffe Arrand is dedicated to providing his guests with simple rustic Italian food at a moderate price. This authentic trattoria, in warm shades of yellow and brown, offers authentic dishes prepared by Executive Chef James Walter. Seafood appetizers include alici anchovies, saffron-marinated mussels, grilled octopus, and baccala croquettes. Spaghetti is flavored with clams, garlic, and white wine. Entrees include frilled swordfish with San Marzano tomatoes, capers, and olives; seared yellow fin tuna with balsamic reduction; and pan-roasted brook trout with pine nuts. Open for lunch and dinner daily, brunch Sun.

Rudi's, 20 High St., Portsmouth; (603) 430-7834; rudisportsmouth .com. Traditional with a twist, that describes this contemporary American restaurant that is proud of its downtown charm and uptown polish. The creative menu is a good match with its salmon burgers and lobster rolls at lunch, and then its more dramatic offerings at dinner: seared Atlantic salmon with mango and sweet chile glaze, grilled mahimahi with cantaloupe salsa crudo, and seared scallops over penne mac and cheese. Rudi's claims to have the only piano lounge in Portsmouth. Open for lunch and dinner Mon through Sat, brunch Sun.

Surf, 99 Bow St., Portsmouth; (603) 334-9855. 207 Main St., Nashua; (603) 595-9293; surfseafood.com. With a name like that, Surf just has to be a premier seafood restaurant. And with two locations, there's just no excuse not to check it out. The magic name behind these two award-winning restaurants is Michael Buckley, the chef and owner with his wife Sarah. Every day the Surf seafood buyers head out to local piers for the freshest seafood available. They handpick only the choicest specimens. With such impeccable ingredients, the chef and his team are able to prepare exquisite dishes, such as Portuguese seafood stew, shrimp vindaloo, Parmesan-crusted flounder, sesame-seared tuna, Cajun tilapia, miso-marinated salmon, and Moroccan-spiced scallops. Surf in Portsmouth has a sushi bar, and Surf in Nashua has a patio of al fresco dining in warm weather. The Portsmouth site is open for lunch Thurs through Sun and for dinner nightly. The Nashua site is open for dinner nightly Tues through Sat.

Lobster Pound

Sanders Lobster Pound, 54 Pray St., Portsmouth; (603) 436-3716; sanderslobster.com. Located on a saltwater back channel in Portsmouth's historic South End, this no-frills lobster pound has been providing locals and tourists with live lobsters since 1952. Three generations of the Sanders family have been involved in the business. The lobsters can be packed live in special stay-fresh containers, or they can be cooked on the premises—just call ahead to place your order. Open Mon from 8 a.m. to 3 p.m., Tues through Sat from 8 a.m. to 5 p.m.

Clam Shack

BG's Boat House, 191 Wentworth Rd., Portsmouth; (603) 431-1074; bgsboathouse.com. It's still a family affair at BG's, founded in 1978 by Bruce and Joanne Graves. This seasonal clam shack has a stylish, well put together menu that has all the required seafood dishes, from chowder and bisque to seafood that's been batter dipped and fried until golden. Light appetite items and mini meals are wisely listed. Full dinners include a crab cake dinner, salt-water smelts, and stuffed haddock. The King of the Ocean is served in 4 ways—as a lobster roll, in a lazy lobster dinner, with steamed clams, and in a boiled lobster dinner. A children's menu is available. Open for lunch and dinner from Mar through Nov, daily in summer, Thurs through Mon in spring and fall.

Seafood Market

Sanders Fish Market, 367 Marcy St., Portsmouth; (603) 436-4598; sandersfish.com. Since 1951, the Sanders family has been selling fish and seafood products sourced from near and far, local and international waters. The quaint store is designed for one-stop shopping with a whole lot more than seafood offered. The staff will pack your food in a cooler if you are on a road trip. They also have a few take-out items, including a "bargain-priced" lobster roll and chowder. A wine shop is located conveniently next door. (They also have a fish truck that goes to the Everett Arena Market in Concord year-round on Friday from 10 a.m. to 4 p.m.) Open Mon through Sat from 9 a.m. to 6 p.m., Sun from 9 a.m. to 5 p.m.

SEACOAST

A curious mix of modest oceanfront homes, miles and miles of sandy beaches, a kaleidoscope of restaurants, and million-dollar residences—that's what makes up New Hampshire's seacoast, less than 20 miles in its entirety.

Heading northward, Seabrook is the southern gateway to New Hampshire. Named for its many brooks winding their way through vast salt marshes to the Atlantic Ocean, Seabrook is home to the state's only nuclear power plant, which can be seen in the distance as you travel up Route 1A. Settled by Quakers, this community still retains a small town atmosphere. With miles of clean beaches, Seabrook has a busy harbor, home to the

Yankee Fishermen's Cooperative that brings in a daily catch of fish and lobster. Much of the oceanfront is a residential mix of year-round homes, beach houses, and seasonal rental cottages. Dozens of restaurants can be found along Ocean Boulevard.

Hampton Beach, Hampton, and North Hampton are the next towns you travel through. This is the heart of New Hampshire's seacoast, an almost timeless stretch of clam shacks and T-shirt shops, much like it was a half a century ago. In the summer, free evening concerts are offered almost nightly, and every Wednesday night a spectacular fireworks display can be seen on Hampton Beach, declared to be one of the cleanest beaches in the United States year after year. Seafood lovers take note—the Hampton Beach Seafood Festival takes place every September with more than 50 local restaurants serving their finest seafood delicacies.

Rye, established in 1623 by a group of fishermen, continues to have an active harbor where visitors can purchase live lobsters that just hours ago were swimming in the Atlantic. Odiorne Point is the largest undeveloped stretch of shoreline on the 18-mile coast. Open daily and year-round, this state park offers sweeping views of the rocky shore and ocean—a great spot for picnics. Island Cruises provides ferry service to the islands, tours of the Isles of Shoals, and educational lobster tours departing from Rye Harbor.

New Castle is the smallest town and the only town in New Hampshire composed entirely of islands. It is a residential and recreational community, home to the famous Wentworth-by-the-Sea hotel (603-373-6566), built in 1874 high atop a hill with a stunningly beautiful view of Little Harbor and the ocean. This amazing resort is known for its contemporary New England cuisine with an emphasis on fresh local seafood.

So many tempting restaurants and never enough time, that's how many visitors feel after cruising along New Hampshire's seacoast.

Seafood Restaurants

Al's Seafood Restaurant and Market, 51 Lafayette Rd. (Rte. 1), North Hampton; (603) 964-9591; alsseafoodnh.com. One of those wonderful New England restaurants that has its own fish market on the premises, Al's Seafood can easily guarantee the freshest seafood possible. You can dine in (by the fireplace in cool weather) or order your food to go. The entire menu is available for takeout. They have an unusual counter service system where you place your order, and meals are delivered to your table by the friendly staff. Seating is first come, first served. What's recommended? For starters the seafood-stuffed mushrooms, followed by the fish chowder and the baked seafood medley. Also getting high praise is Al's famous lobster pie topped with buttery bread crumbs. Open Sun through Thurs from 11 a.m. to 8 p.m., Fri and Sat from 11 a.m. to 8:30 p.m.

Ashworth by the Sea, 295 Ocean Blvd. (Rte. 1A), Hampton; (603) 926-6762; ashworthhotel.com. Step back in time at this historic seaside resort at Hampton Beach, where fresh seafood and lobster are the house specialties. You'll find 3 dining venues to suit every mood and palate. Sophisticated yet casual, Breaker's Restaurant & Bar is known for its lobster mac and cheese and amazing views of the beach, and it's open year-round. The Wharfside Cafe, open seasonally from May through Sept, is a perfect stop before spending your day in the sun and sand. The Sandbar, an outdoor deck, offers ocean views of the Atlantic. There you can enjoy cocktails, lunch, or dinner, with live entertainment—the perfect spot to watch the fireworks every Wednesday night in the summer.

Boardwalk Inn & Cafe, 139 Ocean Blvd. (Rte. 1A), Hampton; (603) 929-7400; boardwalkcafe.net. A hot spot in the summer with never-ending ocean views, the Boardwalk makes local fans happy by staying open year-round. Located right on Hampton Beach, next to the famous Casino Ballroom, this newly remodeled cafe is really an entertainment complex with the Boardwalk Pub offering live entertainment every night of the week. In the summer you can dine on the patio or the upper deck. The menu features New England fare at affordable prices. They are especially known for their french fries baked with melted cheese and bacon bits, a fresh lobster roll (regular and jumbo), and the Captain's Platter, a medley of deep-fried whole-belly clams, haddock, shrimp, and sea scallops. A children's menu is available. Open for lunch and dinner daily.

Bonta Restaurant and Bar, 287 Exeter Rd., Hampton; (603) 929-7972; bonta.net. For an upscale break from classic New England fare, Bonta offers modern Italian cuisine with a creative approach to seafood. For an unusual starter, there's seared rare ahi tuna served with Sicilian-style potato salad. Executive Chef Kevin Riley flavors his pasta dish with chopped fresh clams and pinot grigio butter. The seafood entrees will have you dining with distinction: Mediterranean-spiced halibut, seared sea scallops with walnut gremolata, and pan-roasted salmon with maple-thyme honey. Bonta will remind you of a Tuscan villa, and the dining room has

Old World charm with modern touches. Open for dinner Tues through Sat, brunch Sun.

Carriage House Restaurant, 2263 Ocean Blvd. (Rte. 1A), Rye; (603) 964-8251; carriagehouserye.com. This oceanfront restaurant will surprise you with its freshly made pasta, natural beef, and daily catch seafood. Linguine is used in the shrimp scampi dish flavored with a pinot gris butter. Full and half portions of yellow fin tuna, haddock, grouper, salmon, swordfish, Chilean sea bass, and mahimahi are offered for hearty or light appetites. Signature dishes include haddock piccata, sea scallops Florentine, and a classic French lobster dish flamed in Pernod. Savory sandwiches round out the menu, including a blackened fish fajita wrap. Across the street from Rye Beach, the Carriage House is a casual eatery, located in a charming building. Open for dinner nightly.

Cascade Seaside Restaurant & Deck, D Street, Hampton; (603) 926-5988; no website. Terry Sullivan owns 5 unique eateries on Hampton Beach, offering everything from refreshing shaved ice to foot-long subs. This is where you can soak up some rays on a hot summer day, or watch the Wednesday night fireworks. The Cascade, located at the Casino Water Slide, is a fun spot that's open for breakfast, lunch, and dinner with an extensive menu of coastal favorites. They are especially known for their fish-and chips, steamed and baked seafood, surf and turf, pasta dishes, salads, and sandwiches. The shrimp and scallop Alfredo is definitely worth a try. The expanded deck is so inviting with its bright blue and white market umbrellas and tables, just the place to try what they claim is the best margarita on the beach. Open daily from 7:30 a.m. to 10 p.m.

Galley Hatch, 325 Lafayette Rd. (Rte. 1), Hampton; (603) 926-6152; galleyhatch.com. Ellie, a waitress at the Galley Hatch for the past 30 years, sums it up nicely: "The food is good every time you come, the service is professional but friendly, and there's something for everyone." Still owned and operated by the Tinios family, this landmark restaurant now has a bakery and gift shop on the premises. The main menu consists of classic American fare such as cedar plank–roasted salmon, haddock done in three different ways, broiled sea scallops, boiled or baked stuffed lobster, and a medley of seafood in a rich lobster sauce served in a popover. Lighter fare is on the lunch menu, and a children's menu is also available. Open for lunch and dinner daily.

Luis Sea Fresh Seafood Restaurant & Fish Market, 115 Lafayette Rd. (Rte. 1), Hampton Falls; (603) 967-4790; luisseafresh.com. With its own fish market on the premises, Luis Sea Fresh promises its guests the freshest fish on the seacoast. You can dine in this family-owned restaurant or order takeout. The menu, which has a Portuguese accent, includes stuffed quahogs, lobster rolls, clam chowder, and their famous lobster stew. Other popular items are the sandwiches, pasta dishes, and fried seafood. Early bird specials are offered every day from 3 to 6 p.m. Open for lunch and dinner Tues through Sun from 10 a.m. to 8 p.m.

Master McGrath's Restaurant, New Zealand Road (Rte. 107), Seabrook; (603) 474-3540; mastermcgraths.com. If you're a dog lover, you will love Master McGrath's, named after the greatest greyhound that ever lived in Ireland. He died in 1871, and his picture still hangs in many pubs across the Atlantic. Operated by the Moodie family, this friendly establishment offers many seafood temptations: lobster pie, baked haddock Louisiana style, and haddock Martinique on a bed of scallops with lobster sauce. A children's menu is available. Open for lunch and dinner daily, brunch Sat and Sun.

The Old Salt at Lamie's Inn, 490 Lafayette Rd. (Rte. 1), Hampton; (603) 926-8322; oldsaltnh.com. Built in 1740, Lamie's Inn is home to the Old Salt, a restaurant steeped in history but totally up-to-date when it comes to good food. Fresh seafood is their specialty, served in an authentic colonial atmosphere. The clam chowder is an award winner, and the fish chowder is made with fresh haddock. In unusual sandwiches, the fried haddock is topped with cheddar cheese, and the surf-and-turf burger is fresh ground hamburger flame broiled and topped with lobster meat and lobster sauce. Entrees include an authentic New England clambake and King Neptune's Feast for Two. An early bird menu and a children's menu are available. Open for lunch and dinner daily, brunch Sun.

Purple Urchin Seaside Dining & Patio Pub, 167 Ocean Blvd. (Rte. 1A), Hampton; (603) 929-0800; purpleurchin.net. Two restaurants under one roof with spectacular oceanfront dining, the Purple Urchin is ideal for family and friends in search of truly good food right on Hampton Beach. Start off with Spinney Creek steamers or the seared ahi tuna. In addition to salads and sandwiches, there is seafood galore: lobster, fish-and-chips, oven-roasted haddock, pan-seared salmon, and the rather unusual Atlantic Avenue Bangers (local shellfish drizzled with lobster mornay sauce over mashed sweet potatoes). The open-air bar is a popular spot with an abbreviated menu that includes grilled mahimahi. A children's menu is available. Open for lunch and dinner daily.

Ray's Seafood Restaurant, 1677 Ocean Blvd. (Rte. 1A), Rye; (603) 436-2280; raysseafoodrestaurant.com. In business for more than 50 years and one of the oldest continually operating seafood restaurants on the New Hampshire seacoast, Ray's is devoted to providing their thousands of customers with quality seafood at reasonable prices. This family-style restaurant offers views of Rye Harbor from the lounge and ocean views from the upstairs dining room. On most days you can see the Isles of Shoals from the bright blue upper deck. All that plus sea breezes and delicious food are reason enough to stop in. They catch their own lobsters, so the lobster dinners are a sure bet, as are the lobster quesadilla and lobster-stuffed mushrooms. All the usual fried dishes are on the menu, but it's the baked dishes that will make your mouth water, such as the lobster-stuffed haddock. A children's menu is available. Open for lunch and dinner daily in season, Fri through Sun in winter.

Ron's Landing, 379 Ocean Blvd. (Rte. 1A), Hampton; (603) 929-2122; ronslanding.com. This elegant oceanfront restaurant is in a restored 1920s home. The linen-covered tables have seascape centerpieces and candlelight. Specializing in seafood, the menu is captivating: Norwegian-style seafood fettuccine, swordfish cacciatore, and lobster ravioli tossed with sautéed jumbo shrimp, sea scallops, and lobster claws in a plum tomato sauce. Basic fresh fish is offered baked, blackened, Szechuan style, grilled, broiled, and Bermudian style with a cherry pepper lobster cream sauce. This is a very special restaurant. A children's menu is available. Open Wed through Sat at 4 p.m., Sun at 11 a.m.

Sea Ketch, 127 Ocean Blvd. (Rte. 1A), Hampton; (603) 926-0324; seaketch.com. This seasonal restaurant has a new top-deck bar dotted with bright blue umbrellas for shade, the only place where you get a 360-degree view of Hampton Beach. It's come a long way since it opened in 1973, and fans say the food is better than ever. A multilevel dining destination, it has a beach cafe on the first level and ocean-view dining on the second, third, and fourth floors. The main menu starts off with clam chowder, coconut shrimp, oysters on the half shell, fried calamari, shrimp cocktail, seafood bisque, and steamers. In addition to sandwiches, wraps, and salads, seafood entrees include catch of the day, baked fillet of sole, broiled sea scallops, grilled swordfish, lobster pie, fried clam platter, and much more. A children's menu is available. Open for breakfast, lunch, and dinner May through Columbus Day.

Sharon's Sea Grill, 186 Ocean Blvd. (Rte. 1A), Seabrook; (603) 474-2618; sharonseagrill.com. Open year-round, Sharon's Sea Grill prides itself on using local seafood. You can eat in the yellow and orange dining room, or take your food out to the marsh-view deck in warm weather. Popular dishes include the fried clam basket, baked haddock dinner, and English-style fish and "tips." The fried fish taco wrap gets high marks. Sharon's is located in a small shopping plaza, right next door to a state liquor outlet. Open for breakfast, lunch, and dinner daily in the busy summer season; Thurs through Mon from 7 a.m. to 2 p.m. in the off-season.

Tuna Striker Pub, 7 River St., Seabrook; (603) 474-7063; tuna strikerpub.com. Just about every restaurant on scenic Route 1A has an ocean view, but this is the area's only restaurant actually set on the water. Run by Merrilee Eastman and her son Matt Preston, this open-air restaurant has a definite Key West vibe with wonderful harbor views, especially at sunset. You can watch the Eastman fishing fleet dock and unload their daily catch. Fresh seafood, steaks, and chicken make up the basic menu. Some of the more unusual dishes are scallops and onion rings deep-fried and tossed in buffalo sauce, bacon teriyaki scallops, roasted corn and shrimp chowder, Caesar salad topped with swordfish steak tips, mango grilled swordfish, lobster BLT, and tilapia fish tacos. A children's menu is available. Open for lunch and dinner daily, Apr 1 to Columbus Day. During the spring and fall, open Thurs to Sun from Memorial Day to Labor Day.

Wentworth by the Sea Marriott Hotel & Spa, 588 Wentworth Rd., New Castle; (603) 422-7322; wentworth.com. One of the most luxurious hotels in New England offers a wonderful ocean view. Breakfast, lunch, and dinner are served under the direction of Executive Chef Daniel Dumont. His menu is based on regional favorites, updated New England traditions made with fresh, local ingredients. Lobster and fish are highlights. Within this grand hotel is Latitudes Waterfront, a seasonal restaurant open daily for lunch and dinner from spring to fall. This marina-side restaurant has a teak deck for al fresco summer dining and a bistro-style menu. Almost every dish is a seaworthy celebration: crab and lobster cakes with avocado cream, tomato and crab gazpacho, salmon and heirloom tomato salad, rustic stew of coastal shellfish, hook and line–caught haddock, and the Great Island Lobster Experience with all the fixings of an authentic clambake. Latitudes is open for lunch and dinner daily from spring to early Oct.

Lobster Pounds

Brown's Seabrook Lobster Pound, Rte. 286, Seabrook; (603) 474-3331; brownslobster.com. With scenic marsh and river views, Brown's is a full-service lobster pound with a timber-frame dining hall where you can feast on steamed lobsters and clams, lobster rolls, lobster bisque, and more. This is where you want to be in the summer, especially at sunset. The dining deck overlooks the tidal Blackwater River near Seabrook's popular beach. Brown's has been family owned for more than 50 years and has a sterling reputation. Take-out service is also available. Open for lunch and dinner daily from Apr to Nov; open nightly Fri through Sun nightly from Nov to Apr.

Captain Don's Lobster Pound & Bait Company, 50 River St., Seabrook; (603) 474-3086; captdons.com. Since the 1970s, this is where locals go for their lobsters and bait! Captain Don also offers other catch-of-the-day items, from crabs to steamers. The lobsters are sold live, or if you prefer they will steam your lobsters on the premises and pack them for travel. This is a seasonal operation. Open daily from 6 a.m. to 7 p.m. from Apr 1 to Oct 1.

Little Jack's Seafood Restaurant & Lobster Pool, 539 Ocean Blvd. (Rte. 1A), Hampton; (603) 926-8053; no website. A Hampton Beach tradition, Little Jack's has a large indoor dining area, an upper deck, and picnic tables next to the parking lot. The view from the deck is as good as it gets, plus there's usually a pleasing ocean breeze. Nothing fancy here; be prepared for paper plates even if you order the mussels with pasta. You order your food at a window, and when your number is called, you pick it up and sit wherever you like. The extensive menu offers fried seafood platters, baked or broiled seafood, combo plates, and the house specialty—lobster. Liquor is available. A seasonal operation, it's wise to call to check on the hours. Open for lunch and dinner daily.

Markey's Lobster Pool, Rte. 286, Seabrook, (603) 474-2851; markeyslobsterpool.com. Located near the back dunes of Seabrook, Markey's offers plenty of fresh seafood and is known especially for lobster—steamed or fried, in a toasted roll or creamy bisque. The lobsters come from an on-site lobster pool. In warm weather you can dine on a deck that has a water and marsh view. Tom and Christine Markey opened this family business in 1971, and they urge everyone to "come as you are." The atmosphere is definitely beach casual. Known for its consistently good food and ample portions. Open for lunch and dinner daily from mid-Apr to mid-Oct; closed Mon through Thurs from mid-Oct to mid-Apr.

Petey's Lobster Pound, 1870 Ocean Blvd. (Rte. 1A), Rye Harbor; (603) 427-8441; peteyslobsterpound.com. That summer hot spot, Petey's Summertime Seafood and Bar, now has a lobster pound located just south of the popular restaurant. It's a simple one-room shed at the entrance to Rye Harbor. They catch their own lobsters and sell them live. Shipping is available. You can also order and pick up live lobsters from Petey's restaurant located less than 2 miles away (see page 240). Open daily from 10 a.m. to 6 p.m. from spring to fall.

Ray's Lobster Pound, 1667 Ocean Blvd. (Rte. 1A), Rye; (603) 436-0899; no website. This lobster pound is connected to Ray's Seafood Restaurant right next door (see page 235). They catch their own lobster, so you know they're fresh. Open daily from 11:30 a.m. to 8:30 p.m. in winter, 11:30 a.m. to 9:30 p.m. in summer.

Rye Harbor Lobster Pound, 1870 Ocean Blvd. (Rte. 1A), Rye; (603) 964-7845; no website. A one-room garage right on the dock at Rye Harbor, this lobster pound not only sells fresh lobsters for you to cook at home, they also sell cooked lobsters, and fans rave about the "fluffy chowder" and lobster bisque. Fluffy chowder? Yes, they will ask if you want regular clam chowder or fluffy. Go for the fluffy, which is regular clam chowder topped with a scoop of chopped lobster meat that has been soaked in hot butter and sherry wine. The bisque has chunks of lobster in it. Not exactly a restaurant, and not really a clam shack, but there are picnic tables with a view of the boats moored in the harbor. This is probably the most affordable way to have fresh lobster on the New Hampshire seacoast. It's recommended that you call ahead for hours of operation.

Clam Shacks

Beach Plum #1, 17 Ocean Blvd. (Rte. 1A), North Hampton; (603) 964-7451; lobsterrolls.com. There are two award-winning Beach Plum restaurants, one by land and one by sea. Beach Plum #1 is a cute seasonal operation near the coast and North Hampton State Park. Beach Plum #2 in Portsmouth is just as cute but open year-round with beer and wine available (for details see page 222). The original Beach Plum in North Hampton is a roadside eatery. The outdoor dining area is clean and well kept, with colorful umbrellas providing much-needed shade on those hot summer days. The expanded menu is sure to please everyone, especially lobster lovers—their pricey lobster roll is a foot long and contains 20 ounces of fresh unadulterated lobster meat. In addition, there are all kinds of sandwiches, chowders and soups, and salads. A children's menu is available. And for dessert, they have 78 flavors of ice cream and frozen yogurt waiting to be sampled. Try the blueberry or the strawberry cheesecake for something different. Open for lunch and dinner daily from early Mar to mid-Nov.

Castaways Seafood & Grille, 209 Ocean Blvd. (Rte. 1A), Seabrook; (603) 760-7500; castawaysseafoodandgrille.com. Fans call it paradise, an oasis where they can leave all their troubles behind, at least for a little while. With a tropical motif, it's easy to relax with a cool cocktail in hand as you sit on one of the two large decks that offer arguably the best sunset on the local seacoast. This seasonal operation has an impressive menu with much more than the usual clam shack fare. Appetizers include crab and artichoke dip, a nice prelude to the shrimp Florentine. But fear

not—your favorite fried foods are offered in sandwiches and in lunch baskets served until 4 p.m. These baskets of native clams, calamari, haddock, scallops, and shrimp are partnered with fries and coleslaw. Open for lunch and dinner daily in summer, opening in spring and closing in mid-Oct.

Ceal's Clam Stand, 22 Ocean Blvd. (Rte. 1A), Seabrook; (603) 474-3150; no website. You can't miss it—just look for the little white shack by the side of the road with the very bright red trim. Park right in front of the walk-up windows and check out what's on the big outdoor menu. A local institution, Ceal's has been in business since 1948 with the same family serving chowder, fish-and-chips, seafood platters, and sandwiches on a seasonal basis. Outdoor seating is available. Open weekends only in May and June, for lunch and dinner daily from July to Labor Day (but closed Mon in Aug).

Petey's Summertime Seafood and Bar, 1323 Ocean Blvd. (Rte. 1A), Rye Harbor; (603) 433-1937; peteys.com. A summer hot spot, Petey's is open year-round and now has a lobster pound located just south of the popular restaurant (see page 238). This full-service establishment with ocean views from the upper level is right across the beach from an old shipwreck. You can dine in or take your food out to the colorful picnic area. The menu is quite extensive. If you like, their famous chowder is served in a bread bowl. Deep-fried delicacies include oysters, baby shrimp, and quite possibly the best fried clams in the area. Lobster rolls come in regular and jumbo sizes. For the health conscious, broiled seafood is on the menu. The baked stuffed haddock, shrimp, and scallop platters sound too delicious to pass up. A children's menu is offered as well. Traveling by helicopter? A helipad is on-site. Open for lunch and dinner daily.

Seafood Markets

Al's Seafood, 51 Lafayette Rd. (Rte. 1), North Hampton; (603) 964-9591; alsseafoodnh.com. More than 20 years ago, Al Courchene purchased a small seafood market and take-out stand. Since then Al's Seafood has evolved from a summer destination into a year-round favorite. Al has retired and turned the business over to Debra Boutot and Bret Taylor, who continue to delight customers with the freshest seafood available, locally caught whenever possible. Just about every kind of fish and shellfish is available, from fresh-picked lobster meat to sand-free steamers, from cod and haddock to Chilean sea bass and mahimahi. Lobsters and steamers can be cooked to order, packed to travel, or shipped overnight. Their website provides excellent information on the origin of various seafood, nutritional data, and preparation suggestions. Open daily from 9 a.m. to 8 p.m.

Luis Sea Fresh Fish Market, 115 Lafayette Rd. (Rte. 1), Hampton Falls; (603) 967-4791; luisseafresh.com. Family owned and operated, Luis Sea Fresh offers a wide selection of live lobsters, fresh fish, and shellfish. Local favorites include Atlantic salmon, haddock, and halibut. More exotic fare ranges from Chilean sea bass to mahimahi. A seafood restaurant is also on the premises. Open Mon from 10 a.m. to 3 p.m., Tues through Sat from 10 a.m. to 8 p.m.

Seaport Fish, 13 Sagamore Rd., Rye; (603) 436-7286; seaportfish .com. The only FDA-approved fish market in the area, Seaport Fish is a family-owned company that's been in business for more than 30 years. At least 5 days a week, they bring in fresh fish from the piers of Boston, Portland, and Portsmouth—everything including fresh fish, whole or hand cut into fillets, local and exotic shellfish, side dishes from an on-premise chef, and fresh produce. Open Mon through Sat from 9 a.m. to 7 p.m., Sun from

9 a.m. to 6 p.m. in summer; Sun through Wed from 9 a.m. to 6 p.m., Thurs through Sat from 9 a.m. to 7 p.m. in winter.

Yankee Fishermen's Cooperative, 725 Ocean Blvd. (Rte. 1A), Seabrook; (603) 474-9850; yankeefish.com. The 60 members of this co-op haul in cod, flounder, haddock, lobster, tuna, and shrimp from some of the most productive fishing areas in the Gulf of Maine. Their boats are all day boats, leaving before daybreak to go fishing and returning to port each evening with their catch, the freshest products available. They sell their catch at a retail fish market at Seabrook Harbor. Their website has many recipes for you to try at home. Open daily in summer; Thurs through Sun from 10 a.m. to 6 p.m. in winter.

INLAND (MID- TO NORTHERN NEW HAMPSHIRE)

A completely different world awaits travelers who venture inland on their visits to New Hampshire, called the Granite State because of its extensive granite formations and quarries. Mountain roads such as Kancamagus Highway wind through the majestic White Mountains, dazzling any time of the year but especially in the autumn, when the foliage almost seems to be on fire with color. Railways climb to the top of Cannon Mountain, Loon Mountain, and Mount Washington, the tallest peak in the Northeast at 6,288 feet. Hikers in these regions often come upon graceful waterfalls. This is what the interior of New Hampshire is all about—nature at its breathtaking best. Caves, lakes, and a river that disappears as it snakes through Kinsman Notch—all that and so much more await the curious visitor.

The state sport is skiing, and more than 150 downhill trails can be found at the region's three largest resorts: Attitash Bear Peak, Loon Mountain, and Waterville Valley. Cross-country skiing, snowboarding, and snowmobiling are other popular sports in this winter wonderland.

Lake Winnipesaukee in Central New Hampshire has 253 islands in its 72 square miles of water, ideal for boating and swimming. For more than a century, the lake has been a popular tourist destination, especially in the summer. Strong winds on the lake make for superb sailing. The Mount Washington paddle steamer, which dates back to 1872, still makes round trips on the lake every day in the summer. Other recreation possibilities include biking, hiking, rock climbing, and white water rafting. The main commercial city on the lake is Laconia, home every year to Bike Week, which attracts thousands of motorcyclists to the area.

All these activities are bound to work up anyone's appetite, and there are plenty of restaurants at the ready to serve and satisfy customers. From Pop's Clam Shell in Alton Bay to the Canoe Restaurant on picturesque Lake Winnipesaukee, there's a restaurant, a clam shack, a seafood market just waiting to be discovered.

Seafood Restaurants

Big Catch, 150 Shore Dr., Bristol; (603) 744-3120; no website. A casual restaurant at the foot of Newfound Lake, the Big Catch draws regular customers in by car and boat. This seasonal restaurant specializes in seafood. They are also well-known for their frozen drinks, house-made desserts, and Shane's of Maine ice cream. This is a classic summer lakeside restaurant. Open for lunch and dinner daily from Memorial Day to Labor Day.

Canoe Restaurant and Tavern, 232 Whittier Hwy. (Rte. 25), Center Harbor; (603) 253-4762; magicfoodsrestaurantgroup.com. Picturesque views of Lake Winnipesaukee vie for your attention along with the food of Chef-Owner Scott Ouellette, especially his famous lobster mac and cheese and the award-winning sweet-and-sour calamari. The 5 dining areas include a porch for open-air dining in the summer. Boaters who are docked in town can take the free shuttle to and from the restaurant. The dinner menu is extraordinary: seared ahi tuna, lobster stuffed portabello, flash-fried oysters, and day boat scallops with maple-cider-champagne glaze, just for starters. Entrees include lobster pie, seafood enchiladas, seafood cakes, lobster ravioli, grilled salmon, wild Alaskan cod, and much more. Open for lunch and dinner daily.

Cartelli's Bar & Grill, 446 Central Ave., Dover; (603) 750-4002; cartellis.com. Locals, tourists, and travelers flock to Cartelli's, a downtown gathering place with a menu that has that proverbial "something for everyone." Chef-Owner Mike Cartelli offers classic Italian dishes, steak, pasta, fresh seafood, sushi, burgers, grilled pizza, sandwiches, and pub food, all prepared from scratch. Seafood specialties include mussels in lemon-wine sauce, fried calamari, shrimp scampi pizza, cioppino over fettuccine, haddock Florentine, baked sea scallops, ahi tuna over Asian slaw, grilled Atlantic salmon, and a Cajun salmon Caesar wrap. A children's menu is available. Open for dinner nightly.

Thanks to the Native Americans

Long the ancestral home of Native Americans, the land now known as New Hampshire was first colonized by the English in the early 1600s. In 1629 a settlement built near present-day Rye was named New Hampshire after the English county of Hampshire. Portsmouth was founded one year later. Many classic New England dishes, including the clambake, can be traced back to the Indians who shared their recipes with the early colonists.

Copper Door, 15 Leavy Dr., Bedford; (603) 488-2677; copperdoor restaurant.com. This is one handsome restaurant, starting with the custom-made copper door you walk through to view the stylish dining room with its exposed timber trusses and original artwork of local farm views. The Copper Door also has a beautifully landscaped garden terrace for al fresco dining in the summer. Executive Chef Zack Martineau offers approachable New American cuisine, or upscale comfort food in simpler terms. The prime seafood dishes include pan-seared swordfish with sweet pea butter, cioppino over pasta, cedar-planked salmon with charred tomato pesto, pepper-dusted ahi tuna, wood-roasted haddock with corn-crab hash, and seared sea scallops with fennel salad. A more casual lunch menu and children's menu are available. Open for lunch and dinner daily.

Fish Shanty, 471 Central Ave., Dover; (603) 749-1001; thefish shanty.com. Family recipes and hearty portions are on the menu at this family-owned and -operated restaurant in downtown Dover. The atmosphere is casual, and service is friendly. The menu is fairly extensive and features Greek specialties such as haddock plaki simmered in a sauce of plum tomatoes and peppers. Start off with some fried oysters or the creamy seafood chowder. All kinds of fish are available either baked stuffed, broiled, grilled, or lightly fried. Many seafood entrees are available in small and large portions. The more unusual items include broiled rainbow trout, fried smelts, and the lobster pie baked in a casserole dish and topped with lobster bisque. The gourmet sandwiches are intriguing, especially the grilled scallop melt and the toasted tuna with feta cheese. Luncheon specials, early bird dinners, and a children's menu are also offered. Open for lunch and dinner Tues through Sun.

Jake's Seafood & Grill, 2055 White Mountain Hwy. (Rte. 16), West Ossipee; (603) 539-2805; jakesseafoodco.com. Jake's is named in memory of a Siberian husky found at an animal shelter years ago. Jake loved to eat, and he is remembered every day by the folks at this family restaurant that bears his name. Everything you'd expect at a seafood eatery is on the simple menu, including fried haddock direct from the Boston Fish Pier and fresh whole-belly clams from Maine. Early bird specials are available every day from 4 to 6 p.m. Not to be missed is the Monday night fish fry. A children's menu is available. Open daily from 11 a.m. to 9 p.m.

Jesse's Steaks, Seafood and Tavern, Route 120, Hanover; (603) 643-4111; jesses.com. How does bourbon lime salmon sound? That's what awaits you at this very interesting restaurant that started out in 1976 as a log cabin dinner house. A custom greenhouse was added, and then came the Adirondack lodge and deck. Always expanding and ever improving, the new brick patio now provides a charming spot for al fresco dining. In addition to steak and seafood, Jesse's is known for its all-you-can-eat salad bar and freshly baked Sequoia bread. Entrees include a creamy seafood casserole, sautéed tiger shrimp, and grilled sesame tuna, served with organic brown rice and seasonal vegetables. A children's menu is available. Open for dinner nightly, brunch Sun.

Johnson's Seafood & Steak: Johnson's Northwood, Rte. 4, Northwood; (603) 942-7300. **Johnson's New Durham,** 69 Rte. 11, New Durham; (603) 859-7500; eatatjohnsons.com. The original New Hampshire family restaurant—that is their claim to fame. With two locations in New Hampshire and one in Maine (see page 174), Johnson's are welcome stops along the back roads of New England. Regular customers have high praise for the lobsters and massive ice-cream cones. It all started with a humble dairy bar in Northwood that soon became known for its home-cooked food and warm hospitality. The menu has evolved over the years, but they still promise that same home-away-from-home dining experience. All kinds of seafood are offered baked, breaded, and battered. The lobster pie is topped with crabmeat stuffing. Another good bet is the golden brown Atlantic haddock nuggets. Open daily from 11 a.m. to 9 p.m. Memorial Day to Labor Day; Sun to Thurs from 11 a.m. to 8 p.m., Fri and Sat from 11 a.m. to 9 p.m. Labor Day to Memorial Day.

Lobster Boat Restaurant, 553 Daniel Webster Hwy., Merrimack; (603) 424-5221. 273 Derry Rd., Litchfield; (603) 882-4988. 75 Portsmouth Ave.; Exeter; (603) 583-5183; lobsterboatrestaurant .com. This is the original Lobster Boat, now with sister operations in Litchfield and Exeter and a Li'l Lobster Boat in Tyngsboro, Massachusetts. At each location they work toward presenting a true New England seafood dining experience. This small local chain of restaurants is known for its outstanding food and casual atmosphere. All the basics are on the menu, plus some unusual stand-out dishes: fried lobster fingers with drawn butter, baked mushroom caps stuffed with crab, fish nuggets, charbroiled Cajun swordfish, and lobster chunks and bay scallops over pasta. A scaled-down menu is offered at lunchtime, and a children's menu is available. Open for lunch and dinner daily.

Lobster Tail Restaurant and Lounge, 4 Cobbetts Pond Rd., Windham; (603) 890-5555; lobstertail.net. Many restaurants promote their farm-to-table philosophy. Here it's more like "dock-to-plate" service, and that keeps customers returning again and again to the renovated Lobster Tail. Fresh seafood is delivered daily, and it is used in classic as well as innovative recipes. The extensive menu, which includes jumbo coconut shrimp and swordfish kabobs, is sure to please everyone. The fresh lobster dip with Ritz crackers is a very popular start to dinner. For your pasta course consider the scallop scampi over linguine. In addition to popular fried seafood dishes, specialties focus on lobster and king crab. The baked seafood is special, especially the crab-stuffed gray sole with lobster sauce and the sweet potato-crusted organic salmon. An abbreviated luncheon menu and a children's menu are also available. Open for lunch and dinner daily.

Makris Lobster and Steak House, Rte. 106, Concord; (603) 225-7665; eatalobster.com. The Makris family got started in the restaurant business in the early 1900s, and the legacy continues in Concord, just minutes from the New Hampshire Motor Speedway. With a seafood market on the premises, you can rest assured that your lunch or dinner will be as fresh as it can be. The appealing menu has great variety, starting with the lobster ravioli appetizer and your choice of oyster or lobster stew. Some of the more unusual dishes include fried lobster, shellfish stew, haddock topped with asparagus and snow crab legs, baked stuffed scallops, sautéed Cajun shrimp, and a crab melt (a grilled English muffin with crab salad, sliced

tomato, and melted Swiss cheese). But don't worry—all the classic fried seafood so many people crave is also on the menu. Open for lunch and dinner daily.

Newick's Lobster House, 431 Dover Point Rd., Dover; (603) 742-3205. 317 Loudon Rd., Concord; (603) 225-2424; newicks.com. It began in 1948 when John Newick sold his surplus lobster catch at a roadside stand on Dover Point. Eventually his son Jack built a take-out shack. Both the shack and the menu grew. Today the original Newick's seats 650 people, still on Dover Point overlooking the shores of Great Bay, with a fresh seafood counter on the premises. A working waterfront, you can watch local lobstermen unload their catch on the dock. There are two other locations including one in Maine. The third generation of Newicks is still on the scene, providing guests with all their seafood essentials. Haddock, for example, is prepared at least 10 different ways. Creative dishes include seafood shepherd's pie, seafood provençal, fried lobster tails, and flounder

Dock and Dine

The most delightful way to dine in the summer is to arrive at the restaurant by boat. New Hampshire is blessed with more than a fair share of this type of dining experience. Here are some of the best spots to dock and dine on Lake Winnipesaukee, and they all have seafood on their menus:

In Meredith

The Camp, 300 Daniel Webster Hwy.; (603) 279-3003

Lago's, 1 US 25; (603) 279-2253

Lakehouse, 281 Daniel Webster Hwy.; (603) 279-5221

Town Dock Restaurant, 289 Daniel Webster Hwy.; (603) 279-3445

Mame's, 8 Plymouth St.; (603) 279-4631

In Gilford

Ames Farm, 2800 Lake Shore Rd.; (603) 293-4321

Lyons Den, 25 Dock Rd.; (603) 293-8833

In Alton

Dockside Restaurant, Alton Bay; (603) 875-2110

Pop's Clam Shell, Route 11; (603) 875-6363

flakes. No frills here, just paper plates and plastic utensils and utilitarian chairs and tables covered with red and white checkered tablecloths. Open for lunch and dinner daily.

O's Steaks & Seafood, 62 Doris Ray Ct., Laconia; (603) 524-9373. 11 South Main St., Concord; (603) 856-7925; magicfoodsrestaurant group.com. With two locations, this is the best of both worlds. The Laconia site is at Lake Opechee, and the other site is in downtown Concord. You can sit at the chef's table, where you can watch the staff prepare your meal under the direction of Chef-Owner Scott Ouellette. In the summer

Sandy Point, 1 Sandy Point Rd.; (603) 875-6001

Shibley's at the Pier, Route 11; (603) 875-3636

In Wolfeboro

Garwoods Restaurant, 6 North Main St.; (603) 569-7788

Mise en Place, 96 Lehner St.; (603) 569-5788

Wolfe's Tavern at Wolfeboro Inn, 90 North Main St.; (603) 569-3016

The Wolfetrap, 19 Bay St.; (603) 569-1047

In Center Harbor

Canoe Restaurant and Tavern, 232 Whittier Hwy.; (603) 253-4762

Lavinia's at The Coe House, Route 25B; (603) 253-8617

In Laconia and Weirs Beach

Cactus Jack's, 1182 Union Ave.; (603) 528-7800

Christmas Island Steakhouse, 644 Weirs Blvd.; (603) 366-4664

NazBar & Grill, 1086 Weirs Blvd.; (603) 366-4341

Weirs Beach Lobster Pound, 70 Endicott St. (Rte. 3N); (603) 366-2255

you can dine on the patio. The sophisticated menu tempts you with shrimp toast points, lump crab cakes, shrimp corn chowder, and fried oysters Rockefeller, for appetizers. Entrees are Parmesan-encrusted tilapia, salmon glazed with citrus and soy, seared day boat scallops, seafood risotto, ahi tuna, and Chilean sea bass with creative accompaniments. To go with all that, more than 24 wines by the glass are available, and the exquisite desserts are made on site. Open for lunch and dinner daily.

Pasta Loft, 241 Union Sq., Milford; (603) 672-2270. 220 East Main St., Hampstead; (603) 378-0092; pastaloft.com. Both locations are local hot spots for casual dining with pasta as the star of the show. Seafood aficionados might like the seafood-stuffed portobello mushroom laced with lemon-herb aioli or the seafood fettuccine Alfredo. Specialties include the lobster mac and cheese made with pappardelle pasta. A children's menu is available. Open for lunch and dinner daily.

Restaurant Tek-Nique, 170 Rte. 10, Bedford; (603) 488-5629; restaurantteknique.com. Its name should give you a good idea of what Matthew Trottier, the chef-owner, is all about. His credentials are impressive, and he has trained his staff to be imaginative. Their creative menu reflects that by offering a crispy calamari salad, apple wood-smoked salmon, shrimp and escargot, tuna seared rare and tuna tartare, oysters on the half shell with coconut sorbet, free-form seafood lasagna, salmon with lobster succotash, and pan-roasted jumbo sea scallops with ratatouille. Open for dinner Tues through Sun, brunch Sun.

Shibley's at the Pier, Route 11, Alton Bay; (603) 875-3636; shibleys atthepier.com. Step back in time with a stop at Shibley's. The all-marble bar was a soda fountain in the 1920s. The building that houses this seasonal restaurant is well over 100 years old. The only thing really new is the American cuisine coming out of the kitchen, thanks to the Shibley family, owners since 1993. You can check it out after a relaxing cruise around Lake Winnipesaukee—the tour boat arrives right next door every Tuesday and Sunday in season. You can sit on the deck for a pristine view of the majestic lake. Dine on the steamed mussels with buttery garlic bread, egg noodles with clam sauce, or Asiago-crusted sea bass. A larger, more casual menu is offered every day until 5 p.m. Save room for dessert, especially the fried dough topped with butter, caramel, cinnamon sugar, and powdered sugar. Open for lunch and dinner daily from late Jan to late Oct, with limited hours during winter.

Tinker's Seafood, 545 Hooksett Rd. #6, Manchester; (603) 622-4272; tinkersseafoodrestaurant.com. Clean, bright, and colorful—that's how fans describe this award-winning hometown restaurant, where families have been dining for the past 30 years. And the food is just as eye pleasing, whether it's a mound of golden fried clams or an oversize order of fish-and-chips. Just about every seafood dish imaginable is on the menu, including three different chowders, fried plates, broiled dinners, lobster, and family-style platters. A children's menu and a menu for senior citizens

Weirs Beach

are also available. Open Sun through Thurs from 11 a.m. to 8 p.m., Fri and Sat from 11 a.m. to 9 p.m.

Weathervane Seafood Restaurants, 393 Rte. 101 West, Bedford; (603) 472-2749. 2 Dover Point Rd., Dover; (603) 749-2341. 379 Dover Rd., Chichester; (603) 225-4044. 41 South Broadway, Salem; (603) 893-6269. Weathervane Drive, West Lebanon; (603) 298-7805. 174 Daniel Webster Hwy., Nashua; (603) 891-1776. 279 Lakeside Ave., Weirs Beach, Laconia; (603) 366-9101. weathervane seafoods.com. It all began with a humble take-out stand in Kittery, Maine, and it has grown into a small empire of restaurants throughout New England. In New Hampshire alone, there are 6 Weathervane restaurants and 1 Weathervane's Lobster in the Rough, a seasonal operation (Memorial Day through Columbus Day) on Weirs Beach in Laconia. The year-round locations have similar menus that emphasize classic New England seafood, from founder Bea Gagner's famous clam chowder to fried, broiled, grilled, and baked stuffed seafood. Lobster dishes, sandwiches, and pasta specialties including the house specialty, lobster and asparagus Alfredo, round out the menu. A children's menu is also available. Open for lunch and dinner daily.

Lobster Pounds

Good Tail Lobster Pound, Rte. 3, Glen; (603) 383-0190; goodtail lobster.com. Open year-round, this is the place to go for fresh seafood in the Mount Washington Valley. A quaint cottage with a tin roof, Good Tail offers live Maine lobsters, haddock, tuna, swordfish, salmon, oysters, shrimp, steamers, and littlenecks. A small prepared food menu features lobster rolls, peel-and-eat shrimp, steamers, and clam chowder (in the winter). They suggest that you browse the selection online and phone in your order. They'll have it ready for you to pick up, or delivery is available within 20 miles of the store. In the summer, weekly lobsterbakes are held every Monday at 6 p.m. at Matty B's Mountainside Cafe in Bartlett. Open Mon through Sat from 11 a.m. to 7 p.m. and Sun from 11 a.m. to 5 p.m. from June through Aug; Fri through Sun from 11 a.m. to 7 p.m. the rest of the year.

Shyer's Lobster Pound, 380 S. Broadway (Rte. 28), Salem; (603) 898-2602; shyerslobsters.com. A family-owned business for more than 50 years, Shyer's carries lobsters of all sizes, a full line of fresh fish, and frozen fish items such as salted codfish, salmon burgers, lobster pie, dressed smelts, and scrod entrees ready to heat and serve. Lobster meat, fresh or frozen, is also available. They will steam your lobsters at no extra charge, and they will pack and ship your lobsters for travel. Cash only. Open Mon through Sat from 8 a.m. to 6 p.m., Sun from 8 a.m. to 4 p.m.

Weirs Beach Lobster Pound, 70 Endicott St. (Rte. 3N), Weirs Beach; (603) 366-2255; wb-lp.com. For more than 35 years, this lobster pound has been a local institution for seafood lovers in and around beautiful Lake Winnipesaukee. Thousands of people stop in during Bike Week every June, when motorcycle enthusiasts converge in the Laconia area for food, entertainment, and hospitality. Indoor and outdoor decks overlook the boardwalk and sandy beach. Tables with colorful market umbrellas offer shade for your al fresco dining experience. Back in the 1970s an ingenious steamer to cook lobsters was installed, and it's still in operation. The house specialties are lobster mac and cheese, lobster salad rolls, twin lobster specials, and lazyman lobster, with the meat of two lobsters baked in a casserole dish with a lightly seasoned topping. In addition to seafood, the menu offers heart-healthy items and "A Taste of Italy" specialties. A children's menu is available. Now open year-round, it's wise to call for their seasonal hours.

Seafood Lover's New England

Clam Shacks

Brick House Drive-In, 1391 Hooksett Rd., Hooksett; (603) 622-8091; bhrestaurant.net. A classic seasonal drive-in restaurant, the kind of place that locals grew up with, and now they are taking their children here for seafood "boats" filled with fried haddock, shrimp, clams, scallops, or tilapia. Not to be missed—the house-made potato chips. It really is a red brick house that's been converted into an all-American neighborhood restaurant. Picnic table seating is available in the summer, which makes this a dog-friendly spot. Open daily from 11 a.m. to 8 p.m. from spring to fall.

Clam Haven, 94 Rockingham Rd., Derry; (603) 434-4679; clamhaven.com. A real slice of Americana, Clam Haven is where local teenagers get their first summer jobs, Little League teams go to celebrate a win, and locals celebrate the end of winter when this drive-in restaurant opens for the season. In business for more than 60 years, this popular clam shack is owned and operated by the Metts family. It's easy to fall off your diet here when you're tempted by the Texas-style haddock sandwich and combo plates of various fried foods, all topped with their signature onion rings. This is one of the few eateries in New Hampshire where you can get an order of clam cakes, mostly a Rhode Island thing. And save room for dessert—they offer soft-serve and hard ice cream as well as frozen yogurt with all kinds of toppings. A seasonal operation, open for lunch and dinner daily from Mar through Oct.

Evergreen Clam Shack, 1355 Suncook Valley Rd. (Rte. 28), Center Barnstead; (603) 776-2727; no website. A seasonal mostly take-out restaurant, Evergreen offers fried clams, of course, plus other seafood dishes, hot dogs, burgers, sandwiches, and ice cream. There is a screened-in porch for dining. Fans rave about the "very friendly staff and great food." The Evergreen Clam Shack is on the site of an old ski lodge. No longer an operating ski area, the big hill is popular in winter for sledding. It's recommended that you call ahead for hours of business before going.

George's Seafood & Bar-B-Que, 588 Tenney Mountain Hwy., Plymouth; (603) 536-6330; georgesseafood.com. This is a fun place in the foothills of the White Mountains, not far from Plymouth State University. Dave and Pam Castelot say that their little restaurant is a clam shack at heart with a fish market on the premises. They try to keep their pricing as family

Lake Winnipesaukee, Meredith

friendly as possible. With authentic barbecue on the menu, there's something
for everyone here. The seafood specialties include all the usual dishes, plus
combo plates, baked stuffed haddock, and Atlantic salmon topped with hollandaise sauce. You can eat in or take out. Open for lunch and dinner daily.

High Tide Takeout Seafood Restaurant, 239 Henniker St., Hills-
borough; (603) 464-4202; hightidetakeout.com. It looks like a modest house with a big screened-in porch where you can dine all summer long
on classic summer food. This no-frills family atmosphere is very popular
with the locals. You might be 50 miles from the seashore, but all your favorite beach foods are on the menu: baked and grilled seafood, fried entrees,
combo dinners, chowder, and seafood sandwiches, all served on paper
plates. A children's menu is also available, as well as a playground for the
kids. Stop in on Wednesday night, and you'll step back in time when you
see all the classic cars in the parking lot. Open daily from 11 a.m. to 8 p.m.
from mid-Apr through Columbus Day.

Lobster Claw II, 4 South Main St., Derry; (603) 437-2720; lobster
claw2.com. A combination restaurant and fish market, this humble establishment has won more awards than most businesses can claim. Lee and

John Kratz are the owners, and they aim to please their many customers. They carry the most popular New England seafood products: haddock, scallops, salmon, shrimp, flounder, smelts, lobsters, steamers, oysters, tuna, and some prepared foods such as crab cakes. They welcome special orders—just ask, and they will get whatever you desire. Open in season for lunch and dinner daily; closed Mon.

Pop's Clam Shell, Route 11, Alton Bay; (603) 875-6363; no website. For more than 30 years, Pop's has been serving the Lakes Region with fried clams as its specialty. Their motto is: "It ain't healthy, but it sure tastes good." The outdoor deck is an inviting space with red and white umbrellas and blue tablecloths on the picnic tables, plus a view of Belknap Lakes. It's not unusual to see classic autos from yesteryear parked in front of this seasonal drive-in operation. And dogs are always welcome. Open in season daily from 11:30 a.m. to 8 p.m. It's recommended that you call ahead to check on hours of operation.

Shacketts Seafood Shack, 256 W. Shore Rd., Bristol; (603) 744-3663; shacketts.com. Located on the shores of picturesque Newfound Lake, Shacketts is more than just a seafood shack—it's also a full-service supermarket where you can get some of Shacketts's famous donuts and fudge, pick up some cold beer, fill your propane tank, rent a kayak, and even put gas in your boat. Both the market and seafood shack are seasonal operations, family run for almost 70 years. Seasonal hours.

Town Docks, 289 Daniel Webster Hwy., Meredith; (603) 279-3445; thecman.com. A member of the impressive Common Man restaurant group, this is a seasonal operation that offers lakeside outdoor dining and an outdoor tiki bar on Lake Winnipesaukee. You can get there by car or boat, with free docking. There's plenty of seafood on the take-out menu, starting with New England clam chowder and lobster corn chowder. Peel-and-eat shrimp, steamed clams and mussels, crab cakes, and calamari are among the appetizers. Signature sandwiches include a lobster roll, fried clam roll, crab cake sandwich, tuna roll, and fishwich. Classic entrees include a fisherman's platter, fried scallops, and grilled Atlantic salmon. Lobster lovers can have a steamed lobster, a complete New England shore dinner, or a lobster tail with grilled bourbon steak tips. Fresh lobsters weighing up to 2 pounds each are available if you prefer to cook at home. Open seasonally for lunch and dinner daily.

Woodman's Seafood & Grille, 454 Charles Bancroft Hwy., Litchfield; (603) 262-1980; woodmans.com. Woodman's world-famous clam shack in Essex, Massachusetts, now has a satellite operation in New Hampshire as the exclusive caterer for Mel's Funway Park in Litchfield. The site has a huge tent with covered picnic tables and a tiki bar with an amusement park on the premises. Woodman's to-die-for fried clams and award-winning chowder are on the menu, as are other seafood delicacies. Children eat free with the purchase of a dinner plate Sept through Apr. Hours of operation change with the seasons, so it's wise to call ahead. Open for lunch and dinner daily in summer; open for lunch and dinner Wed through Sun in winter.

Seafood Markets

Donahue's Fish Market, 20 Plaistow Rd., Plaistow; (603) 382-6181; donahuesfishmarket.com. Everything from fresh flounder to fish cakes is available at Donahue's, which gets its seafood almost daily from Gloucester, Massachusetts. Fish is brought in whole and cut in house to ensure freshness. All the deli items, including ready-to-go dinners, are made on the premises. Lobster rolls and chowders are available. A separate take-out menu offers seafood in sandwiches, fried, baked, and grilled. Open Mon through Sat from 9:30 a.m. to 7 p.m., Sun from 9:30 a.m. to 5 p.m. Take-out hours are Mon through Sat from 11:30 a.m. to 7 p.m.

Free Range Fish & Lobster, 2076 Wakefield Rd., Sanbornville; (603) 522-6868; freerangefish.com. With locations here and one in Portland, Maine, this market fills a local void for fresh fish in the greater Wakefield area. Live Maine lobsters and other seafood are delivered from the Portland operation (see page 168). The lobsters are from the Gulf of Maine and unloaded on the docks of Casco Bay. Fresh fish is purchased early in the morning every day off the docks in Portland, New Bedford, Gloucester, and Boston. The seafood varies and is subject to availability. They also process the seafood. Check their website for daily specials. Lobsters may be ordered online and are shipped overnight in sturdy boxes with ice/gel packs. They sell only sustainable seafood and mostly fresh. If it's previously frozen, it is prominently marked. Open daily from 10 a.m. to 6 p.m., Fri from 10 a.m. to 7 p.m.

Buying Right Off the Boats

"From our boat to your table" is their motto. The *F/V Rimrack* is a harvester of local, wild caught fish and shrimp that pulls into the dock landings at Rye Harbor with its daily catch. People in the know go online (rimrackfish.com) to check on availability, prices, and landing times. They show up with their own containers and plenty of ice to keep the seafood fresh. Buying seafood directly off fishing boats such as the *F/V Rimrack* supports New Hampshire fishermen and sustainability. Operated by the Sullivan family, the website also offers recipes. Make sure you check out the Captain's Log.

Fresh Fish Daley, 146 Front St., Exeter; (603) 772-5011; freshfish daley.com. The longest-running local fish market, Fresh Fish Daley also sells organic produce. They're happy to take your order over the phone, and they'll have it ready for you to pick up. They'll even extend their regular business hours to suit your schedule—just give them advance notice. All their fresh fish, soups, chowders, and ready-to-go items are listed with prices on their website. Customer favorites are calamari salad, albacore tuna salad, and freshly made fish sticks. Open Mon through Fri from 10 a.m. to 6 pm., Sat from 10 a.m. to 5 p.m., Sun from 11:30 a.m. to noon.

George's Seafood & Bar-B-Que, 588 Tenney Mountain Hwy., Plymouth; (603) 536-6330; georgesseafood.com. This is a combination fish market/clam shack/barbecue joint. On the market side of things, they offer lobster, steamers, oysters, haddock, scallops, shrimp, salmon, calamari, and chowder by the quart. They are happy to take special orders for items such as tuna loin and swordfish. Open daily at 11 a.m.

Milford Fish Market, 251 Elm St., Milford; (603) 673-4200; milfordfish.com. They claim to have the freshest seafood "this side of Boston." Fans say that prices here are lower than the supermarkets, and the selection is better. With a restaurant on the premises, you can have lunch (try the Cajun catfish) and watch the fresh fish being delivered. If you have any special requests, it's a good idea to call ahead. Open Sun through Thurs from 11 a.m. to 8 p.m., Fri and Sat from 11 a.m. to 9 p.m.

Newick's Lobster House, 431 Dover Point Rd., Dover; (603) 742-3205; newicks.com. Since 1948, Newick's has grown from a roadside lobster stand on Dover Point into a huge restaurant, still on Dover Point overlooking Great Bay. Just inside the main entrance is a gift shop and fresh seafood counter. With the working waterfront in full view, you can trust that the fish and shellfish on ice are as fresh as they can be. Open daily from 11 a.m. to 9 p.m.

Tinker's Seafood, 545 Hooksett Rd. #6, Manchester; (603) 622-4272; tinkersseafoodrestaurant.com. For 30 years award-winning Tinker's has been known for the freshest seafood in the Manchester area. Their seafood arrives daily from the Ipswich Shellfish Company. All the basics are available, from calamari to swordfish. Frozen appetizers and dinner entrees are also available. You can call in your order, and you can have live lobsters shipped anywhere in the nation with next-day delivery. Open Sun through Thurs from 8 a.m. to 8 p.m., Fri and Sat from 8 a.m. to 9 p.m.

NEW HAMPSHIRE EVENTS
Spring & Fall
New Hampshire Restaurant Week, restaurantweeknh.com. Restaurant week is celebrated at restaurants throughout the state from early to mid-March (and again in November), and seafood always plays an important role on the special prix-fixe menus offered.

May
Golden Clam Award, waterville.com/events. The annual event is held in late May, usually on Memorial Day weekend, in Waterville Valley. As many as 10 Waterville Valley–area restaurants compete in hopes of winning the coveted "Golden Clam Award." Attendees get to sample all the chowders, and they are given a ballot to vote for their favorite. Local microbreweries share their varieties of summer ales under the Town Square tent during the entire event.

June
Chowderfest, prescottpark.org/chowder.cfm. New England's oldest chowder-tasting event is held in early June, kicking off the Prescott Park Arts Festival in Portsmouth. Thousands of seafood lovers attend with more than 500 gallons of piping hot chowder available for sampling, provided by more than a dozen local restaurants. The crowd votes for their

favorite chowder and determines which restaurant wins the best chowder title. Many restaurants use this popular event to try out new recipes, while others serve up their tried-and-true chowders—everything from a spicy seafood chowder to a smoked scallop chowder. Judges also give an award for their favorite chowder and for the best booth. Sponsored by *Taste of the Seacoast* magazine, this taste-testing event also features live music in a beautiful waterfront setting.

September
The Hampton Beach Seafood Festival, hamptonbeachseafood festival.com. Seafood lovers should not miss this late-summer event. The Hampton Beach Seafood Festival offers all kinds of New England seafood prepared by more than 50 of the best restaurants located on the New Hampshire seacoast. More than 150,000 are expected at this annual 3-day event, declared "One of the Top 100 Events in North America" by the American Bus Association. In addition, more than 80 arts and crafts vendors offer locally made products under a massive tent.

The New Hampshire Fish & Lobster Festival, prescottpark.org. This is a wonderful interactive event that celebrates centuries of fishing traditions along the coastline. Attendees can board local fishing boats for an up close look, and they can learn about the Gulf of Maine ecosystem. They get to taste fresh local seafood, learn how to prepare it, and watch top chefs compete in a cook-off. Sea shanties and tales from yesteryear round out the festivities that take place in mid- to late September at Prescott Park along the historic waterfront in Portsmouth. Admission to this "fishtival" is free, with a minimal fee for tastings. The generous support of Smuttynose Brewing Company has made this event accessible to the whole community.

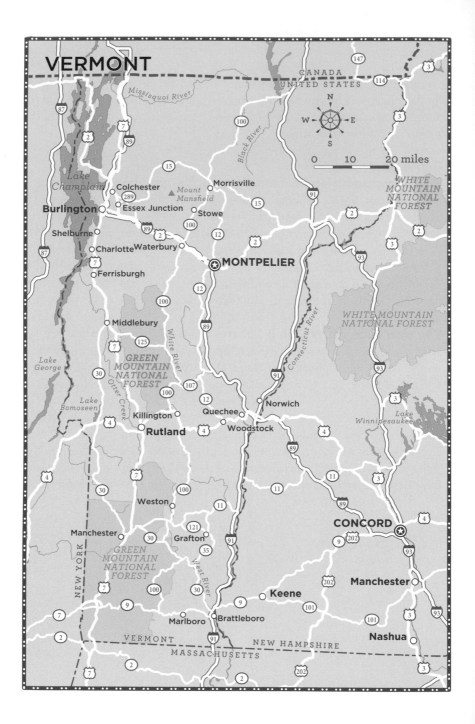

Vermont

Vermont, perhaps more than any other New England state, brings to mind images of covered bridges in fall, ski lodges in winter, and maple syrup farms in spring. Summer is a blend of hiking in the mountains and spending lazy days by the lake. Most people, especially food lovers, think only of Vermont cheddar cheese and Ben & Jerry's premium ice cream when asked what the state is famous for. As the only landlocked state in New England, Vermont has no ocean coastline, no quaint fishing villages, no strong connection to seafood in general. It is here, quite possibly, that a guide to seafood restaurants, lobster pounds, clam shacks, and fish markets is needed much more than anywhere else.

But anyone who has visited Vermont, and certainly those who live there, are aware of all that the state has to offer. Residents are to be commended for taking extraordinary measures to preserve its picture-postcard character. People who have chosen to make Vermont their home do so

Vermont Food News

For up-to-date information on restaurants, events, local products, and lodging, check out these online sources:

diginvt.com: Dig In Vermont is a direct route to the state's agricultural and culinary experiences that are open to the public, from farmers' markets to restaurants using local ingredients to make comfort food. More than 100 restaurants are listed in addition to wineries and breweries.

vermontlife.com: *Vermont Life* is a quarterly publication devoted to all things Vermont, from restaurants to the arts. Every season this is the go-to source for what's happening throughout the state.

visitvt.com: Visit Vermont is an excellent resource for vacation planning, provided by the Vermont Chamber of Commerce. The restaurant listing includes bistros, cafes, fine dining, and farm-to-table restaurants.

A lighthouse on Lake Champlain

because of the quality of life. There are no big cities, only the wonderful big town of Burlington with its many galleries, craft shops, and appealing restaurants. The state—with three general regions that become more rural as you travel north—is home to many organic farmers, artisan bakers, and skilled food producers.

Vermont may not have the depth and breadth of Maine or Massachusetts when it comes to seafood restaurants, but here and there are well-stocked and reputable fish markets and a wide variety of independent restaurants waiting to be discovered, from ski town saloons with train motifs to modern American pubs with sophisticated fare and waterfront establishments that promise you a spectacular sunset to go with your delicious dinner.

SOUTHERN VERMONT

The southern part of Vermont is easily the most visited part of the state, with its easy access from New York and Massachusetts. That's where you'll find the foothills of the beautiful Green Mountains, spectacular during foliage season in early fall. This is also the start of ski country with Okemo, Mount Snow, and Stratton drawing skiers of all ages.

Southern Vermont has three major towns: the artsy Brattleboro, the collegiate Bennington, and the sophisticated Manchester, with its trendy outlets. Farther north is the storybook village of Woodstock, more skiing in Killington, and Rutland, with its Victorian downtown. For a beautiful view of the Green Mountains, a trip up the Mount Equinox Skyline Drive is a must.

After a day of browsing art galleries or shopping in unique stores, you'll work up an appetite, one that can be satisfied in all kinds of restaurants in this region, from rustic to elegant.

Seafood Restaurants

Anchor Seafood House & Grille, 8 South Main St., Wilmington; (802) 464-2112; anchorseafoodrestaurant.com. An accurate replica of an 1850s building that housed a maple syrup cannery is home to the Anchor, as it's called by locals. This family-run restaurant is known for its consistent food and attentive service. Popular dishes include the Caesar salad with blackened swordfish and sesame-encrusted tuna with Asian ginger sauce. Food is served in the cozy dining room and in the handsome marble and oak cabaret bar room. More casual food can be found on the lunch menu. For anyone doubting that great seafood can be found in southern Vermont, the Anchor will convince them otherwise. A children's menu is available. Open for lunch and dinner daily.

Bennington Station, 150 Depot St., Bennington; (802) 442-7900; benningtonstation.com. It's hard not to like a restaurant inside a former train station. The historic depot has been transformed into a chef-owned and -operated dining establishment. Dinner options include Dover sole, broiled deep-sea scallops, shrimp scampi, porcini-encrusted Norwegian salmon, house-aged sirloin paired with shrimp scampi, seafood in garlic lobster cream sauce tossed with penne pasta, and baked scrod. Lighter fare, including a lobster roll and salmon burger, is also offered. A children's menu is available. Open for lunch and dinner Tues through Sun; closed Mon.

Casey's Caboose, 2841 Killington Rd., Killington; (802) 422-3795; no website. This is the quintessential ski-town saloon and very popular with locals. Many folks love the train theme, while some say it's dated. Casey's offers a pretty ambitious menu for a pub: mussels, calamari, and crab cakes for appetizers; house-smoked trout pasta, a mélange of seafood over linguine, sesame-crusted Atlantic salmon, broiled rainbow trout with maple-chive butter, blackened catfish, Maine lobster, and Alaskan king crab legs for entrees. Open for dinner nightly.

Dover Forge Restaurant, 183 Rte. 100, West Dover; (802) 464-5320; doverforge.com. Two miles south of the Mount Snow Resort is this warm and rustic restaurant built around an impressive forge hearth. The menu promises something for everyone, from the basic fish-and-chips to seafood fra diavolo in a spicy marinara sauce. On the premises is the One More Time Billiards Parlor & Tavern, which has a more casual menu. Open for lunch and dinner Sun, dinner only Mon through Sat.

Leslie's Tavern, On the Green, Rockingham; (802) 463-4929; lesliestavern.com. "A hidden gem, an oasis, a welcome respite" . . . that's how Chef-Owner John Marston and his wife Leslie describe their authentic inn in the Bellows Falls area. Since 1986 classic regional New England cuisine has been on the ever-changing menu, along with touches of French, Italian, and Thai cooking. Popular appetizers include the New England clam chowder, Cajun-style shrimp with tasso cream, crab cakes with lemon beurre blanc, and jumbo sea scallops with maple-mustard cream. Entrees range from jumbo sea scallops and shrimp over penne pasta to gray sole stuffed with crabmeat. A children's menu is available. Open for dinner Wed through Sun.

Lil' Britain Fish & Chips Shop, 116 North St., Bennington; (802) 442-2447; lilbritain.com. It's almost like being in London. Owners Kevin and Sarah Wright are Brits, and they claim that fish-and-chips are in their blood. Much like the way America has a coffee shop on every corner, the English are known for their fish-and-chips shops. Of course that is the number one dish at this small downtown storefront. You can also get shrimp-and-chips, scallops-and-chips, combo plates, a fish sandwich, chowder, and British specialties such as bangers and mash. In a rush? Get it to go. Open for lunch and dinner Tues through Sat.

The Marina, Putney Road (Rte. 5), Brattleboro; (802) 257-7563; vermontmarina.com. Waterfront dining with amazing sunsets awaits you at The Marina, a casual restaurant with outdoor seating in warm weather. Start off with the big mug of clam chowder served with Vermont

Beyond the Sea

Let's be honest: if you travel to Vermont, you haven't gone there for the seafood. Fortunately there are a number of restaurants, markets, and events where we seafood lovers can get our fix, as detailed in this book. But while in Vermont, here are three things not to be missed:

- The fresh apple cider and warm cider donuts made at the Cold Hollow Cider Mill, 3600 Waterbury-Stowe Rd. (Route 100), Waterbury Center; (800) 327-7537.

- A cooking class at The Essex, Vermont's Culinary Resort & Spa, 70 Essex Way, Burlington; (800) 727-4295.

- The 30-minute guided tour (with taste samples) of Ben & Jerry's ice cream factory, 1281 Waterbury-Stowe Rd., Waterbury; (866) 258-6877.

oyster crackers or the smoked trout with crackers. Follow that up with one of the many salads, topped with grilled tilapia or salmon. Or, if you're really hungry, go for the lobster and scallop pie topped with puff pastry. The inexpensive nightly specials are hard to beat. Open for lunch and dinner daily, brunch Sun. Hours change with the seasons.

TJ Buckley's, 132 Elliot St., Brattleboro; (802) 257-4922; tjbuckleys .com. A 20-seat restaurant inside a classic old railroad dining car in the funky arts town of Brattleboro makes this one of the most romantic spots to dine in Vermont. Chef-Owner Michael Fuller has been dazzling customers for more than 25 years in his open kitchen, just a few feet away from his guests. This is where you will find North Country cooking at its best: crab cakes with garlic aioli, a smoked trout tartlet with chèvre, diver scallops with crispy pork belly, and wild king salmon seared and steamed in lobster stock. This is one of the most unusual dining experiences you will find in Vermont. Open for dinner Wed to Sun in summer, Thurs to Sun in the off-season.

Woodbridge Cafe Restaurant & Coffeehouse, Route 4 West, Woodstock; (802) 332-6075; woodbridgecoffeehouse.com. For breakfast, try the crabmeat omelet. At lunch, the seafood chowder goes well with a big cheese panini. Come dinnertime, there's much to consider: fisherman's platter, baked scallops, baked haddock, crab cakes, coconut shrimp, and fettuccine Alfredo with shrimp. This is a BYOB establishment, so plan on bringing some beer or wine in a cooler. Open Mon through Thurs from 7:30 a.m. to 3 p.m., Fri and Sat from 7:30 a.m. to 8 p.m.

Woodstock Inn, 14 The Green, Woodstock; (802) 448-7900; woodstockinn.com. There is something very special about this classic New England inn. Go there for dinner in the Red Rooster restaurant, and you'll want to stay the night, or better yet, the weekend. This is a four-diamond eating establishment with a very creative culinary team preparing seafood stew and fish tacos for lunch and seared day boat scallops with lobster risotto for dinner. End the night with a nightcap in the warm and inviting Richardson's Tavern. Outdoor porch seating is available in warm weather. A children's menu is available. Open for breakfast, lunch, and dinner daily.

Lobster Pound

Bill Austin's Lobster Pound, 42 Maple St., Chester; (802) 875-3032; wmaustin.com. This is as strange as it gets, even for Vermont. Bill Austin's antiques and refinishing business is housed in an enormous old Victorian house, with more than 10,000 square feet of items (including taxidermy), the kind of place where you can wander around for hours. On the premises is a 1950s soda fountain serving dessert and coffee. In the basement you'll find a lobster pound with live lobsters crawling over one another in circulating tanks of water, plus fresh shrimp, scallops, oysters, clams, crab, fish, and more. Open daily from 9 a.m. to 6 p.m. (until 9 p.m. on Fri).

Seafood Markets

Adam's Fish Market, 92 Putney Rd., Brattleboro; (802) 257-9900; adams-seafood.com. In business for more than two decades, Adam's has been striving to provide customers with the freshest fish possible. Offerings include a wide variety of fish, live lobsters, steamers, freshly made chowders, and their famous lobster rolls. Open Mon, Tues, Wed, and Fri from 10 a.m. to 6 p.m., Thurs from 10 a.m. to 7 p.m.

Woodstock Farmers' Market, 9979 W. Woodstock Rd., Woodstock; (802) 457-3658; woodstockfarmersmarket.com. A unique concept, this where you can buy seafood, meats, groceries, and prepared foods; where you can shop online for artisan cheese and foods; and where you can grab a bite to eat at lunch or dinner. The fresh seafood selection includes New England staples such as cod and gray sole, as well as regional catches such as swordfish, striper, tuna, sablefish, wild and farm-raised shellfish, and Maine lobsters They also offer peeled and de-veined shrimp, smoked salmon, and seafood pâtés. Open Tues through Sat from 7:30 a.m. to 7 p.m., Sun from 9 a.m. to 6 p.m.; closed Mon.

CENTRAL VERMONT

The midsection of Vermont is often referred to as Champlain Valley in recognition of the vast Lake Champlain, called New England's Great Lake or "an inland sea." Summer residents on the lake include the Royal Lipizzaner Stallions, a historic breed of milk-white horses known in the past for their bravery in wartime and now for their graceful equestrian performances.

Farther north is the college town of Burlington, where you can visit the shops on Church Street and the Lake Champlain Maritime Museum. Weather permitting, plan on a lake cruise on board the *Spirit of Ethan Allen III*. The 45-acre Shelburne Museum includes a full-size Lake Champlain steamship and a 1920s carousel.

Fans of the 20th-century poet Robert Frost will want to hike the Robert Frost Interpretative Trail near Ripton, where Frost spent his last 22 summers. The 1.2-mile path winds through meadows and forests, marked by plaques embossed with some of his poems, including the famous "Road Not Taken." Such a wide variety of things to do in Central Vermont is matched by the many restaurants in this region, offering everything from impeccably fresh sushi to creative cuisine in waterfront locations.

Seafood Restaurants

Asiana House, 191 Pearl St., Burlington; (802) 651-0818; asian noodleshop.com. The ethnically diverse selection at this hot spot ranges from Korean barbecue to Indonesian satay. But it's the sushi that brings the crowds in, hungry for the torched salmon roll with avocado, crispy crab maki, and spicy tuna maki. Everything goes well with one of the premium sakes on the menu. This downtown restaurant has only a dozen tables, so it fills up fast. At peak times prepare to wait. Outdoor dining is available in warm weather. Open for lunch and dinner daily.

Blue Paddle Bistro, Route 2, South Hero; (802) 372-4814; blue paddlebistro.com. Nestled in the beautiful Lake Champlain islands, this is a special place, created especially for foodies by owners Mandy Hotchkiss and Phoebe Bright. Mandy is the host and sommelier, while Bright is the chef. The food is exquisite without being pretentious. Crab cakes are served with chutney-mango tartar sauce. The ravioli is stuffed with crabmeat and topped with a crab cake. Sea bass with chile-maple glaze, lobster and prosciutto in a light lemon butter cream, grilled marinated shrimp, and soy-glazed salmon are the seafood stars on the menu. Outdoor dining is offered in summer. Open for dinner nightly in summer, Wed through Sun in the off-season.

The Ice House Restaurant, 171 Battery St., Burlington; (802) 864-1800; icehousevt.com. Being on the waterfront and having 35 years of experience makes the Ice House a "must visit" restaurant. During the 1800s, this really was the icehouse that provided large chunks of ice from frozen Lake Champlain for the nonelectric refrigerators of yesteryear. The views from the covered decks are worth the trip; the innovative food is a bonus, from the Atlantic salmon finished with a Vermont apple cider reduction to the lobster risotto served with sautéed shrimp and lobster claws. Open for lunch and dinner daily.

Little Harry's, 121 West St., Rutland; (802) 747-4048; littleharrys .com. The locals have spoken, and they are raving about this hidden gem for its eclectic menu, generous portions, and competitive pricing. "Warm and cozy . . . awesome food . . . top-notch . . . outstanding . . ." These are just some of the accolades. The large menu features lobster-stuffed mushrooms, crab cakes, shrimp wrapped in wontons, green curried mussels, calamari, and the very hot "red red" shrimp for appetizers. Dinner possibilities are the roasted salmon with Cajun crab stuffing, grilled jerk scallops, cod oven poached in white wine, sautéed shrimp with stuffed pasta purses, scallops casino on a bed of roasted red pepper fettuccine, pan-blackened fish of the day with tropical fruit salsa, and good old fish-and-chips. A children's menu is available. Open for dinner nightly.

The Scuffer Steak & Ale House, Church Street Marketplace, Burlington; (802) 864-9451; thescuffer.com. It might be a steak house, but the seafood deserves equal recognition, starting with the crab cakes drizzled with lemon caper aioli, crispy fried calamari with a sweet Thai chile sauce, steamed mussels, shrimp cocktail, and New England clam chowder. The seafood selections are worthy of your attention: pan-roasted salmon, grilled swordfish with pineapple salsa, a mixed seafood broil, shrimp scampi over linguine, and whole Maine lobster with drawn butter. Fish-and-chips, a lobster roll, and a children's menu are also available. Outdoor seating is available in warm weather. Open for lunch and dinner daily.

Shanty on the Shore, 181 Battery St., Burlington; (802) 864-0238; shantyontheshore.com. With a history that dates back to 1775, the Shanty on the Shore opened in 1985. Today it proudly offers top-notch seafood you can't find anywhere else in town and the only raw bar on this side of Lake Champlain, according to its website. Original wood beams create a rustic setting with bright blue nautical touches and a sweeping view of the harbor. The mostly seafood menu has lots to tempt you, from Portuguese mussels to buffalo shrimp and Rhode Island calamari for appetizers. The clam chowder and lobster bisque are served in a bread bowl, if you like. Shanty classics include roasted deep-sea scallops and maple-ginger salmon, all kinds of fried seafood dishes, and lobster in various presentations, including lobster and shrimp au gratin. Lighter fare is available midday. Open for lunch and dinner daily.

Splash at the Boathouse, College Street, Burlington; (802) 343-5894; splashattheboathouse.com. How can you not like a seasonal restaurant that sounds like summer fun? Located on the waters of Lake Champlain, Splash draws folks from all over, including boats from as far away as Quebec, Canada. If you dine outside under one of the colorful umbrellas, you'll see that you are on a floating dock. All this is the vision of well-known local caterer Barbara Bardin, who opened Splash in 2003. Everything you'd expect at a modern American restaurant is on the menu, including some unusual dishes: coconut-mango crab cakes, fish tacos, and a grilled salmon sandwich. A children's menu is also available. Open for lunch and dinner daily in summer only.

Windjammer Restaurant, 1076 Williston Rd., Burlington; (802) 862-6585; windjammerrestaurant.com. For more than 35 years, The

Windjammer has been Burlington's premier steakhouse and seafood restaurant. Now partnering with Wood Mountain Fish Company in Boston, Executive Chef JJ Vezina has access to seafood so fresh that it was swimming just 12 hours earlier. The chef is especially known for his accompanying sauces. House specialties served in handsome and comfortable surroundings include salmon dolce, encrusted with sweet potato and finished with a ginger root–honey glaze, and a broiled seafood platter with herb butter. A children's menu is available. Open for lunch and dinner daily.

Seafood Market

Mehuron's Market, 5901 Main St., Waitsfield; (802) 496-3700; mehurons.com. Tom Mehuron is the third generation of his family to own and operate this full-service market with a reputable seafood department. Back in 1941, folks used to go to Mehuron's to get their animals slaughtered and buy ammunition. The business has evolved from a country store to a modern-day market, but old-fashioned friendly service is still in place. Seafood is delivered fresh three times a week, everything from ocean fish to lobsters. Open Tues through Fri from 8 a.m. to 7 p.m., Sat from 8 a.m. to 4 p.m.

NORTHERN VERMONT

Largely unspoiled, northern Vermont gets far fewer visitors because of its remoteness. Long and winding roads connect timeless villages with breathtaking views at every turn.

The big draw in this region is the capital city of Montpelier, where the New England Culinary Institute can be found. A wonderful vacation can be had at any time of the year at one of the ski resorts near Stowe Mountain, or perhaps at a charming bed-and-breakfast. Side trips can take you to quaint farms where apple cider is made fresh on the premises, and to Cabot Creamery, famous for its award-winning cheddar cheese. The number one tourist destination in Vermont is the Ben & Jerry's Ice Cream Factory in Waterbury, where you get to sample everything from Cherry Garcia to Chunky Monkey.

The uppermost reaches of Vermont are called the Northeast Kingdom, which consists of very rural farm country and a paradise for cross-country skiers. After a day of touring this remote part of the state, you'll be ready to head back to more populated areas, where an abundance of restaurants stand ready to serve you some real Vermont hospitality.

Seafood Restaurants

Ariel's Restaurant, 29 Stone Rd., Brookfield; (802) 276-3939; arielsrestaurant.com. The menu at Ariel's is always in tune with the seasons. This family-owned restaurant is a short drive south from the state capital, Montpelier. Owners Lee Duberman and Richard Fink have created a romantic and comfortable haven where the food is quite imaginative: mussels in red curry sauce, grilled whole branzino (rarely seen on menus), and seafood with green curry and Thai rice noodles. Open for dinner Wed through Sat from May to Oct; Fri and Sat from Dec to Mar; closed Apr and Nov.

Bayside Pavilion, 15 Georgia Shore Rd., St. Albans Bay; (802) 524-0909; baysiderestaurant.net. This is one of those small-town restaurants right next to Lake Champlain, perfect for an after-dinner stroll. It started out in 1921 as Barker's Restaurant, a well-known summer destination. Bayside is now known for its Thursday night lobster special and beer-battered fish-and-chips every Saturday. The menu includes mussels, crab cakes, country fried breaded codfish sandwich, and seafood entrees: grilled salmon, fresh sea scallops, crab-stuffed jumbo shrimp, and a seafood combo. Outdoor dining is available on the rustic deck in warm weather. Open for lunch and dinner daily.

Cornerstone Pub & Kitchen, 47 N. Main St., Barre; (802) 476-2121; cornerstonepk.com. This is a modern American pub, owned by Keith Paxman and Rich McSheffrey, with an intriguing menu. For starters, consider the blackened swordfish tacos and poutine, a regional specialty (house-cut fries topped with cheddar cheese curds, braised short rib, and gravy). Entrees include pan-seared diver scallops with butternut squash risotto and traditional fish-and-chips utilizing line-caught haddock in a beer batter. Craft beers round out your dining experience. Open for dinner Tues through Sat.

East Side Restaurant & Pub, 47 Landing St., Newport; (802) 334-2340; eastsiderestaurant.net. This is the kind of restaurant where customers are always asking the chef for recipes—it's that good. People rave about the baby blues scallop casserole, a tasty combination of scallops, garlic, mushrooms, and blue cheese. On the shores of Lake Memphremagog, which extends into Canada, the East Side is known for its hearty comfort food. Fireside favorites include oyster bruschetta and sweet chipotle shrimp. Creative entrees include honey-baked scallops and maple-grilled salmon. The mountain view from the wraparound deck is serene and tranquil. Open for lunch and dinner daily.

Harrison's Restaurant & Bar, 25 Main St., Stowe; (802) 253-7773; harrisonstowe.com. In the heart of historic Stowe village near the beautiful Green Mountains, Harrison's has more than 35 years of experience making locals and visitors feel welcome upon arrival and satisfied when they leave. The diverse menu is sure to please all, starting with the classic fish-and-chips. For more sophisticated palates, there's the pecan-encrusted ahi tuna. Lighter fare includes shrimp tacos. The lower-level dining room is a cozy spot with quiet booths and a roaring fireplace on cold winter days. The barn-board walls are covered with historical photos of the area. Open for dinner nightly.

Hob Knob Inn, 2364 Mountain Rd., Stowe; (802) 253-8549; hob knobinn.com. Family owned and operated, the Hob Knob Inn was built in 1937 as Stowe's first ski lodge. Now completely restored, guests can enjoy fireside dining in the winter, when the on-premise restaurant reopens

every December. A typical dinner might be scallops wrapped in bacon for starters and ginger-rubbed Atlantic salmon or jumbo lump crab cakes over fresh baby greens for the entree. Open for dinner Thurs through Sat for the winter ski season.

Jeff's Restaurant, 65 N. Main St., St. Albans; (802) 524-6135; jeffsmaineseafoodrestaurant.com. Fresh seafood plus regional ingredients just about guarantee a positive dining experience in this downtown restaurant with 2 dining rooms and jazz playing in the background. "Stylishly Vermont" is the motto here. A typical dinner might include coconut-crusted shrimp or fish chowder followed by grilled or blackened swordfish, tuna, or salmon. Craving pasta? Try the shrimp and sea scallops in vodka cream sauce over penne. Right next door is Jeff's Market, offering fresh fish and prepared foods. Open for dinner Tues through Sat.

Ray's Seafood Market Restaurant, 7 Pinecrest Dr., Essex Junction; (802) 879-3611; raysseafoodmarket.com. For more than half a century, the Dunkling family has been providing customers with fresh seafood and shellfish through its Ray's Seafood business, which has grown over the years to now include a popular restaurant. You can eat in or take out seafood chowder, clam chowder, oyster stew, buckets of fish nuggets, shrimp cocktail, stuffed clams, crab cakes, seafood stuffed mushrooms, bacon-wrapped scallops, coconut shrimp, and the rather unusual cheddar cheese shrimp jammers. All kinds of fried seafood are available a la carte, in a sandwich roll, or in baskets with your choice of side dishes. Broiled and baked seafood dinners are also available, as well as king crab leg and lobster dinners. Open for lunch and dinner daily.

Stonegrill Restaurant & Pub, 116 Rte. 15 West, Morrisville; (802) 888-4242; stonegrillvt.com. Healthy and hearty eating is the promise at Stonegrill, where the menu changes with the seasons and an effort is made continuously to use fresh local ingredients. A unique dining experience is offered, imported from Australia. Food is served on a heated stone that allows diners to sear their filet mignon or tuna steak to the desired temperature. Conventionally prepared food is also available, such as baked haddock or a fried seafood combo. More casual fare is available midday. Open for breakfast, lunch, and dinner daily.

Clam Shack

Cajun's Snack Bar, Montgomery Center, 1594 Rte. 100, Lowell; (802) 744-2002; no website. Simply put: These are the best fried clams in Vermont, according to fans. Other fried seafood platters feature scallops, shrimp, oysters, and haddock. With a nod to Louisiana, the menu offers oyster or crawfish po' boys and a Cajun catfish wrap. "From the bayou" menu items include fried alligator, frog legs, catfish, and crawfish dinners with outstanding fries. This is a kid-friendly, affordable restaurant with outdoor dining in warm weather and majestic views. It is set in a rustic cabin with a front porch and bright red roof. A seasonal operation with classic car shows on Wednesday night in the summer. Open for lunch and dinner daily in summer; closed from fall to late spring.

Seafood Markets

Ray's Seafood Market, 7 Pinecrest Dr., Essex Junction; (802) 879-3611; raysseafoodmarket.com. It's almost easier to list what they don't offer at Ray's Seafood Market. If it's not in stock, they'll be happy to special order it for you. In addition to lobster and ocean fish, Ray's brings in freshwater fish from Lake Champlain. A full list of market items can be found on their website. Their mobile seafood van travels to Bristol every Wednesday from spring through late fall. Open daily from 10 a.m. to 6 p.m. in winter; Mon through Fri from 10 a.m. to 6 p.m., Sat and Sun from 2 to 6 p.m. in summer.

Stowe Seafood, 504 Mountain Rd., Stowe; (802) 253-8004; stoweseafood.com. "Bringing the best of the ocean home to the mountains" is their motto. Considered an excellent source of fresh seafood, Stowe Seafood on any given day might offer house-marinated Hawaiian salmon as well as Atlantic, Alaskan, and organic salmon. All the basics are in stock: shrimp, squid, calamari, mussels and clams, steamers, and diver and sea scallops. More exotic fare includes Chilean sea bass, mahimahi, wahoo, arctic char, gray sole, and grouper. As always, they have live lobsters, swordfish, bluefish, haddock, and halibut on ice. Open Mon through Sat from 10 a.m. to 6 p.m., Sun from noon to 5 p.m.

Vermont Meat & Seafood Market, 104 Cornerstone Dr., Williston; (802) 878-2020; vtmeatandseafood.com. Live Maine lobsters, Scottish salmon, grouper, yellow fin tuna, ahi tuna, raw shrimp, shucked oysters, clams, mussels, and oysters—that's what this retailer of seafood, meats, and wine has in stock on a regular basis. The market focuses on quality local products and premium national items. Open Mon through Thurs from 11 a.m. to 7 p.m., Fri and Sat from 10 a.m. to 7 p.m., Sun from noon to 5 p.m.

The Uncommon Market, 1 School St., Montpelier; (802) 223-7051; uncommonmarket.net. A full-service, city-style delicatessen and small market that specializes in groceries, specialty foods, local products, hand-cut steaks, and fresh seafood. Sharon Allen and her husband Peter Foote, with their daughter Chelsea, own the market where folks can get their breakfast, lunch, or dinner. On any given day the seafood might include day boat haddock, arctic char, swordfish, cod, red snapper, yellow tail sole, salmon, yellow tail tuna, scallops, shrimp, mussels, and oysters. Open Mon through Fri from 6:30 a.m. to 8 p.m., Sat from 8 a.m. to 8 p.m., Sun from 9 a.m. to 7 p.m.

Vermont Events

April/May
Vermont Restaurant Week, vermontrestaurantweek.com. This week is celebrated at restaurants throughout the state in late April/early May, and seafood always plays an important role on the special prix-fixe menus offered.

Mid June
Stowe Wine & Food Classic, stowewine.com. This is a three-day annual event held at the Trapp Family Lodge, a premier resort in Stowe. Festivities include beer and wine tastings, food pairings, a gala dinner, live auction, and cooking demonstrations.

Recipes

Simple Steamed Lobster

Guilford Lobster Pound in Guilford, Connecticut, is a family-owned business established in 1991 by Captain Bart Mansi and his wife Janice. Mansi has been lobstering in Long Island Sound since the 1970s. He leaves the dock at the Guilford Lobster Pound around 4 a.m. daily aboard his 42-foot lobster boat, *Erica Page*, named after their daughter. The catch is brought back to the lobster pound, where it's weighed and sorted by size. Customers get not only the freshest lobsters in the area, they also get these Mansi family recipes.

In a large stockpot over high heat, bring 2 inches of water and a lemon cut in half to a full boil. Add the lobsters. Bring the water back to a full boil, cover, and steam for 12 to 18 minutes (for lobsters weighing between 1¼ to 1½ pounds).

How to Care for Your Lobsters

Refrigerate lobsters when they arrive, either in the crisper or loosely on the shelf. Cook them even if they appear motionless. After cooking, the tail should curl up under the body, and the meat should be firm. Eat lobsters as soon as possible, the fresher the better.

Do not put lobsters in the bathtub or sink with tap water. They will drown in fresh water.

Captain Bart's Steamed Lobster

This recipe is the same as the recipe for Simple Steamed Lobster, but instead of water and lemon, use a bottle of champagne to steam the lobsters. Yes, you read it right: champagne.

Grilled Lobster

In a small pan over medium heat, melt 1 stick of butter. Add 4 cloves of minced garlic and 2 tablespoons of chopped fresh dill. Reduce the heat to low and let the flavors meld. Split the lobsters down the middle so they are halved. Place the lobsters meat side down on a hot grill for 4 to 5 minutes. Turn the lobsters over and baste with the butter mixture. Cook another 4 or 5 minutes until lobster meat is white, basting constantly. Serve with grilled corn on the cob.

Lobster Lady's Stuffed Lobster

MAKES 4 SERVINGS

4 fresh lobsters (1½ pounds each)
3 sleeves Ritz crackers, finely crushed
1½ sticks butter, melted
1 (8-ounce) bottle clam juice
2 (6-ounce) cans crabmeat
1 (6-ounce) can chopped clams
2 tablespoons freshly chopped parsley
Pepper, to taste
Butter, for baking and serving
Lemon slices, for garnish

1. Preheat oven to 350°F. Split the lobsters down the middle.

2. In a bowl, combine the crushed crackers with the melted butter. Add the clam juice, crabmeat, chopped clams, chopped parsley, and pepper. Mix well so that mixture is moist but not wet. If too wet, add more cracker crumbs.

3. Place the stuffing in the lobster body and down the tail. Top with a few pieces of butter. Bake for 35 minutes, or until lobster meat is firm and white. Serve with melted butter and fresh lemon slices.

Lobster Cooking Instructions

1. Boil water in a large pot.
2. Add sea salt seasoning.
3. Place live lobsters in pot.
4. When water begins to boil again, cover and cook according to weight chart.
5. Melt some butter for dipping and enjoy!

Cooking Chart

Size	Cooking Time
1–1½ pounds	10–12 minutes
1½–2 pounds	13–14 minutes
2–3 pounds	16–18 minutes
3–4 pounds	20–22 minutes
4–6 pounds	23–25 minutes
7–10 pounds	30–35 minutes
10–15 pounds	40–45 minutes

Grilled Littleneck Clams

Place the clams on a hot grill and close the cover to the grill. Allow the clams to cook until just opened. Brush the opened clams with your favorite sauce—BBQ, melted butter with chopped garlic, hot sauce, or just melted butter. Close the grill for another few minutes until clams are piping hot. Serve immediately.

Steamer Cooking Instructions
1. Rinse steamers carefully in cold water.
2. Put 1 inch fresh water into a large pot.
3. Place steamers in pot and cover with lid.
4. Boil on high until the shells fully open.
5. Melt some butter for dipping and enjoy!

Dad's Famous Stuffed Shrimp

Baked stuffed shrimp is a very popular dish in Rhode Island, often appearing on restaurant menus. On special holidays, especially Christmas Eve, home cooks prepare this dish as a special treat for their family and friends. This particular recipe, where the jumbo shrimp is stuffed with even more seafood, is from R&D Seafood in Woonsocket, Rhode Island.

MAKES 4 SERVINGS

12 jumbo shrimp
4 ounces bay scallops
4 tablespoons butter, divided
½ cup water
4 ounces crabmeat
½ cup crushed Ritz crackers
½ cup crushed Saltines
Paprika, optional

1. Peel and devein the shrimp, leaving the tails intact. Remove and discard the large vein running along the back, or outside curve, of the shrimp. Preheat oven to 375°F.

2. Cut the scallops into small pieces. In a small saucepan, combine the scallops, 2 tablespoons of the butter, and the water. Boil the scallops until cooked through, about 1 minute. Drain, reserving the liquid.

3. Shred the crabmeat, and melt the remaining 2 tablespoons of butter. Combine the crabmeat, scallops, Ritz crackers, Saltines, and melted butter. Mix well. Mix

in the reserved liquid, in small amounts, until the stuffing reaches the desired consistency.

4. Split each shrimp along its back and arrange on a greased cookie sheet. Place an equal amount of stuffing on each of the shrimp. Sprinkle with paprika, if desired. Bake for 20 minutes, or until done.

Rhode Island Clam Chowder (Clear Chowder)

There are all kinds of seafood on the menu at Iggy's Doughboys, with two locations in Rhode Island: Oakland Beach in Warwick and Point Judith in Narragansett. But hands down the most popular items are Iggy's famous clear Rhode Island chowder and clam cakes. Many fans even dip their clam cakes in the chowder before devouring them.

MAKES 4 SERVINGS

2 tablespoons olive oil
1 large onion, chopped (about 2 cups)
3 stalks celery, chopped (about 1 cup)
1¼ pounds Red Bliss potatoes, cut into ½-inch dice (about 4 cups)
2 cups clam juice
1 tablespoon Worcestershire sauce
1 teaspoon fresh thyme or ½ teaspoon dried thyme
Enough water to cover above ingredients
1 (18-ounce) can Iggy's chopped clams
Freshly ground black pepper, to taste

1. Heat the oil in a large soup pot over medium-high heat. Add the onions and celery. Cook, stirring occasionally, until the vegetables begin to soften, about 8 minutes.

2. Add the potatoes, clam juice, Worcestershire sauce, thyme, and water. Bring to a boil and simmer until potatoes are soft, about 30 minutes.

3. Add the chopped clams just before serving. Season with pepper to taste.

Rhode Island–Style Clam Cakes

1 POUND OF IGGY'S FRITTER AND CLAM CAKE MIX WILL MAKE 2 TO 3 DOZEN CLAM CAKES.

1 pound Iggy's Fritter and Clam Cake Mix
  (mix can be ordered online at iggysdoughboys.com)
1½ cups cold water
1 cup minced clams, with juice (canned or frozen; thaw if frozen)
Minced onion, black pepper, other spices, to taste (optional)
Oil, as needed for deep-frying

1. In a large bowl, combine the clam cake mix with the water. Mix until smooth. Add the minced clams and clam juice. If desired, add minced onion, black pepper, and other spices. Mix well. Let stand for 5 to 10 minutes. Gently mix again to remove air pockets. Do not overmix.

2. Use a No. 40 or No. 60 ice-cream scoop to drop the clam cake mixture into hot oil (350°F). Fry for 3 to 4 minutes, turning gently after 2 minutes, until golden brown. Using a slotted spoon, remove the clam cakes from the hot oil and drain on paper towels. Serve immediately.

Clam cakes or fritters can also be griddle fried.

Crab Cakes

MAKES 6 CRAB CAKES

1 (6-ounce) can jumbo lump crabmeat
1 medium red onion, chopped fine
1 red pepper, chopped fine
1 bunch scallions, chopped fine
2 cups crushed Saltine crackers
2 eggs
1 tablespoon mayonnaise
Old Bay Seasoning, to taste
Dry mustard, to taste
Salt and pepper, to taste
1 tablespoon butter
Tartar sauce for serving

1. In a large bowl, combine the crabmeat, onion, red pepper, scallions, crushed Saltines, eggs, mayonnaise, and seasonings, all to your own taste. Mix well. Form the mixture into patties.

2. In a large skillet, melt the butter. Fry the patties for 4 minutes on each side. Serve with tartar sauce.

Boston Baked Beans

The rich history of Durgin-Park in Boston, Massachusetts, can be traced all the way back to 1742. The landmark restaurant has had a series of owners through the years, and little has changed—including this recipe for Durgin-Park's famous Boston Baked Beans, still served in an authentic bean pot. Chef's note: Albert Savage, who has been the head chef at Durgin-Park for more than 35 years, says it is imperative that you keep a watchful eye on the beans in the oven. Add water as necessary to keep the beans moist, but not too much, which would flood the beans.

MAKES 10 SERVINGS

    2 pounds dry beans, California pea beans preferred
    1 teaspoon baking soda
    1 pound salt pork
    1 medium onion
    ⅔ cup molasses
    4 teaspoons salt
    ½ teaspoon pepper
    8 tablespoons sugar

1. Soak the beans in water overnight. In the morning, parboil them for 10 minutes with the baking soda. Then run cold water through the beans in a colander or strainer.

2. Preheat oven to 300°F. Dice the rind of the salt pork into 1-inch squares, cut in half. Put half on the bottom of a 2-quart bean pot with the whole onion. Pour the beans into the pot. Put the rest of the pork on top.

3. Mix the remaining ingredients with 1 quart hot water. Pour over the beans. Put in a preheated 300°F oven for 6 hours.

Uncle John's Lobster Thermidor

MAKES 8 SERVINGS

8 tablespoons butter, divided
½ pound sliced mushrooms
3 tablespoons flour
2 cups heavy cream or milk
¼ cup dry sherry
4 cups cooked lobster meat
Salt
⅓ cup freshly grated Parmesan cheese

1. Preheat oven to 450°F. Butter a shallow baking dish.

2. Melt 5 tablespoons of the butter in a saucepan. Add the mushrooms and cook until they are softened. Remove from heat and set aside.

3. Melt the remaining butter, stir in the flour, and cook until smooth and blended. Slowly stir in the cream or milk, and cook over low heat, stirring until the sauce is smooth and thickened. Add the sherry and cook 1 minute more. Remove from heat and add the lobster and salt to taste.

4. Spoon mixture into the buttered baking dish, sprinkle with cheese, and bake about 10 minutes, until the cheese is melted and lightly browned. Serve over rice or puffed pastry with peas on the side.

Lobster Pie

MAKES 4 SERVINGS

 5 (1-pound) lobsters or 1½ pounds lobster meat
 ½ pound butter
 2 tablespoons lemon juice
 3 cups crushed Ritz crackers
 Parsley for garnish
 Lemon wedges for garnish

1. Preheat oven to 450°F.

2. Steam the lobsters in salted water 12 to 15 minutes, or until done. Let cool. Over a bowl that can hold the juices, pick out the meat from the tails, knuckles, and claws. Reserve the tomalley.

3. Melt the butter in a frying pan. Stir in the tomalley and lemon juice; remove from heat. Stir in the crushed crackers. Add enough reserved lobster juice so the mixture is moist and thick, somewhat like turkey stuffing.

4. Divide the lobster meat among 4 individual casseroles. Cover with the cracker mixture, patting it on evenly. Bake at 425°F until the top begins to brown, about 10 minutes. Garnish with parsley and lemon wedges.

Easy, Perfect Baked Haddock

MAKES 4 SERVINGS

½ stick butter, melted
¾ sleeve Ritz crackers, crushed
Dash of black pepper or lemon pepper, to taste
4 haddock fillets
1 tablespoon lemon juice
½ teaspoon dried or fresh parsley (optional)

1. Preheat oven to 350°F.

2. Melt the butter in a glass bowl. Add the crushed crackers and pepper and combine gently.

3. Spray a shallow baking pan with cooking spray. Put a few cracker crumbs on the bottom of pan. Lay the haddock in the pan. Cover with the remaining cracker crumb mixture. Sprinkle the lemon juice and parsley over the fish.

4. Bake for 20 minutes. Watch closely, as fillet size varies greatly. Don't overcook. Remove from the oven when the fish is white and flakes easily.

Broiled Scallops

MAKES 4 SERVINGS

2 pounds bay or sea scallops
1½ tablespoons garlic salt
2½ tablespoons melted butter, plus more for serving
2½ tablespoons lemon juice

1. Preheat the broiler.

2. Rinse scallops and place in a shallow baking pan. Sprinkle with garlic salt, melted butter, and lemon juice.

3. Broil 6 to 8 minutes, or until scallops start to turn golden. Remove from oven and serve with extra melted butter on the side for dipping.

Shrimp Scampi

MAKES 4 SERVINGS

  1½ pounds jumbo shrimp, peeled and deveined
  Kosher salt and freshly ground black pepper, to taste
  2 tablespoons unsalted butter
  2 teaspoons minced garlic
  ¼ cup dry white vermouth
  1 tablespoon freshly squeezed lemon juice
  ¼ teaspoon grated lemon zest
  2 teaspoons finely chopped parsley

1. Put the shrimp in a large pie pan or plate and pat completely dry with a paper towel. Arrange the shrimp so they lie flat and are evenly spaced. Season with salt and pepper.

2. Heat a large skillet over medium heat. Add the butter. When the foaming subsides, raise the heat to high and invert the plate of shrimp over the pan so the shrimp fall into the pan all at once.

3. Cook the shrimp without moving them for 1 minute. Add the garlic and cook for 1 minute. Turn the shrimp over and cook 2 minutes more. Transfer the shrimp to a bowl.

4. Return the skillet to the heat, and pour in the vermouth and lemon juice. Boil the liquid until slightly thickened, about 30 seconds. Scrape up any browned bits from the bottom of the pan with a wooden spoon. Stir the zest and parsley into the sauce.

5. Pour the sauce over the shrimp. Season with salt and pepper to taste, and toss to combine well.

Steamed Mussels

MAKES 4 SERVINGS

4 pounds mussels
2 tablespoons olive oil
1 shallot, minced
2 garlic cloves, shaved
4 sprigs fresh thyme
½ cup dry white wine
1 lemon, juiced
1 cup chicken broth
Pinch of red pepper flakes
1 tomato, peeled, seeded, and cut into large dice
½ cup roughly chopped parsley
2 tablespoons butter
Garlic bread for serving

1. Rinse the mussels under cold running water while scrubbing with a vegetable brush. Discard any broken shells.

2. Heat the oil in a 6- to 8-quart stockpot. Sauté the shallot, garlic, and thyme to create a base flavor. Add the mussels and give them a good toss.

3. Add the wine, lemon juice, chicken broth, and red pepper flakes. Cover the pot and steam over medium-high heat for 5 minutes, until mussels open.

4. Toss in the tomato, parsley, and butter. Re-cover the pot and steam for another minute to soften. The tomatoes should keep their shape. Serve with plenty of grilled garlic bread to soak up the broth.

Chunky Clam and Bacon Dip

Captain Marden's Seafoods got its start in 1945, and today it's still a thriving family business in Boston. The Marden family always found that the best recipes were those passed along to them by relatives, neighbors, friends, and customers, so they created an online recipe swap shop.

MAKES 2½ CUPS

4 ounces thick-sliced smoked bacon, diced

⅓ cup chopped red onion

3 scallions, white and light green parts, coarsely chopped

6 ounces chopped clams (meat from about 12–14 top neck or larger clams)

8 ounces sour cream

8 ounces cream cheese, at room temperature

1 red bell pepper, roasted and coarsely chopped, or 1 roasted red pepper from a jar

Pinch of red pepper flakes

2 tablespoons coarsely chopped Italian (flat-leaf) parsley

Ground white pepper and coarse (Kosher) salt, to taste

1. In a large skillet, sauté the bacon over medium-high heat until crisp. Drain the fat from the pan, and add the onion, scallions, and clams. Sauté until the clams are just cooked through, about 1 minute. Remove from heat and set aside.

2. Combine the sour cream, cream cheese, roasted bell pepper, red pepper flakes, and parsley in a large mixing bowl. Mix with an electric mixer on low speed or work with the back of a large spoon until smooth and well blended.

3. Add the contents of the skillet along with all the pan juices to the sour cream mixture, and stir well. Season to taste with pepper and salt. Serve immediately with chips or crudités, or cover and refrigerate until ready to serve (the dip will keep for several days). This mixture is also delicious tossed with diced cooked potatoes for a terrific summer potato salad.

Mussels with Tomatoes, Herbs, and Garlic (Moules Provençale)

MAKES 2 SERVINGS

1 tablespoon olive oil
2 onions, chopped
1 celery stalk, chopped
1 garlic clove, chopped
1 teaspoon chopped fresh basil, plus extra to garnish
1 tablespoon tomato paste
1 pound ripe plum tomatoes, peeled and chopped, or 1 (14-ounce) can
  chopped tomatoes
Salt and pepper, to taste
1 teaspoon sugar
2¼ pounds mussels, cleaned
½ cup dry white wine

1. To make the sauce, heat the olive oil in a large saucepan; add the onions, celery, garlic, and basil; and cook over low heat for 5 minutes, or until softened but not browned.

2. Mix in the tomato paste, tomatoes, salt, pepper, and sugar and simmer gently for 30 minutes.

3. Place the mussels and wine in a casserole dish over high heat and bring to a boil. Cook for only a few minutes, until the mussels have opened (about 5 minutes), stirring frequently to ensure they are evenly cooked. Pour off the cooking liquid, discard any mussels that have not opened, and return the opened mussels, in their shells, to the casserole dish.

4. Pour the hot sauce over the mussels and heat through. Sprinkle with chopped basil and serve at once.

Scampi Rockefeller

MAKES 4 SERVINGS

½ pound large uncooked shrimp, shelled and deveined
Salt and pepper, to taste
1 tablespoon olive oil
6 large garlic cloves, chopped
1 bunch green onions, chopped
½ (10-ounce) package ready-to-use fresh spinach leaves, stemmed
1 bunch basil leaves, coarsely chopped
2 tablespoons grated Romano cheese
½ teaspoon hot pepper sauce (such as Tabasco)
½ teaspoon (or more) white wine vinegar
3 tablespoons Pernod or other anise-flavored liqueur

1. Preheat oven to 450°F. Lightly oil a 9-inch glass pie plate. Arrange the shrimp on the prepared plate. Season lightly with salt and pepper.

2. Heat the oil in a heavy medium-size skillet over medium-high heat. Add the garlic and green onions, and sauté until softened, about 2 minutes. Add the spinach to the skillet. Cover and cook until the spinach is tender and wilted, stirring occasionally, about 4 minutes.

3. Mix in the basil, cheese, hot pepper sauce, and vinegar. Season with salt and pepper. Remove from heat; mix in the Pernod. Spoon the spinach mixture evenly over the shrimp.

4. Bake until the shrimp are just cooked through, approximately 8 minutes.

Shrimp & Artichoke Casserole

MAKES 2-4 SERVINGS

1 (14-ounce) can artichoke hearts, drained and quartered
¾ pound cooked peeled shrimp
½ pound fresh button mushrooms, sliced and sautéed until limp
2 tablespoons butter
2 tablespoons flour
1 cup cold milk
Salt and pepper, to taste
1 tablespoon Worcestershire sauce
¼ cup dry sherry
Dashes of salt and pepper
Chopped parsley (optional)
¼ cup grated Parmesan cheese
Paprika, to taste

1. Preheat the oven to 375°F.

2. Arrange the artichokes in an 8x13-inch buttered baking dish. Spread the shrimp over the artichokes. Layer the sautéed mushrooms on top of the shrimp.

3. Melt the butter in a double boiler or small saucepan. Slowly stir in the flour, blending well over low heat. Whisk in the cold milk until smooth. Slowly bring to a boil for 2 minutes, stirring constantly.

4. Add the Worcestershire sauce, sherry, parsley (optional), salt, and pepper to cream sauce. Pour the mixture over the contents of the baking dish.

5. Sprinkle the top with Parmesan cheese, and dust with paprika. Bake for 20 minutes.

Baked Sole with Creamy Dill Sauce

MAKES 2 SERVINGS

    2 pounds fillet of sole
    2 teaspoons lemon juice
    Salt and pepper, to taste
    ½ cup mayonnaise
    ½ cup sour cream
    1 teaspoon dried dill
    1 teaspoon chives
    4 tablespoons Captain Marden's Cracker Crumbs
    Paprika, to taste

1. Preheat oven to 400°F.

2. Butter a shallow baking dish and place the fish in it. Sprinkle with the lemon juice, salt, and pepper.

3. In a small bowl, mix together the mayonnaise, sour cream, dill, and chives. Spread over the fish. Sprinkle the fish with the cracker crumbs. Dust with paprika. Bake for 20 minutes.

Swordfish, Bacon, and Cherry Tomato Kebabs

MAKES 4 KEBABS

¾ pound swordfish steak (about ½ inch thick)
1 large garlic clove, minced
2 teaspoons fresh lemon juice
2 teaspoons olive oil
8 slices bacon
12 cherry tomatoes

4 (10-inch) wooden skewers, soaked in water for at least 30 minutes
Lemon wedges, as a garnish

1. Prepare your grill.

2. Cut the swordfish into 1-inch pieces. In a shallow dish, toss the swordfish with the garlic, lemon juice, and oil to coat. Cover and refrigerate for 20 minutes.

3. In a skillet, cook the bacon over moderate heat until pale golden but still soft; transfer to paper towels to drain, reserving the fat.

4. Thread the swordfish, bacon, and cherry tomatoes onto 4 water-soaked 10-inch wooden skewers. Brush the kebabs with some of reserved bacon fat and grill on an oiled rack set about 6 inches over glowing coals for 3 to 4 minutes. Turn the kebabs and grill 3 to 4 minutes more, or until the swordfish is just cooked through.

5. Serve the kebabs with lemon wedges.

Deviled Maine Lobster Cakes with Fresh Tomato and Cilantro Salsa

The folks at the Hurricane Restaurant in Kennebunkport, Maine are so proud of their cuisine, they give away their cooking secrets. Not only do they include a recipe in every newsletter, they also have an online recipe file from past newsletters, as well as some special requests they've received from diners. If you have a favorite Hurricane Restaurant dish you'd like to re-create in your own kitchen, drop them a line. They'll see if they can pare it down to a servable size and add it to their recipe file.

MAKES 4 SERVINGS

For the fresh tomato salsa:
¾ cup diced plum tomatoes
1 tablespoon minced fresh cilantro
2 tablespoons diced celery
¼ cup diced red onion
2 tablespoons diced green pepper
2 scallions (white and green parts), diced
¼ teaspoon salt
¼ teaspoon prepared horseradish
¼ teaspoon white vinegar
1 teaspoon granulated sugar
1 teaspoon Worcestershire sauce
1 jalapeño pepper, seeded and finely diced

For the lobster cakes:
1 tablespoon diced green peppers
1 small white onion, diced
1 tablespoon diced red bell pepper
2 tablespoons diced celery
1 teaspoon black pepper
½ teaspoon salt
4 drops (more or less to taste) Tabasco sauce
4 cups fresh bread crumbs
1 pound fresh Maine lobster meat
1 egg
½ cup butter, melted
Fresh cilantro, for garnish
Lemon wedge, for garnish

1. To prepare the lobster cakes, sauté the vegetables in a frying pan until transparent. Add the seasonings. Mix in the bread crumbs, lobster meat, egg, and butter. Form into 1-ounce patties and refrigerate until ready for use. May be done 1 day in advance.

2. To prepare the fresh tomato salsa, mix all the salsa ingredients and refrigerate overnight in a plastic container to marry the flavors.

3. Melt additional butter in a skillet, and brown the lobster cakes on both sides. Serve with fresh tomato salsa and garnish with a fresh sprig of cilantro and a lemon wedge.

Farnum Hill's Cider Fish

Unusual and delicious, this dish from Farnum Hill Cider in Lebanon, New Hampshire, calls for simmering fish fillets in cider, preferably the Summer Cider, Farmhouse Cider, or Semi-Dry Cider from Farnum Hill. The recipe can easily be doubled and redoubled.

MAKES 2-3 SERVINGS

 3 cups apple cider, preferably from Farnum Hill
 2-3 fish fillets (cod or sole)
 2 large shallots, finely chopped
 ¼ cup plain yogurt
 1 tablespoon flour
 4 tablespoons butter, cut into small pieces
 Salt and pepper, to taste

1. Bring the cider to a boil in a nonreactive skillet. Add the fish fillets and shallots to the skillet. Return to a boil, then reduce to a simmer. The fish fillets may be rolled and pinned with a toothpick before cooking if you'd like to fit more in the pan.

2. When the fish is done (after 8 to 12 minutes, depending on the thickness of the fillets), remove from the pan and keep warm.

3. Bring remaining liquid back to a boil and reduce to approximately 1 cup. In a bowl, combine the yogurt and flour, mixing well. Whisk this mixture into the reduced liquid. Remove the pan from the heat and whisk in the butter, piece by piece. Season to taste with salt and pepper. Pour this sauce over the fish and serve immediately.

Scallops and Apple-Smoked Bacon with Maple Cream

Something about the apple-smoked bacon and the maple cream make this a wonderful fall appetizer. The key to success with this recipe is cooking the scallops quickly and not a minute too long. This is just one of the dishes you get to explore when you dine at Leslie's Tavern in Rockingham, Vermont.

MAKES 8-10 APPETIZER SERVINGS

2½ cups heavy cream
⅓ cup Vermont maple syrup
1½ tablespoons Dijon mustard
½ teaspoon grated nutmeg
Salt and pepper, to taste
1 pound apple- or maple-smoked bacon
Olive oil, as needed
2 pounds fresh dry sea scallops
Chopped chives, for garnish

1. Combine the cream and maple syrup in a medium saucepan. Bring to a boil and then simmer until reduced to about half (stir frequently to prevent boiling over). Stir in the mustard, nutmeg, salt, and pepper and remove from heat.

2. Slice the bacon into julienne slices, and sauté to render the fat. Drain off the fat from the bacon and add the bacon to the cream mixture.

3. Heat a large sauté pan to high and add some olive oil. Let the oil get hot and then add the scallops. Sear on both sides (about 3 minutes per side for large scallops). The scallops should be slightly rare in the middle. Transfer the scallops to plates. Pour maple cream over the scallops and sprinkle with the chopped chives.

Appendix: Sportfishing Opportunities in New England

Many a seafood lover enjoys a day spent out on the water fishing with a pro, and there are hundreds of charter boats available for half-day and full-day excursions. In Rhode Island alone, the smallest of the New England states, there are 66 sportfishing boats for your consideration when visiting the Ocean State. Based on the season and what species are running, professional charter boats and guides can bring you to the best fishing spots. Species vary by location but include striped bass, bluefin tuna, yellow fin tuna, flounder, fluke, bluefish, swordfish, halibut, sea bass, cod, and many other game fish. Customarily all bait and tackle are provided, and the crew cleans the fish for you. All you have to do is enjoy your day at sea, whether you're a novice or an experienced fisher. Here's a state-by-state sampling of the many sportfishing opportunities in New England.

Connecticut

Coastal Fishing Charters
40A Cross Rd.
Waterford, CT 06385
(203) 943-6738
fish-ct.com

Destiny Fishing Charters
Port Clinton Marina
Clinton, CT 06437
(203) 640-6995
destinyfishingcharters.com

Tiderunner Charter
Pine Island Marina
916 Shennecossett Rd.
Groton, CT 06340
(413) 427-1198
tiderunnercharter.com

Westport Outfitters
609 Riverside Ave.
Westport, CT 06880
(203) 341-9490
westportoutfitters.com

Rhode Island

Block Island Fishworks
PO Box 1373, New Harbor
Block Island, RI 02807
(401) 466-5392
bifishworks.com

Cast a Fly Charters
1089 Frenchtown Rd.
East Greenwich, RI 02818
(401) 864-3794
castaflycharters.com

Coastal Charters Sportfishing
63 Ormerod Ave.
Newport, RI 02871
(401) 207-4095
coastalcharterssportfishing.com

Flukin Sportfishing Charters
33 State St.
Galilee, RI 02882
(401) 692-9058
flukin.com

Frances Fleet
33 State St.
Galilee, RI 02882
(401) 783-4988
francesfleet.com

Hot Reels Sport Fishing Charters
54 Kilvert St.
Warwick, RI 02886
(340) 227-3451
hot-reels.com

Patterson Guide Service
12 Juniper Ct.
Bristol, RI 02809
(401) 396-9464
patteronguideservice.com

Seven B's V
30 State St.
Galilee, RI 02882
(401) 789-9250
sevenbs.com

Massachusetts

Adventure with Magellan Deep Sea Fishing Charters
715 Rte. 28
Harwich Port, MA 02646
(508) 237-9823
capecodsportsmen.com

Capawock Charters of Martha's Vineyard
14 Capawock Rd.
West Tisbury, MA 02575
(617) 448-2030
capawock.com

First Light Anglers Charters
75 Essex Ave.
Gloucester, MA 01930
(978) 948-7004
firstlightanglers.com

Got Stryper
43 Chatfield Ln.
Chatham, MA 02669
(508) 680-6317
gotstryper.com

Mass Bay Guides
80 Old Dock St.
Scituate, MA 02066
(781) 545-6516
massbayguides.com

Midnight Charter
83 Merryknoll Rd.
Weymouth, MA 34105
(781) 335-3298
charterfishboston.com

Nantucket Outfitters
Nantucket, MA
(917) 584-5270
ackoutfitters.com

Reel Pursuit Fishing Charter
28 Constitution Rd.
Charlestown, MA 02129
(617) 922-FISH (3474)
bostonfishing.com

Seaduced Fishing Charters
18 Lonetree Rd.
Dennisport, MA 02639
(508) 394-6546
seaducedfishing.com

Tuna Hunter Fishing Charters
75 Essex Ave.
Gloucester, MA 01966
(978) 407-1351
tunahunter.com

Maine

Captain Doug Jowett
61 Four Wheel Dr.
Brunswick, ME 04011
(207) 725-4573
mainestripedbassfishing.com

Captain John Ford
PO Box 10318
Portland, ME 04104
(207) 471-5858
mainesaltwaterfishing.com

Coastal Fly Angler
10 Cranberry Ridge
Freeport, ME 04032
(207) 671-4330
coastalflyangler.com

Rip Tide Charters
1 Georgia St.
York, ME 03909
(207) 363-2536
mainestriperfishing.com

Seafari Charters
7 Island Rd.
Kittery, ME 03904
(207) 439-5068
seafaricharters.com

Super Fly Charters
255 Arboretum Park Dr.
Warren, ME 04864
(207) 691-0745
superfly-charters.com

Sweet Action Charters
38 Capital Island Rd.
Southport, ME 04576
(207) 318-4898
sweetactioncharters.com

Tidewater Fishing Charters
PO Box 7101
Kennebunkport, ME 04014
(207) 229-0201
tidewaterfishing.com

South End Charter Company
1870 Ocean Blvd.
Rye Harbor, NH 03870
(603) 205-1806
southendcharters.com

The Ultimate Catch
147 Green Mountain Rd.
Effingham, NH 03882
(603) 539-2106
theultimatecatch.com

New Hampshire

Adventure Charters
Hampton State Pier
1 Ocean Blvd.
Hampton Beach, NH 03842
(603) 926-4648
adventurefishingcharters.com

Al Gauron Deep Sea Fishing
State Pier
Hampton Beach, NH 03842
(603) 926-2469
algauron.com

Atlantic Deep Sea Fishing
1870 Ocean Blvd.
Rye Harbor, NH 03870
(603) 964-5220
atlanticwhalewatch.com

Seacoast New Hampshire Sportfishing
26 Neptune Dr.
Rye, NH 03870
(603) 394-5807
seacoastnhsportfishing.com

Vermont

Fishing Champlain Guide Service
980 W. Lakeshore Dr.
Colchester, VT 05446
(802) 734-7092
fishingchamplain.com

Green Mountain Fishing Guide Service
593 Rte. 140
Tinmouth, VT 05773
(802) 446-3375
greenmtnguide.com

Lake Champlain Fishing Charters
10 King Hill Rd.
Readsboro, VT 05350
(802) 423-7632
champlainfishingcharters.com

VT Lake Region Fishing Service
5672 Rte. 30
Sudbury, VT 05733
(802) 345-0799
VTLakeRegionFishingService.com

Index